HITLER'S NUCLEAR WEAPONS

HITLER'S NUCLEAR WEAPONS

The Development and Attempted Deployment
of Radiological Armaments by Nazi Germany

by
Geoffrey Brooks

LEO COOPER
LONDON

First published in Great Britain in 1992 by
LEO COOPER
190 Shaftesbury Avenue, London WC2H 8JL
an imprint of
Pen & Sword Books Ltd,
47 Church Street, Barnsley, South Yorkshire S70 2AS

Copyright © Geoffrey Brooks, 1992
ISBN 0 85052 344 3

A CIP catalogue record for this book is available
from the British Library

Typeset by Yorkshire Web, Barnsley, South Yorkshire
in Times Roman 10 point

Printed by
Redwood Press,
Melksham, Wiltshire

CONTENTS

For my sons Louis Leon and Anthony Emil
and in grateful memory of Werner Karl Heisenberg

ACKNOWLEDGEMENTS

The evidence for the existence of Hitler's nuclear weapons came to light in Wolfgang Hirschfeld's book *Das Letzte Boot* (Universitas Verlag, Munich 1989), an account of his captivity in the United States shortly after the Second World War. I am indebted to him for his unvarying kindness and assistance in responding urgently and at great length to all the questions which I put to him.

I must also express my great appreciation to the German Historical Institute, Bloomsbury, London; to the Science Museum Library, South Kensington, London, and to Dr Albert Miller and his staff at the Kernforschungszentrum, Karlsruhe, Germany, without whose freely given help this work could not have been completed.

Geoffrey Brooks
London, 1992

INTRODUCTION

'The first serious mention of the possibility that the atomic bomb might not be used came after V-E Day, when Under-Secretary of War Patterson asked me whether the surrender in Europe might not alter our plans for dropping the bomb on Japan.... A little later some of the scientists began to express doubts about the desirability of using the bomb against Japan. President Truman knew of these diverse and conflicting opinions. He must have engaged in some real soul-searching before reaching his final decision.'

'The development of nuclear energy in Nazi Germany never got beyond the laboratory stage.'

General Leslie R. Groves, US Army;
Chief of Military Intelligence of
Enemy Activities;
Head of Manhattan Project 1942-47.
Now It Can Be Told
Harper, New York 1962.

WHAT DID THE AMERICAN atomic physicist, Robert J Oppenheimer, mean when he said that the atom bombs dropped on Hiroshima and Nagasaki in 1945 came from *German* arsenals?

Following pressure from a CNN television documentary team in 1983, the United States Naval Archive disclosed a loading list which admitted a consignment of 550 kilos of uranium aboard the surrendered German submarine *U-234* at Portsmouth, New Hampshire, in May, 1945. However, the authorities declined to discuss the matter further, claiming the protection of their atomic secrecy legislation. Since the Americans were perfectly open about accounting for the uranium seized by their forces in mainland Europe at the war's conclusion, what is the reason for the inordinate secrecy surrounding this particular half-ton?

The question is: is it really true that the atomic energy project in Nazi Germany failed?

Wolfgang Hirschfeld's book *Das Letzte Boot* (Universitas Verlag, Munich 1989) is an account of his captivity in the United States following the surrender of the U-boat on which he served as Senior Radio Operator in the rank of Warrant Officer (Telegraphy). Hirschfeld himself certainly did not understand the significance of what he saw as he watched the submarine being loaded at Kiel and unloaded at Portsmouth, New Hampshire, but as an inveterate diarist, he duly noted the event with precision.

1

When I read a copy of his book, my knowledge of one particular aspect of nuclear physics, together with my understanding of the circumstances of the voyage of *U-234*, immediately convinced me that the cargo aboard *U-234* was Hitler's nuclear weapons.

Wolfgang Hirschfeld is a most important character in this history, for without his account, Hitler's nuclear weapons would have remained a secret for ever; it was a happy coincidence that such a keen observer should have been aboard *U-234* on her maiden war voyage.

The destination of *U-234* had been Tokyo; the undertaking was unique in the history of war simply because the destinies of two great warring nations, the United States and the Empire of Japan, hinged upon whether or not the submarine arrived there.

Hirschfeld was born in Berlin on 20 May, 1916, and after a period as a deckhand aboard a Baltic fishing trawler enlisted in the German Navy in December, 1935. Upon completion of basic training at Stralsund, he served with the Wireless Monitoring and Observation Service (B-Dienst) before returning to Fleet duty aboard minesweepers in September, 1937.

By the outbreak of war two years later, he was Petty Officer (Class III) and in charge of the wireless office of the Torpedo boat *T-139*. *T-139* was a relic from the Great War and with the exception of Hirschfeld, the entire crew were reservists.

During the first six months of the European conflict, the boat was stationed in the Kattegat on contraband control duty. On returning to Kiel for a refit at the beginning of April, 1940, Hirschfeld was ordered to report aboard the 6,000 ton light cruiser *Karlsruhe* waiting to sail at Wilhelmshaven.

On that Sunday afternoon Hirschfeld sent a junior radio operator to Kiel railway station with his seabag, properly labelled, and then he joined his colleagues at a farewell party he had thrown. Leaving it to the last moment before setting off for the train-ferry at Kiel-Garden, he found time always against him, and he swears to this day that the ferry sailed a minute early, causing him to miss it. He waited in great agitation for the next, and on finally arriving at the other bank, sprinted up the steps to the railway platform from where, bathed in sweat, he watched the red tail-lamps of the last train to Wilhelmshaven slowly dwindling in the distance. He gave chase along the sleepers of the track until rugby-tackled by two military policemen.

He did not know it then, but it was the decisive moment for his future life.

With the permission of the commander, he returned to *T-139* in order to await the morning express, but that evening the German fleet sailed for Norway as Operation Weserübung unfolded, and Hirschfeld remained on *T-139* in his old position for the duration of the emergency. *T-139* embarked troops at Warnemünde for the invasion and landed them in southern Norway, afterwards returning safely to Kiel.

Meanwhile the cruiser *Karlsruhe* had been torpedoed and sunk off Christiansand by the British submarine HMS *Truant*. All her surviving telegraphists were remustered en masse to the wireless office of the battleship *Bismarck*. Hirschfeld's name had been erroneously included on the crew list of the *Karlsruhe* and Lieutenant-Commander Schwarten of *T-139* had omitted to inform the Admiralty that Hirschfeld was remaining at his old posting. It was, therefore, presumed that Hirschfeld had been drowned on the *Karlsruhe*.

It was some time before the error was discovered, and when it was, Hirschfeld was placed at the disposal of the U-Boat Arm. He now became the NCO in charge of the wireless office of the Type IXb submarine *U-109* which commissioned at Bremen in December, 1940, and sailed for the Atlantic from Cuxhaven on 7 May, 1941.

It therefore came about that Hirschfeld stood on the conning tower of *U-109* on the early morning of 27 May, 1941, and watched the gun flashes of the distant battle as the *Bismarck* fought the Home Fleet. Once the British had gone, they searched the storm-lashed seas for survivors and found none. Every member of the radio crew of the *Bismarck* went down with the ship.

Hirschfeld sailed on five further long-distance missions aboard *U-109* under the command of the Knight's Cross holder, Lieutenant-Commander Heinrich Bleichrodt. Three of these missions were to the coast of North America, and in January, 1942, *U-109* was one of the five boats of the first wave of German submarines attacking shipping close to the United States coastline in Operation Paukenschlag. *U-109* was a moderately successful boat and sank fifteen merchant vessels in her six cruises.

On 7 October, 1942, Hirschfeld was declared unfit for U-boat service by the Flotilla Surgeon and sent to the hospital at Lorient for treatment of a serious skin infestation. There they burnt his skin with Cignolin-Vaseline and peeled it off, but the fungus had eaten down very deep and the treatment had to be repeated several times. He was not released from hospital until the beginning of December, 1942, by which time *U-109* had sailed on her seventh mission. He was unfit for U-boat service until further notice, and could not be transferred to another boat; he was therefore attached to the staff of the signals centre at Kernevel as Cipher Room Supervisor, from where he was able to follow the progress of the Atlantic battle-front. He learned that *U-109* sailed from Lorient on her ninth war patrol on 28 April, 1943, under Lieutenant Joachim Schramm, her first lieutenant on the sixth voyage, and was sunk on 4 May, 1943, by a Liberator bomber of RAF Coastal Command whilst approaching a convoy 900 miles west of Brest. There were no survivors.

At the beginning of 1943, the Signals Officer of the Second U-Flotilla, Lieutenant Gugelmeier, called Hirschfeld to Lorient and informed him that he had been selected as a candidate for the rank of Warrant Officer, but that he would have to continue with the flotilla until the new course started. He was promised that, on successful completion of the course, he would be returned to the signals centre at Kernevel.

In Chapter Three of this book Hirschfeld's story is continued.

When I asked Hirschfeld what he knew of the German nuclear programme in the Hitler era, he told me, 'All I know now is that the project under Professor Werner Heisenberg failed either to build nuclear weapons or even make a reactor go critical. I think they were going to use heavy water. That is history, isn't it?'

Supposing I told you that no scientist has ever been so maligned as Heisenberg; that we should all bow the knee to him for what he did for us?'

Hirschfeld gave me a sceptical glance.

'But if as you maintain, *U-234* was shipping Hitler's nuclear weapons to Japan, what should we be thanking him for?'

'The point is, it wasn't Heisenberg's, but a second, secret project which succeeded.'

'And why has that been concealed then?'

'From the German point of view, probably to give them a chance to answer, in defence of the atrocities, "At least we didn't kill half a million innocent civilians with two atom bombs. We didn't test atom bombs on people'."

'And from the American point of view?'

'There are three obvious reasons. To conceal the complete failure of the intelligence mission *Alsos*, which rampaged across a defeated Germany and missed what they were suppose to be there looking for. Secondly, and understandably, to denigrate the achievement of German science under Hitler, for political propaganda. And thirdly, to prevent the American public from knowing how close the civilian population came to a terrible disaster caused by the over-confidence of their government.'

Hirschfeld indicated that I should continue.

'There is a true hero in this story, and we must give him centre-stage. So I will start by telling you about the activities of a very courageous gentleman, to whom we all owe very, very much. I'll start by telling you about the German physicist, Werner Karl Heisenberg....'

CHAPTER 1

The Official Uranium Project Of The National Socialist State.

'Under a dictatorship, active resistance can only be practised by those who pretend to collaborate with the regime. Anyone speaking out openly against the system thereby indubitably deprives himself of any chance of active resistance.

For if he only utters his criticism from time to time in a politically harmless way, his political influence can easily be blocked... if, on the other hand, he really tries to start a political movement, among students for instance, he will naturally finish up a few days later in a concentration camp. Even if he is put to death, his martyrdom will in practice never be known, since it will be forbidden to mention his name.... I have always been very much ashamed when I think of the people, some of them friends of my own, who sacrificed their lives on 20 July, 1944, and thereby put up a really serious resistance to the regime.

But even their example shows that effective resistance can only come from those who pretend to collaborate.'

> Werner Karl Heisenberg (1901-76); Robert Jungk, *Brighter than a Thousand Suns*, Victor Gollancz Ltd and Penguin Books Ltd.

HE WAS ONE of the greatest of all theoretical physicists, but in addition to his enormous contribution to the world's scientific knowledge, he prevented the introduction of radioactive warfare to the European battlefield and almost certainly denied Hitler the means to accomplish Nazi Germany's war aims.

Werner Karl Heisenberg was born in Würzburg, Germany on 5 December, 1901. His father, August Heisenberg (1869-1930), who was a teacher at the Altes Gymnasium in Würzburg and a private lecturer in mediaeval and modern Greek at the city's University, originated from a family of master craftsmen in Osnabrück and married Anna Wecklein, the daughter of the rector of the Maximilians Gymnasium in Munich in 1899. Werner was their second son.

In April, 1910, August Heisenberg succeeded his teacher, Krumbacher, in the Chair of Greek at the University of Munich, and in September of the following year, Werner entered the highly regarded Maximilians Gymnasium which was still under the rectorship of his grandfather.

Proving himself to be a diligent, ambitious and outstanding student, he soon showed an extraordinary aptitude for mathematics, teaching himself differential and integral calculus, working with elliptic functions and studying abstract number theory. By the time he was 13, he was also an accomplished pianist and could perform master compositions.

His father, an infantry officer in the reserve, was mobilized at the outbreak of war in 1914 and remained absent from the family home for the duration of the conflict. When shortages of fuel and food towards the end of the war brought about the temporary closure of his school, Werner volunteered for land service in 1918 in order to supplement the family's meagre resources and helped with the harvest on a farm near Miesbach in Upper Bavaria.

Defeat and the abdication of the Kaiser led to revolutionary unrest across Germany, and in Bavaria a socialist republic was declared on 7 November, 1918. Overthrown by a soviet republic on 7 April of the following year, an appeal to Berlin brought the intervention of the army and the republic was restored a month later after a period of serious disorder. During the fighting in Munich, Werner Heisenberg joined many fellow students in volunteering to support the moderate socialists. He served with the 11th Cavalry-Rifle Brigade carrying messages and manning an observation post on the roof of the Catholic seminary opposite the University.

He had a great affinity for the outdoors and spent much of his leisure time hiking and camping in Germany and abroad. He was a member of the new Boy Scout movement until the enforced disbanding of independent scouting organizations by the Nazis in 1933. He loved hiking, skiing and mountain climbing, and enjoyed the beauty of nature.

His final Gymnasium examination results for the certificate of matriculation were considered brilliant, and he was accepted as a scholar at the prestigious Maximilianeum Foundation from where he entered the University of Munich during the 1920/21 winter semester.

Dissuaded from reading pure mathematics, his first choice, he chose theoretical physics instead and obtained admission to Professor Arnold Sommerfeld's seminar composed of advanced students and post-doctoral researchers. In three years of university study, he attended lectures covering the entire discipline of theoretical physics including quantum and relativity theory, but he showed so little enthusiasm for laboratory work and lectures in experimental physics that his course lecturer was almost inclined to fail him. He completed his doctoral dissertation in Munich in July, 1923, successfully treating the problem of the onset of turbulence in vortices which had defied all the previous attempts of mathematicians and physicists to resolve it. Because of his indifferent performance in experimental physics, however, he received his doctorate 'cum laude' only, rather than 'magna' or 'summa cum laude'.

Heisenberg became the Assistant to Max Born[1] at the University of Göttingen in December, 1923, and worked with Born on atomic and molecular models. By July of the following year he had obtained his *Habilitation* which qualified him as a University lecturer. He was then 22 years of age.

With the assistance of a Rockefeller scholarship in 1924, he spent long periods in Copenhagen at Niels Bohr's Institute[2] where he investigated with Bohr the most difficult problems of atomic theory. This helped him to obtain a thorough understanding of quantum physics which Bohr himself had founded. He also learned to speak English and Danish.

The centrepiece of what, after 1913, was known as the 'old quantum theory' was Bohr's model of the planetary atom in which electrons circled the nucleus in well-defined orbits, but new research had undermined the model because the theory was unable to describe the properties of complicated atoms and molecules. Furthermore, the discovery of a phenomenon known as the Compton Effect in 1922 had contradicted classical radiation theory, and the inability of radical theoreticians to account for these difficulties led to a 'crisis' in theory in the mid-Twenties.

In June, 1925, while recuperating from hay fever on the island of Heligoland, Heisenberg demonstrated a method of accounting for certain stationary states in atomic systems, and his solution, analogous to that of a simple planetary atom, initiated the programme for the development of the quantum mechanics of atomic systems.

Some months later his deliberations appeared under the title *Respecting the Quantum-Theoretical Reinterpretation of Kinetic and Mechanical Relationships*[3] in the periodical *Zeitschrift für Physik* and he proposed a reinterpretation of the basic concepts of mechanics.

In May, 1926, Heisenberg accepted the position of Lector at Niels Bohr's Copenhagen Institute, where he lectured in Danish on contemporary physical theories. In October, 1927, he was called to the Chair of Theoretical Physics at the University of Leipzig, creating there a leading centre for atomic and quantum physics research.

Two of the many students who studied under Heisenberg were Carl-Friedrich von Weizsäcker and Victor Weisskopf, both of whom were to play a greater or lesser role in later events.

In the year of his appointment at Leipzig, Heisenberg postulated his Uncertainty Principle, a proposition of far-reaching consequence for philosophy and science, which challenged Einstein's insistence that the universe should be viewed as a place both orderly and predictable.

Thus Heisenberg took his honoured place in a branch of science which the Nazis were to impugn as 'Jewish physics'.

Sir Isaac Newton's basic assumption had been that time was absolute and that it flowed always from past to present in the manner of a river. Einstein's 1905 Special Theory of Relativity proclaiming that all motion is relative excepting the speed of light, which is an absolute constant no matter what its source, abolished Newton's law. Moreover, by virtue of the equation $E = mc^2$, he dismissed the previously held view that mass and energy were separate and distinct, proving mathematically that they were actually interchangeable, since mass varies with velocity.

It has now been proved in large-particle accelerators that the mass of a proton accelerated through a tube several miles in length increases many thousands of times as its velocity becomes a significant fraction of the speed of light.

In his 1915 General Theory of Relativity, Einstein postulated that there was no such thing as gravity but rather the curved geometry of the universe in which heavenly bodies indent space and pull objects of less mass towards them.

However, the corollary of his equations indicated an unstable universe which astronomical observations were subsequently to confirm. This concept of an expanding or collapsing, non-static universe was an interpretation unpalatable to Einstein, who now attempted to force his theory to accommodate his personal predilection for an isotropic universe, stable and permanent, by the invention of a cosmological constant.

In 1922 the Russian mathematician Friedman solved Einstein's equations both with and without the constant, and demonstrated that the universe is expanding and may be either finite or infinite depending upon whether the density of matter is greater than, or less than, a certain level respectively.

In 1929 the astronomer Hubble discovered the dispersal of the galaxies at the rate directly proportional to their distances from the Milky Way and proved Friedman's version of Einstein's General Theory. This now strongly suggests that at the beginning of the universe there must have been a 'singularity' in which all matter whatsoever was contained in a single point.

While general relativity conceives of the 'singularity', there is a contrary system considered to be of equal importance to general relativity but which cannot be reconciled with it, and that is quantum mechanics, which appears to suggest that the subatomic world is without independent structure except for that defined by intellect.

Einstein's General Theory of Relativity formulated in 1915 modified Newton's 17th century law of gravity to conform with Maxwell's theory of electrodynamics, but these classical theories involved quantities which where continuously variable and which could be measured in theory with arbitrary accuracy. When the two theories were applied in an attempt to construct a model of the atom, they predicted that the negatively charged electrons, which were assumed to orbit the nucleus of the atom in the same way that the earth orbits the sun, would radiate electromagnetic waves. If that was true, it implied that those waves would deplete the electrons of energy, eventually causing them to spiral into the nucleus to bring about the collapse of the atom.

In order to rectify this problem, Heisenberg enunciated his Uncertainty Principle, which states that certain pairs of quantities such as the position and momentum of a particle, cannot be measured simultaneously with accuracy. Thus the electron is no longer to be considered the speck of matter of classical physics, but an entity smeared out around the nucleus of the atom, for the location of any particle at a particular instant can only be described by a system of probabilities.

Whereas Einstein insisted that the world is predictable, Heisenberg's Uncertainty Principle and quantum mechanics declare only the uncertain and random distribution of atomic and nuclear particles which are unpredictable and cannot be shown to obey causal laws. The theory has withstood every test devised for it, and today's physicists hold the quantum system to be of equal importance to general relativity.

While the latter allows for the 'singularity' at the beginning of time, quantum mechanics refutes any attempt to define the location, velocity and mass of any single particle. Therefore in order to understand the workings of the universe from its inception, relativity must ultimately be reconciled with quantum mechanics in the hope of finding the elusive field theory to explain how the universe works.

In the year 1933 Heisenberg received the award of the 1932 Nobel Prize for Physics, but declined to acknowledge that he accepted the award on behalf of the German Führer and Chancellor, Adolf Hitler, giving as his reason for doing so the fact that there was no existing precedent.

In the years following 1933 Heisenberg became recognized as the principal spokesman for modern theoretical physics. The number of his students decreased, but he continued to present systematic lectures covering the entire discipline, including the politically disfavoured special and general theories of relativity.

Soon after the accession to power of Adolf Hitler, a doctrine known as Aryan physics began to flourish in Germany. Two leading physicists, the 1905 Nobel Prize winner, Philipp Lenard, and the 1919 Nobel Prize winner, Johannes Stark, two of the few scientists of any note to join the Party out of conviction for its policies, imbued Hitler with the notion that atomic physics, quantum theory and the relativity theories of Einstein were a Jewish sedition and the 'outgrowths of alien mentalities'[4].

Einstein's theories were denigrated as 'Jewish world bluff' and National Socialist dogma now proceeded to reject any science or philosophy based on them, encouraging instead a restoration of the classical physics rooted in the previous century which excluded relativity and quantum theory.

When relativity theories were attacked in an article published in the Nazi Party organ *Völkischer Beobachter* on 26 February, 1936, Heisenberg prepared a paper also signed by Professor Geiger and seventy-six other professors of physics, including a number of Party members, expressing his concern to the Reichsminister for Education, Bernhard Rust, at the official policy of discrediting theoretical physics.

The nomination of Heisenberg as the leading candidate to succeed to the vacant Chair at the Faculty of the University of Munich the following year brought the controversy to the boil and the vehemence of the opposition to him from supporters of German physics rallying around its protagonists, Lenard and Stark, became markedly more hysterical.

The swell of protest culminated in an unsigned article entitled 'White Jews in science', attributed to Johannes Stark which appeared in *Das Schwarze Korps*, the journal of the SS, in its edition of 15 July, 1937.

> 'Just how secure the "White Jews" feel themselves to be is demonstrated by the behaviour of the Professor of Theoretical Physics at Leipzig, Professor Werner Heisenberg, who in 1936 managed to smuggle an article into an official party organ describing Einstein's relativity theory as "the obvious basis of further research" and also "one of the principal tasks for German youth in science in the further development of the understanding of systems in theory".
>
> At the same time he attempted to browbeat centres of authority by canvassing the support of German physicists for his evaluation of the theory.

In 1928 this protegé of Sommerfeld, and vessel of the spirit of Einstein in the new Germany, became Professor in Leipzig at twenty-six at an age, therefore, when he had scarcely had time to complete his research training.

He began his incumbency by dismissing the German assistant at his Institute and replaced him first with the Viennese Jew, Beck, then the Zürich Jew, Bloch. His seminar was attended predominantly by Jews until 1933 and the inner circle of his admirers today still consists of Jews and foreigners.

In 1933 Heisenberg received the Nobel Prize at the same time as the Einstein boys, Schrödinger and Dirac − proof of the way Jews influence the Nobel Committee against National Socialist Germany − and should be seen in the same light as the distinction given to Ossietski[5].

Heisenberg paid his own tribute in August, 1934, by refusing to sign the Declaration of German Nobel Prize winners for the Führer and Reichskanzler. His answer was: "Although I personally am in favour, political affirmations by scientists seem wrong, since it was never the practice in the past. Therefore I won't sign."

This answer identifies the Jewish spirit of its author, who considers the unity of the people and national responsibility of scientists to be improper.

Heisenberg is only one example of many. They are all vessels of Jewishness in German intellectual life and must disappear as must the Jews themselves.'

Johannes Stark contributed his opinion in a footnote to the article warning that

'...whilst the influence of the Jewish spirit has been removed from the German Press, literature and art as well as from German jurisprudence, it still has its defenders and protagonists among Aryan associates of Jews and those who have been pupils of Jews.

In this situation, the *Schwarze Korps* renders great service if by virtue of its courageous and important utterances it directs public awareness to the damage to which German intellectual life and the education of its academic youth are being exposed by White Jews.'

Realizing now that he was in serious danger, on 21 July, 1937, Heisenberg responded with a letter to SS-Reichsführer Heinrich Himmler, handed by his own mother to Himmler's mother for forward transmission to ensure its receipt by the addressee; there had been a loose connection between the families since Heisenberg's maternal grandfather, Nikolaus Wecklein, and Himmler's father had been professorial colleagues at the same Munich High School:

'I must request a decision on the basic principle... I will naturally submit my resignation if the view of Herr Stark corresponds with that of the Government. But if that is not the case, as I have been expressly assured by Reich Education Minister Rust, then I request you as SS-Reichsführer to defend me effectively against such attacks in this newspaper.'

During the next twelve months Heisenberg was frequently summoned to hearings in Berlin. Many interrogations were conducted in the notorious Gestapo prison on the Prinz Albrecht Strasse, from where he would return exhausted and distressed.

These frightening interviews were attended by an SS physicist well disposed towards Heisenberg who saw to it that he was not brutally treated.

On 21 July 1938, exactly a year since his letter, Himmler exonerated Heisenberg:

'Precisely because you were recommended to me by my family, I caused your case to be examined with special care and intensity. I take pleasure in being able to inform you that I do not approve of the attacks made against you in the article in *Das Schwarze Korps* and I have therefore ensured that there will be no further attacks on your person. However, I consider it right to mention that in front of your audience in future, you should clearly distance yourself from the human and political identity of the researcher when recognizing scientific research results.'

A scientific nonentity, Müller, acceded to the Munich Chair of Physics, while Heisenberg resumed academic life at the University of Leipzig.

The dogma of Aryan physics, which categorized atomic physics as a pseudoscience, ensured the suppression of public interest in the subject in pre-war Germany.

In contrast to the United States, where many modern laboratories were being constructed and equipped with the high voltage particle accelerators indispensable for training and research, Nazi Germany had only two adequately equipped laboratories, both run privately by the Kaiser Wilhelm Society for the Advancement of Science. These establishments were the Institutes at Heidelberg and Berlin Dahlem, where small high-voltage installations were available for nuclear research.

The cyclotron[6] had been developed by E.O. Lawrence at Berkeley in 1930, but in 1938 the first German model, privately funded and primarily intended for medical research, was still in the course of design and would not enter service until the fourth year of the war.

The progress, however, in experimental nuclear physics elsewhere in the world which had resulted from the introduction of these particle accelerators had been limited by the apparently insoluble problem of exploiting the tremendous energies latent in the nucleus of the atom. It was, therefore, a most laudable feat that the situation should be remedied early in 1939 by shoestring chemical research in Germany.

The heaviest element occurring in nature is uranium. Its component isotopes are the rare, fissile U^{235} forming 0.7 per cent of the atoms and the predominant U^{238} which account for virtually all the remainder.

Generally speaking, the nuclei of atoms of moderate size are more tightly held together than the largest nuclei. In the Thirties, physicists expected that if the nucleus of a heavy atom could be split into fragments of lesser mass, a formidable amount of energy would be obtained from the fissioning by the release of the binding energies of the nucleus.

In an article appearing in the scientific journal *Die Wissenschaften* on 6 January, 1939,[7] Otto Hahn and Fritz Strassman[8] announced that their experiments at the Kaiser Wilhelm Institute for Chemistry in Berlin had demonstrated nuclear fission in uranium.

They had observed that when a U^{235} isotope of uranium was struck by a neutron, the new U^{236} compound resulting from the collision was highly unstable and split up almost instantaneously. As this fission occurred, the highly charged fragments repelled each other with a violent kinetic energy; by virtue of their energies they were also very radioactive.

In the 22 April, 1939, edition of the scientific periodical *Nature*, Professors Joliot, von Halban and Kowarski, a team of experimental physicists at the College de France, reported findings to the effect that at least two neutrons eject during fission, followed in the succeeding few minutes by a small supplementary number from the fragments under decay..

This significant bulletin meant that since the collision between one neutron and a U^{235} nucleus brought about the creation of more than two fresh neutrons, it was probably possible to arrange for the surplus to cause a chain reaction.

Calculations had previously shown that if such was the case, then a formidably large quantity of energy would be gained from the combustion of one gramme of uranium fuel, and this would be 2×10^6 times as remunerative in terms of heat energy released as 1 gramme of coal.

The usefulness of nuclear energy for generating steam in power plants was self-evident, but in addition to driving turbines, its application in warfare as an explosive of monstrous force was also apparent.

In normal circumstances, the vastly predominant isotope of natural uranium, U^{238}, absorbs most of the free neutrons in the material and thus prevents the chain reaction cascade.

By the simple expedient, however, of depleting the uranium of most of the U^{238} isotopes, the opportunities for millions of neutrons to encounter millions of U^{235} atoms for an instantaneous chain increase are so enhanced that once a critical amount is present, the nuclear explosion occurs.

Thus, in an atom bomb, two lumps of fissile material of sub-critical mass, which in aggregate exceed a critical mass, are transported to the detonation site and are fired together by means of a conventional explosive. A single fission sets off an uncontrollable chain reaction within 10^{-7} second.

Within 48 hours of the publication of the French announcement, German scientists languishing in impoverished centres of learning, acutely aware of the financial possibilities of selling the energy and explosives aspects of nuclear physics to the appropriate departments of government, put pen to paper in a quest for the money.

Paul Harteck was born in Vienna on 20 July, 1902, the son of a senior civil servant and one-time Vice President of the Austrian Patent Office. He was educated at a Benedictine high school in the capital and showed an early aptitude for science. In 1921 he graduated in chemistry at the University of Vienna, and at the age of twenty-six obtained his PhD at the University of Berlin.

After two years as Assistant Professor at the University of Breslau, he became the Assistant to Professor Fritz Haber at the Kaiser

Wilhelm Institute for Physical Chemistry at Berlin Dahlem, making there his discovery of parahydrogen.

In 1933 he was awarded a Rockefeller scholarship and elected to study nuclear physics (which he felt 'would become important') under Lord Rutherford at the Cavendish laboratory, Cambridge; he had 'got the fever for it'[9] in the university of Berlin colloquia at which Einstein, Planck, Schrödinger and Max von Laue presided.

In 1934 he jointly wrote with Oliphant and Rutherford an important paper on fusion entitled 'Transmutation Effects Observed with Heavy Hydrogen' which reported on experimental work into thermo-nuclear fusion processes. In connection with the research, Rutherford had set Harteck the task of producing a quantity of heavy water (D_2O); after weeks spent passing an electric current through a small electrolytic cell, he achieved his objective. The quantity obtained was minute in comparison with all the gallons of water employed in the process. It served as a salutary introduction to a material which was to engage his energies for the best part of four years during the Second World War.

Following his return to Germany in 1934, Professor Harteck was appointed Director of the Institute of Physical Chemistry at the University of Hamburg.

He was a member of the Nazi Party and his group of five co-workers was known as the 'Hamburg Bomb Group'.

A letter jointly signed by Harteck and Dr Wilhelm Groth dated 24 April, 1939, took the liberty of drawing the attention of the Heereswaffenamt[10] to:

> 'the newest developments in nuclear physics which, in our opinion, will probably make it possible to produce an explosive many orders of magnitude more powerful than conventional ones... that country which first makes use of it (nuclear fission) has an unsurpassable advantage over the others.'[11]

Asked after the war why he wrote this letter, Harteck explained that it was simply because his group received no support from the State and were impecunious. Recognizing that the postulated explosive would be attractive to the War Office, they approached them hoping for funds for the research. The only other financial assistance granted them for nuclear investigations had come from the Hamburg Society of Authors.

The letter drew no windfall for Harteck; he heard no more of the matter until September.

The German universities were controlled by the Reich Education

Ministry. Acting on a letter from the theoretical physicists, Joos and Hanle, at Göttingen suggesting the enormous significance of recent developments in nuclear physics in Europe, the Ministry called upon the President of the Reich Bureau of Standards and head of the physics section of the Reich Research Council, Professor Abraham Esau, to undertake an investigation into nuclear fission.

At a secret conference at the ministerial offices in Berlin on 29 April, 1939, those present were addressed on the subject of German and other research into the possibility of constructing a nuclear reactor, after which the chairman, Esau, declared his intention to requisition all existing stocks of uranium material in Germany, to obtain a prohibition of its export, and proposed the formation of a research group composed of the country's leading physicists to operate under his personal overlordship. It scarcely needs to be added that Esau was an old Nazi; he had been a career professor at Jena where he had specialized in high frequency electronics.

During the Thirties uranium itself had found few applications, but its ores yielded radium and the major extraction plant for the process was in Belgium. The British Government, having rightly assumed that there must be a substantial dump of uranium compounds in Belgium, now took steps to ascertain the quantity and gave some thought as to whether it ought not to be removed from its close proximity to Germany.

Sir Henry Tizard, Chairman of the Committee on the Scientific Survey of Air Defence and a Director of the Imperial College of Science and Technology, recommended that the Government should either attempt to purchase the uranium or obtain an option on it; on 26 April, 1939, only four days after the publication of the French findings in *Nature*, enquiries with the Treasury and the Foreign Office revealed that the only uranium stock in Belgium was held at the premises of the Union Minière du Haut Katanga Company which had an English Vice-President, Lord Stonehaven.

It was arranged for the President of Union Minière, M. Edgar Sengier to meet Sir Henry Tizard in London on 10 May, but by then the initial excitement at the uranium possibilities had subsided and the British Government had quietly dropped the idea of an outright purchase of the stock. In the event, Sengier refused to grant Britain an option either on the ores in Belgium or at the Company's mines at Shinkolobwe in the Congo. He also informed Tizard that existing stocks of uranium oxide in Belgium were very small, only a few tons divided between different places.[12] Sengier was in no doubt as to the potentiality of uranium as he had had the matter explained to him by his friends the

Joliot-Curies; he now cynically advised Sir Henry Tizard that although he expected Belgium to remain neutral in a probable future conflict involving Germany, he was undertaking to notify London of any abnormal enquiries for uranium from a particular source.

At the conclusion of the meeting, Tizard reminded Sengier that he should not forget that he controlled 'something which might mean a catastrophe to your country and mine if this material were to fall into the hands of a possible enemy'.

General Leslie Groves, the executive head of the Manhattan Project in the United States, stated[13] that this remark made a lasting impression on Sengier, but it is perfectly clear that he lied to the British about the huge stockpile of uranium oxide warehoused at Oolen near Brussels, which he intended to make available to the Germans. This was a purely business decision, made to ensure that Union Minière would maintain its pre-eminence in Western Europe in the event that Hitler emerged victorious in a war on the Continent. A balance was obtained by sending instructions to Katanga to flood the mines and dismiss the labour force as soon as the available ores had been shipped from Lobito to the United States.[14]

Finally, in October, 1939, Sengier transferred his offices to New York, where he remained for the duration of the war. Groves[15] writes that Sengier also gave òrders that the stock at Oolen was to be removed to the United States too, but it appears that no such intention actually existed on the part of Sengier and the uranium remained where it was.

After the war Groves recommended the award of the Medal of Merit, the highest civilian award made by the United States Government, to M. Edgar Sengier for his services to the United States, Belgium and the free world: 'As a Belgian, Sengier fully appreciated the absolute necessity of an Allied victory. It was his broad, statesman-like attitude that made it possible for us to reach an agreement satisfactory to all.'[16]

The agreement was certainly satisfactory to Hitler, who had not even been consulted.

On 31 August, 1938, Heisenberg wrote to his former lecturer, Sommerfeld:

> 'As early as last summer, Professor Betz of Columbia University presented me with an invitation to go there, either for one seminar or permanently. In response to his letter, I wrote that I preferred to stay in Germany and that for the time being, I would only come for a short period.'

In another letter, to his mentor, Niels Bohr, he made it clear that he was tortuously uncertain as to which course he should follow: how much better it would be if he had no alternative but to emigrate, if fate would intervene to decide the matter for him, as it had done with so many of his friends!

But his marriage in 1938 had added to his dilemma, while his personal involvement in the fight against the philistine Aryan physics remained a powerful force to bind him to Germany, for it seemed that to desert his followers now might amount to a betrayal of them to whom he was a teacher and philosopher.

When Columbia University repeated its offer the following year, however, he saw that the European war was inevitable and decided to pay a last visit to his friends before the deluge broke.

He visited New York and Chicago for two months beginning in mid-May, 1939, and at the Symposium on Cosmic Rays at the University of Chicago between 27 and 30 June presented his latest results on the theory of cosmic ray showers.

One of the reasons for his trip had been to explain his decision to remain in Germany in the coming war; he believed that friendships could outlast political differences between nations. His Italian colleague, Fermi, at least was able to express a degree of understanding for his decision whilst dissenting from it; but other 'friends' in the American physics community were not convinced.

It has often been said that Heisenberg's decision to remain in Germany was motivated by his belief in and desire for a Nazi victory; since he was a nationalist strongly and emotionally attached to his homeland, the assumption has been that he was dedicated to Hitler's triumph.

But Heisenberg was not persuaded that his expatriation could affect the war to Hitler's disadvantage; by leaving his university position and Germany, he could save his personal reputation and his family, but at the expense of the community of Jewish physics theorists, and students and the doctrine itself. Moreover, in defecting to the United States, he would almost certainly incur an obligation to invest his energies in the development of atomic weapons, and the prospect of collaborating in a project to construct atom bombs which would almost inevitably be dropped on German cities, if ready in time,[17] was unappealing to him.

In a letter to his wife after returning from internment in England following the capitulation, he wrote:

> 'Since 1933 it had been clear to me that a terrible tragedy was unfolding: only I could not imagine its extent or end.

At the time I had stayed in Germany to be there when it was over, and to help. That is what I told my friends during the summer of 1939, and the best among them understood it well.'

No braver decision did any scientist, in Germany or outside it, ever make than this. In August, 1939, Heisenberg returned to Hitler's Germany aboard the almost empty liner *Europa*. Within a year he would save the European continent and the world, for in the absence of Heisenberg, Harteck would have won the war for Hitler.

The letter from the Hamburg physical chemists, Harteck and Groth, received by the War Office in April, 1939, had not been acknowledged, but had been forwarded to the research branch of the Heereswaffenamt under Professor Erich Schumann. From him it had been delegated to the Army's explosives consultant, Dr Kurt Diebner.

Diebner had graduated at the University of Halle in 1931 with a thesis on the ionization of alpha rays and had worked on the construction of a particle accelerator at the Bureau of Standards laboratory, but since 1934 had been discontentedly engaged on conventional explosives research with Dr Friedrich Berkei. Now having obtained Army funding to initiate research on uranium, Diebner built a small nuclear physics laboratory at Gottow in the Kummersdorf rocket and explosives research park outside Berlin.

The War Office was ill-disposed towards the Education Ministry's parallel nuclear programme under Professor Esau and in September ordered the Bureau of Standards to discontinue its involvement. This instruction was conveyed to Esau by SS-Brigadeführer Professor Rudolf Mentzel, his departmental superior.

Esau held a quantity of uranium oxide which he had obtained the previous summer, and persisted with private experiments at Göttingen until three physicists working for his uranium club, Joos, Hanle and Mannkopf, were simultaneously conscripted, Hanle even being subjected to the indignity of being called for by the military police at 2 o'clock in the morning.

Esau admitted defeat and surrendered his uranium stock to the Army.

Hitler ought to have been able to achieve all his military objectives within the first three years of war using weapons built on the atomic principle, but the seed of his ultimate defeat was sown at a secret conference of fifteen nuclear physics experimentalists held at the Hardenbergstrasse offices of the Heereswaffenamt in Berlin on the morning of Saturday, 16 September, 1939.

Under the chairmanship of Dr H Basche, a senior civil servant and Diebner's superior at the War Office, the purpose of the meeting was to study the feasibility of a German uranium project for power and weapons production.

Professor Paul Harteck has stated that Dr Basche asked him outright to take responsibility for the whole programme. He declined the suggestion on the grounds that he believed the project could only be directed effectively by a group consisting of the various heads of disciplines, and not one man. As he was to realize later, this decision was a fatal error of judgment. Throughout the war, Harteck was to demonstrate clearly that of all the nuclear scientists at the disposal of Hitler, he alone had the necessary vision, the energy, the innovative intellect and the commitment to have created a monopoly of nuclear power for the Nazi Government.

Furthermore, there can be little doubt that he would have been quickly accepted by the scientific community as having the necessary qualities and pedigree to assume overall control of the programme.

A further development immediately compounded this disaster. Despite spirited opposition, it was grudgingly agreed to co-opt the theoretical physicist, Werner Heisenberg, to attend the next conference scheduled for 26 September, with a view to having him elaborate the theory of the chain reaction in uranium. The upshot of this decision was to invite the participation of the greatest of all the German scientific mathematicians who, while pretending to collaborate in the project, would set out to ensure that in five and half years of endeavour, it achieved nothing worthwhile. Of all the secret opposition to Hitler, that of Heisenberg was to prove the most insidious and the most effective.

The co-ordinating head of the project, Professor Schumann, recommended to the Heereswaffenamt that a 'Nuclear Physics Research Group' be formally established, its activities to be disguised as 'the creation of new energy sources *for R-rocket propulsion*'[18] under the stewardship of Diebner. The wording of the camouflage is significant and will appear again later in another context.

As a conscripted military reservist, Heisenberg had served two months in the previous two summers in the Gebirgsjäger. Obeying a mobilization order late on 25 September, he travelled by train from Urfeld to Berlin and reported to Hardenbergstrasse 12, Berlin, at ten a.m. on the morning of 26 September, to be informed that his call-up telegram had been a deception and that he was to report next door to an atomic physics group.

He had been inducted into a conference of atomic physicists

21

considering the possible applications of nuclear energy under the tutelage of Professor Schumann whose address to the assembly was couched in terms emphasizing the defensive aspect of the enquiry. Since the German Reich was now at war, it was of the greatest importance that Germany should be forewarned of all possible eventualities; this was the purpose of the technical appraisal they were undertaking. Even a negative conclusion was valuable, for the military could then be reassured that no unpleasant surprises were in store.

The experimentalists were commissioned to undertake a variety of materials measurements in specified areas of research, while Heisenberg was given the written task:

> To 'consider whether, under the known circumstances of the characteristics of fission processes in uranium, a chain reaction is at all possible, and if so, please commit your ideas to paper.'[19]

Professor Schumann also announced that the War Office proposed the Kaiser Wilhelm Institute for Physics at Berlin Dahlem to be the scientific centre of its uranium research project. The Director of the Institute, Peter Debye, was Dutch and was thus debarred from taking part in State research as a non-national; declining to accept German citizenship, he placed himself on indefinite leave and accepted a guest professorship at Cornell University in January, 1940.

His position was filled provisionally by Diebner, who was considered to be a physicist of the second rank, but he was a Nazi Party member, which was the determining factor in his appointment.

It was immediately recognized by Dr Karl Wirtz and Heisenberg's former pupil and close friend, Professor Carl Friedrich von Weizsäcker, two of Debye's former collaborators, that inherent in this arrangement was a great danger that the uranium project was vulnerable to penetration by political functionaries, as had happened elsewhere.

Accordingly they intrigued to have Heisenberg invited to join the Institute as a scientific adviser, travelling from his University at Leipzig to Berlin once per week, his visits enabling him to interfere where necessary in undesirable developments in research in Berlin and elsewhere.

Dr Karl Wirtz[20] and Heisenberg[21] both said later that Diebner actually appreciated the weakness of his own position and understood that the survival of the Institute rested on having a scientifically competent and authoritative Directorship. Therefore, he had no hesitation in agreeing to the plan to have Heisenberg offered the succession to Debye in due course and welcomed the interim weekly arrangement.

Whereas the majority of physicists were willing to affiliate with the Heereswaffenamt group, a large proportion of them were not prepared to remove from the regions to relocate under the one roof at Berlin Dahlem, and thus from its inception the programme was structured with a Headquarters and three principal provincial satellites:

Kaiser Wilhelm Institute for Physics
Berlin Dahlem and Gottow Research Centre

Diebner	Von Weisäcker
Czulius	Bopp
Berkei	Fischer
Hartwig	Wirtz
Herrmann	Pose

Institute of Theoretical Physics
University of Leipzig

Heisenberg
Döpel and wife

Kaiser Wilhelm Institute for Medical Research
Heidelberg

Bothe
Jensen, P.
Ritter

Institute of Physical Chemistry
University of Hamburg

Harteck
Groth
Knauer
Süss
Jensen, J.

The investigation of the possible practical applications of the chain reaction in uranium had not previously attracted Heisenberg who found experimental work almost an anathema. His specialist field was the contemplation of problems in quantum mechanics and astrophysics, and for that reason his co-workers admired him for the apparent ease with which he embraced reactor theory and so became the pathfinder for German uranium research.[22]

Heisenberg's commission from Professor Schumann was completed within two months, and on 6 December, 1939, he submitted his findings in the first of two pioneering papers, *G-39 The Possibility of Obtaining Energy from Fission in Uranium.*[23]

The nuclear reactor is an engineering structure in which a chain reaction is controlled for the purpose of providing steam for electrical generators, and radioisotopes for medical and industrial tracer research. The first American reactors were built for plutonium extraction, i.e. weapons purposes.

Heisenberg's primary aim was to stress the power aspect of the reactor and to conceal the fact that there was only evidence to the contrary that a chain reaction could be controlled. This was to ensure that the direction of the project did not become exclusively concentrated on the development of the U^{235} bomb, which he was obliged to admit certainly might be feasible, if stupendously expensive.

Principally because all reactors incidentally produce fiercely radioactive waste and plutonium (although it was not appreciated until 1940), the evidence tends to suggest that Heisenberg and his colleague von Weizsäcker must have decided at a fairly early stage that it would be in the best interests of all concerned if the reactor project was not to succeed. The National Socialist government examined all new developments in science for their military application and it could not be guaranteed that the State would not abuse radioactivity for weapons purposes, a fact to be later confirmed.

The ponderous experimentation which occupied the official programme for the entire war had as its objective the establishing of criteria for the geometry of uranium elements in the bulk of the moderator (the heavy water), and the critical quantities of both. Some idea of the inertia surrounding the project can be gained from the fact that it took five years to put into effect Heisenberg's correct suggestion in the 1939 paper that graphite was better than water as the neutron reflector around the core of the reactor.

Since it was he who, as senior theoretical physicist had drawn up the guidelines for the uranium project for the duration, he tended to continue to dominate what went on thereafter. Heisenberg claimed at the end of the war that his small, intimate circle had purposely striven to keep the research in their own hands in order to prevent the development of nuclear weapons by Nazi Germany. Little else but sabotage can indeed explain its poor progress.

The nuclear physics in this book is basic and the reader should not experience difficulty in understanding the science contained in the narrative, once the following descriptive passages have been absorbed:

* Uranium, which is the heaviest element occurring in nature, being half as heavy again as lead, is composed of

two principal atoms or isotopes occurring in the approximate proportions:

U^{235} 0.7 per cent
U^{238} 99.3 per cent

* An atom can be conceived of as a microplanet orbited by a cloud of electrons. At its centre is the nucleus, which is composed of protons and neutrons bound tightly together by nuclear forces into a roughly spherical volume.

* U^{235} is the fissile atom, and is the only naturally occurring material which can be fissioned, or 'split', by neutrons of all energies. When a neutron arrives in close proximity to a U^{235} atom, the equilibrium of the nucleus becomes disturbed, and the nucleus may fission, usually into two fragments.

* Together with a gamma radiation emission, the fragments expel an average of 2.6 neutrons, each having a powerful kinetic energy of 3MeV. These prompt neutrons emerge within one ten-millionth of a second, but a longer-lived small fraction of delayed neutrons are liberated a little later.

* The natural function of the majority U^{238} isotope is to prevent such fissions. If any of these loose neutrons should approach close to a U^{238} atom at an energy of between 6eV and 200eV, then it will almost certainly be captured, and be absorbed into the nucleus of the U^{238} atom. As the trough of the energy band, or 'resonance', is 6eV, however, a neutron possessed of a lesser kinetic energy than this will escape and so possibly proceed to initiate further fissions.

* Thus, in order to enhance the probability of further nuclear transformations with the U^{235} atoms in natural uranium, it is desirable to decelerate neutrons to a very low energy. This is achieved in a reactor by geometrically spacing the uranium fuel elements through a moderating substance of lighter atomic structure, such as heavy water, or pure carbon.

During excursions between the uranium fuel elements, which the neutrons leave at speed and later re-enter with much reduced energy, they undergo repeated elastic collisions of the 'billiard-ball' type with the atoms of the moderator, at which they shed energy without being absorbed.

* A chain reaction is a series of progressive nuclear transformations involving the splitting of the U^{235} nuclei, in which a geometric increase in the neutron population occurs from one generation to the next. A reactor goes critical when each transformation causes on average one further transformation.

Heisenberg had been commissioned to enquire into whether a chain reaction was possible; his December 1939 thesis launched into an immediate consideration of reactor materials and combinations.

The Heavy Water Reactor

> 'Natural uranium can be employed by using it in conjunction with another substance which slows down the neutrons from the uranium without absorbing them.
> Ordinary water is not suitable for this purpose. On the other hand, it would seem that heavy water and very pure carbon satisfy the requirements. Slight impurities in them can spoil the reaction.'

Heavy water (D_2O or deuterium oxide) is four times more efficient at slowing neutrons than the purest carbon and thus a much smaller reactor is required. Neutrons collide with deuterium molecules in heavy water and lose energy but are not absorbed by them, and for this reason it is exceptionally efficient as a moderator.

Ordinary water (H_2O) is unsatisfactory because its hydrogen molecules absorb neutrons.

Heavy water is ordinary water from which all hydrogen atoms have been removed, but the acquisition of ponderable amounts of the fluid requires a major industrial plant for the separation which is formidably expensive:

> 'A combination of heavy water and uranium would bring about a neutron multiplication and would lead to energy production.
> For this reactor assembly, however, large quantities of heavy water are required which would involve very substantial expense.'

His initial impression of the critical size of such a reactor proves to be rather on the small size:

'One can roughly calculate that with a uranium-heavy water mixture of 1000 litres of heavy water and 1200 kilos of uranium.

This would be within a sphere of 60cm. radius and surrounded by a reflector of ordinary water. A spontaneous energy supply would be achieved at a stationary temperature of 800°C.'

Pure Carbon Reactor

'Pure carbon is also suitable for the slowing down of neutrons.

It can be estimated that from a reactor three metres cubed in size, one would obtain the reaction and energy.

For this apparatus, one would need about 30 tons of pure carbon and 25 tons of uranium oxide.'

By 'carbon', Heisenberg essentially had in mind bricks of electro-graphite, which is the relatively soft jet black material widely used in pencils and which can be machined, although, as will be seen, there are carbon compounds which may be used to moderate reactors of a different kind. Graphite contains a number of foreign atoms such as cadmium and boron which give a high probability of absorption for neutrons and it would have been difficult to prepare this form of carbon in a very pure state under the conditions prevailing in wartime Germany.

The first American reactor used 385 tons of graphite bricks and 46 tons of mixed uranium substances (6 tons of uranium metal powder and 40 tons of uranium oxide and uranium dioxide).

The Most Favourable Reactor Design Of All

'But the *most favourable design of reactor* based on existing figures would be 4cm. thick layers of uranium oxide sandwiched between two 5cm. thick linings of heavy water.

Between each sandwich would be a gap of about 10-20cm. filled with pure carbon.

The reactor would be surrounded by a reflector of pure carbon.'

The volume of this design would be 1.2 cubic metres; it would need only 2 to 3 tons of uranium, 600 litres of heavy water and 1 ton of pure carbon.

In his supplementary paper of 29 February, 1940, Heisenberg elaborated on the first two assemblies whilst confessing to some misgivings in respect of the pure carbon reactor. As to his 'most favourable design', he would not comment on that further, he said, but pass it to his close colleague, Professor Carl-Friedrich von Weizsäcker for further evaluation, and that for some reason is the last we hear of it.

One would presume that its disappearance was occasioned by an appreciation of just how close this would approach the critical point; Germany had a stock in excess of 600 litres of heavy water by August, 1942, and the graphite would have been forthcoming in this quantity.

It is also highly significant that as early as December, 1939, it was thought that the most favourable reactor design would incorporate a reflector of pure carbon. The reflector is the substance enclosing the core of a nuclear pile against which escaping neutrons are scattered back into the reaction. All but two of the official project's experiments used ordinary water or solid paraffin as a reflector. Not until January, 1945, was graphite eventually tried as the tamper, even though the 1939 idea had not only been subsequently validated by Professor Walther Bothe's analysis at Heidelberg in 1941, but had actually been confirmed as the outstanding reflector. As has been remarked upon, this was one of the many inconsistencies which interfered with the progress of the research and which can only have been intentional.

Enrichment Of Isotopes-Reactors

'The surest method of realizing energy production from the fissioning of uranium lies in enriching the U^{235} isotope.

The greater the enrichment, the smaller the reactor. The enrichment of U^{235} is the only means whereby a compact reactor one cubic metre in size can be designed.

It is clear from the appended tables that an enrichment of 30 per cent (i.e. from 0.7 per cent to 0.9 per cent) is sufficient to render possible the production of energy using uranium with ordinary water.

If the isotope is enriched by 50 per cent (i.e. from 0.7 per cent to 1 per cent), success is practically certain.'

The natural ratio of the two companion isotopes U^{235} and U^{238} in a lump of uranium is 0.7 per cent to 99.3 per cent. Where the uranium is depleted of some of its U^{238} isotopes, the marginally smaller quantity of the element now consists of U^{235} and U^{238} in a different ratio, nowadays of the order of about 1.5 per cent to 98.5 per cent at the least, which allows the use of ordinary water as the moderator in the core instead of heavy water. This is possible because the increase in the number of U^{235} atoms in the uranium compensates for the relatively weak absorption of neutrons by the hydrogen atoms in ordinary water.

As in the case of the heavy water reactor and the pure carbon reactor mentioned previously, the material requirements had been underestimated. This may be accounted for by the preparation of inaccurate cross sections for the absorption of neutrons in uranium oxide and in other nuclear materials, a point which will be repeated in another context shortly.

The two uranium isotopes are chemically identical, and separation can be achieved only by the use of physical methods depleting microscopic quantities of U^{238} from each sample of uranium hexafluoride gas, and very formidable separation plants, requiring fantastic industrial and technical development and a huge labour force, are necessary for the purpose.

The question of enriching the U^{235} isotope in tons of uranium in order to make possible an ordinary water reactor was never a serious proposition. By the end of the war, four years of laboratory experiment had resulted in working prototypes of two designs (see Glossary), but the resources required to set up the project were possibly beyond Germany's capabilities.

Enrichment Of Isotopes-Explosives

'Enrichment...is the only method of producing those explosives which exceed by many powers of magnitude the most destructive explosives known.'

If a chain reaction was possible, then the explosion would be possible, the intensity of which would depend on the rate of liberation of energy compared with the rate at which that could be transferred out:

'An increase in temperature results from enriching the U^{235} isotope.
'If the U^{235} isotope were to be enriched sufficiently to obtain a temperature T corresponding to a neutron energy of approximately 300eV...'

A common measurement for neutron energy is temperature in °K, which is synonymous with °C at high levels. 300ev corresponds to a temperature of $3.48 \times 10^{6°}$K, or 3.5 million °C.

'... then by virtue of the equation $T = 300° \left(\dfrac{R}{\pi\, l\, 300°} \right)^4$ and since diffusion length l varies with $\sqrt[4]{T}$, then the optimum radius of the mass for an instantaneous increase in temperature to $10^{12°}$C and the release of all available fissile atoms at once, would be:

$$R = 10\,\pi\, l \text{ cms}$$

(where l = diffusion length, i.e. the mean distance travelled by a neutron between release at fission, to absorption and fission in another U^{235} nucleus.)
At 300eV the fission cross section of U^{235} is 5×10^{-24} cm^2 and above 300eV neutron energy the diffusion length does not increase with temperature.
This explosive transformation of the U^{235} atoms can only occur in almost pure U^{235}, because the capture bands of the U^{238} isotopes, even where U^{238} is present in only small quantities, still absorb the neutrons.'

The weapon would have been a spherical bomb of almost pure U^{235} of critical radius $10\,\pi\, l$ cm = $31.4\, l$ cm.
This formula, however, is not a formal expression of critical size.
The two important factors on which the calculation is based are the exponential growth in the neutron flux with time and the fission cross section for U^{235} (the average number of neutrons in a beam of 1cm^2 which interact to produce fission on the nuclei of a given area), and neither of these are stated by Heisenberg.
No indication exists as to what Heisenberg had calculated the neutron diffusion length to be for his formula. In forming an opinion as to the critical size of his reactor designs, Heisenberg had underestimated the critical mass of the uranium by 60 per cent and by inference he may also have underestimated the critical mass of the U^{235} bomb initially as well.
The actual critical size of the U^{235} bomb with a reflector of beryllium is 14 kilos of highly enriched uranium, and to amass a quantity of this magnitude in wartime Germany would have been virtually impossible. However, if Heisenberg had misinformed himself as to a critical size substantially less, then this would account for his persisting concern about the U^{235} enrichment question, highlighted on the occasion in 1940

when he was shown a blueprint for a highly efficient isotope separator by the inventor Manfred von Ardenne.

It is significant that both Otto Hahn and von Ardenne reported that when answering the latter's enquiry on the subject, Heisenberg warily informed von Ardenne that 'only a few kilos of U^{235}' was required for a bomb.

In the transcripts of secretly taped conversations of interned German physicists at Farm Hall, Huntingdonshire, in the summer of 1945 (Public Records Office, Kew WO 208/5019), when asked to explain how the Americans could have built the Hiroshima bomb, Heisenberg is on record as having supposed:

'I rather think Harteck was right and that they have just put up 100,000 mass spectrographs or something like that. If each mass spectrograph can make one milligramme a day, then they have got 100 grammes a day.'

The principle on which von Ardenne's invention was based (see Glossary) was the mass spectrograph. But why so many of them?

Because Heisenberg produced a variety of figures for the critical mass of the U^{235} bomb, it seems reasonable to assume that he either deliberately falsified the neutron diffusion length from time to time, or was unable to decide conclusively upon it.

In 1940 he advised von Ardenne that the critical mass was 'just a few kilos'. By February, 1942, it had become 'the size of a pineapple', as he told Wehrmacht chiefs at a conference in Berlin. He confided to fellow internees at Farm Hall in August, 1945, that it was '400 kilos with a heavy reflector', and incredulous British interrogators learned that it would actually be in the region of 'forty tons' when they asked him for his figures at about the same time.

Following the suggestion that it might need 100,000 mass spectrographs to produce enough enriched uranium for one bomb,

Heisenberg: 'That would give them 30 kilos a year.'
Hahn: 'Do you think they would need as much as that?'
Heisenberg: 'I think so certainly, but quite honestly I have never worked it out.'

It is for the reason that a sphere small for its mass loses a significant number of neutrons at its surface at detonation that a hypothetical U^{235} bomb of only a few kilos cannot be exploded (although in theory it can be detonated by compressing the explosive material to a point at which its density exceeds the critical value, i.e. by imploding it). This fortuitiously served to convince those interested in the matter in Germany that the U^{235} bomb was not feasible for a technical reason. No evaluation of the critical mass of a plutonium bomb was undertaken.

Heisenberg considered it right to ensure that the dangers of the working pile were clearly understood:

> 'An extraordinarily intensive neutron and gamma radiation goes hand in hand with energy production. Even in achieving only 10kW power, 10^{15} neutrons and gamma rays are created every second. The radiation is, therefore, 100,000 times greater than that produced in a large cyclotron. Even if a substantial amount of this radiation is absorbed in the core of the pile, nevertheless the working reactor would obviously require the provision of the most comprehensive biological shielding against radiation. This applies especially at the "switching-on" of the machine, i.e. at criticality.
> At the moment when the temperature reaches the stationary value of 100°C, 10^8 calories are used to produce heat leaving an excess of $5 \cdot 10^{19}$ neutrons and gamma rays liberated.'

The most interesting and decisive component of his report is the section which Heisenberg omits to include at all, and it is from this point that the evidence begins to accumulate to the effect that he was a saboteur of Nazi science. Was this omission material, and was it left out from the report for a purpose prejudicial to the success of the project?

He was in a unique position to sabotage the uranium work, since, as the acknowledged senior theoretical physicist, he had been entrusted with the task of formulating the theory from the outset and, having set the guidelines, continued to influence the experimental side of matters until Germany's final surrender.

In the preamble to his report, Heisenberg cited as his principal source of reactor theory an article published in the scientific periodical *Die Naturwissenschaften* on 9 June, 1939, (vol.27, pages 402-410) under the title *Can Technical Use be Made of the Energy Content of Nuclei?* written by the physicist Dr Siegfried Flügge of the Kaiser Wilhelm Institute for Physics at Berlin Dahlem. Under a sub-title *The Control of Chain Reactions* (page 407), Flügge had stated:

> 'The decisive question for the technical application of the mechanism is manifestly this: is it possible to slow the chain

cascade? Adler and Halban (*Nature* Vol.143, 1939, p.739) have entered the debate and suggested the addition of cadmium salts to the mixture beforehand. In the absence of the cadmium, the reaction would soar straightaway to a stationary temperature of 100,000°C.'

Adler and Halban had warned:

> 'The danger that a system containing uranium in high concentration might explode once the chain starts, is considerable.'

The two Frenchmen had suggested that if the first generation of neutrons at the critical point could be kept as small as 1007, then it would be 0.01 seconds before that generation doubled itself and the energy it liberated; it therefore seemed at least theoretically possible to prevent the reactor blowing up by previously leaving in the reactor core an absorbent, such as cadmium.

We now know that the idea of the instantaneously explosive chain reaction in a reactor is grounded in an error of theory caused by the failure to take into the mathematical reckoning the small fraction of relatively long-lived neutrons which are emitted up to a minute after the fission process. These delayed neutrons play the decisive role in the safe controlling of modern atomic energy plants and without them nuclear reactors would not be feasible.

It is to be remembered that this was a fact not known to Heisenberg who believed until after the war, when the Americans let him into the secret, that a critical pile was a large, immobile bomb. In his report G-161 *Observations on the Planned Half-Technical Experiment with 1½ tons of Heavy Water and 3 tons of Uranium Metal* dated 31 July, 1942, the first occasion when he gave voice to the stability problem, Heisenberg pointed out that everything depended on the resonance bands of the U^{238} isotope at the critical instant:

> '...if the breadth of the resonance capture bands is not sufficient to stabilize the assembly, apparently no other process exists to prevent the chain reaction avalanche....in a large reactor this entire proceeding would occupy 0.16 seconds, and involve the immediate fissioning of practically the entire neutron inventory.'

Was his belief that no means existed by which it would be possible to control a chain reaction in a nuclear reactor, which would correspondingly explode a sixth of a second after it went critical, a material detail for his report? And was it unreasonable to conceal that belief from the authorities for two and a half years?

The thing speaks for itself. It was not only a material detail, it was the central pillar of what he had been given to report on. All the geometrical experimentation with uranium and materials was completely valueless if, at the end of the day, the beautiful assembly disintegrated in a blinding flash and a cloud of radioactive débris. It was not a problem to be resolved at the verge of success; it belonged at the very beginning of the project itself. Heisenberg was a saboteur of Nazi science, and this is the first concrete evidence of his work.

Contemplating a hypothetical reactor stabilized at its equilibrium temperature, Heisenberg remarked that the machine would still present an enormous number of operational problems for the extraction of heat energy because it would automatically shut down at certain peaks of temperature and then only resume when the temperature had fallen again. This occurred because of the expansion of materials on heating, resulting in a lowering of density and an alteration in the various cross sections.

An additional effect of the increase in temperature of the reactor is an increase in the width of the energy bands of the U^{238} nuclei owing to the nuclear Doppler Effect. The widening of the capture peaks of the U^{238} isotopes causes the interception and absorption of far more neutrons, resulting in a lessening of the fission occurrence until the reaction collapses altogether.

It was Professor Harteck of the Hamburg 'Bomb-group' who had suggested to Heisenberg that uranium and moderator should be segregated into a heterogeneous design which would be more favourable for the production of an efficient reactor than a homogeneous lump and upon reading Heisenberg's two papers issued in December, 1939, and February, 1940, Harteck immediately saw that the corollary of Heisenberg's comment on temperature was that a very low temperature moderator would not only benefit from the nuclear Doppler Effect, since the capture bands of the U^{238} isotopes would be reduced in subzero temperatures, but would also produce no heat. Thus all the troublesome engineering arrangements inherent in an energy-producing reactor, such as heat transfer, core and fuel cooling and temperature control, were obviated.

So if such a reactor produced no heat and thus no energy, what useful purpose would it serve?

The answer is that it would produce radioisotopes and the intensely radioactive decay products of nuclear fission. Radioisotopes do have modern applications in medicine, biochemistry, biology and industry, but Professor Harteck saw only one use for the dry-ice reactor.

He has admitted[24] that his purpose was to procure for Hitler an abundance of radioisotopes to shower down on the population of Allied cities. The radiation bomb.

A radiation bomb is a device packed with reactor materials with a conventional explosive at its centre which is designed to scatter radioactive material over a wide area for the purpose of causing death, radiation sickness, chronic disease and genetic injury to persons.

In order to understand the effect of deliberately showering a densely populated city with processed reactor waste, it must first be appreciated that radiation kills largely by disrupting the delicate chemistry of living tissue in the body by a process known as ionization. This means that the normal molecular and atomic structure of the human body is altered. If the changes are sufficiently severe, the casualty will die before the biological system has had time to repair the damage. There is no set dosage; it very much depends on the circumstances and the levels received.

The product can be sprayed by an aircraft or delivered by rocket, but the probable ordnance would have been an aerial bomb. A shielded casing containing a core of 800 kilos of conventional high explosive surrounded by 200 kilos of dust mixed with the radioactive fission products from an atomic reactor would give a bomb of just over one ton in mass. A mix of shorter-life nuclides with long-life particles would give high activity for average unit mass so as to ensure that even a small mass of the material would cover a large area with a deadly blanket of radiation. The device would be dropped from an aircraft and deployed by parachute to air-burst for maximum contamination at a height of about a hundred feet from the ground, ideally in dry conditions.

Persons within a 275-metre radius of the point of explosion of the bomb could expect to receive a radiation dosage which would cause death within a period ranging from ten days afterwards to instantaneously. The principal causes would be cerebro-vascular damage affecting the central nervous system and heart and blood vessels. Those surviving the longer period would eventually succumb to gastro-intestinal damage.

Persons further than 275 metres from the point of scatter would receive a dosage which, while not automatically fatal, would probably damage bone marrow and lymphatic tissue so seriously that death would ultimately claim them within one month.

The maximum initial extent of contamination from the point of scatter likely to cause fatality within the first month would be a circle of one mile radius.

This takes no account of the infliction of possible long-term bodily disorders to persons receiving low dosages outside the zone, nor does it contemplate the effect of the radiation dust drifting with the elements afterwards.

Once disseminated, the contamination might continue for centuries, gradually spreading through the atmosphere or by sea and river to surrounding countries.

The initial countermeasure would be the evacuation of the affected area at once. The question of resettlement might be considered a few hundred years later, once the radioactive material had decayed to a safe level.

The radiation bomb was and is the most fiendish weapon of mass terror ever conceived for use against a civilian population and no protection exists against it. It became an attractive nuclear option for the Nazis because substantial quantities of radioactive matter are produced through the breaking-down of the uranium fuel during the normal fission cycle. The waste is cheap and plentiful, and no exposed acreages of separation plant and factory complexes, nor huge financial investment, nor a massive labour force would be required to develop and produce it.

The effect of dropping reactor waste on the population of a city as a means of instilling terror would almost certainly have been sufficient to have had the desired result against any of the Allied belligerents in 1940 and 1941, including the United States which, for both political and ecological reasons, would then have been the most likely recipient of the ordnance, as she was intended to be later.

What are the best indications of the nature and size of Hitler's nuclear weapon?

The eventual V-4 radiation weapon was a one-ton aerial bomb containing 850 kilos of high explosive in a warhead packed around by twelve pumpkin-sized bomblets holding the radioactive matter, totalling 150 kilos in all. This would have exterminated all human life within two to three kilometres from the point of impact.

Against which states would the radiation weapon have been used? Hitler had consistently maintained that Britain and her Empire was a factor in world equilibrium, and that, 'to rub her nose in the mud of defeat would not benefit Germany, only Japan, the United States and others.'

36

Accordingly the war aim of Germany with respect to Britain was to convince the British Government by force and political persuasion that the continuation of the war served no useful purpose, and that Britain should seek to conclude a negotiated peace with Hitler in which he was allowed a free hand on the continent of Europe.

Hitler had no original quarrel with the United States either, but Roosevelt had declared his policy to be the giving of all possible material aid to Britain. The American effort clearly infringed the duty which the United States owed to Germany under the conventions of neutrality then in force and was *ipso facto* a continuing act of war against Germany.

In the event, Hitler refrained from making war upon the United States during the period when he was engaged in attempting to destroy Britain's ability to continue the struggle, even though the assistance rendered to Britain by the United States was critical for Britain's survival. Nowhere was this more apparent than in the Atlantic battle, where Churchill had made it clear that the 'gradually maturing' and ultimately deadly danger was the steady and increasing diminution of Britain's sea tonnage.

The amount of damaged shipping far exceeded the resources available for repair, and with the yards becoming ever more congested, Britain was always falling further behind.

By offering shipyard facilities on her Eastern seaboard and naval protection to merchant vessels, in addition to the enormous supply of contraband war materiel and other essential commodities to the British Isles, the United States had become the major obstacle to a satisfactory conclusion of hostilities with Britain.

It will thus be appreciated how a swift, overwhelming blow against the United States, forcing a permanent cessation of their interference in the European conflict, would have most satisfactorily resolved Hitler's problem in the West.

The dropping of a large radiation bomb on a metropolitan area with heavy population density, such as Manhattan, might have eventually resulted in a million fatalities and seriously impaired the functioning of the city of New York as a whole. The importance of the effect on the American people and their government of the overwhelming and complete surprise of the bomb cannot be overestimated.

The German ultimatum would have required the United States to adopt isolationism as a policy and to act with strict neutrality towards the European belligerents, as she was actually required to do by international law. Whether the President would have capitulated immediately to the Nazi demand or whether further bombings would have been necessary is a matter for speculation, but probably the one would have been sufficient in the face of public tumult. Inevitably, the Americans would also have had to accept the permanent presence of a Gestapo uranium inspectorate on their territory to ensure the Nazi monopoly of the uranium weapons in perpetuity.

The enforcement of a policy of isolationism and strict adherence to neutrality upon the United States would by itself have been so detrimental to the ability of Britain to persevere with the war against Germany that the British Government would have had no realistic alternative but to seek terms from Hitler with little further commotion. The threat of the radiological weapon, the use of which in close proximity to German-held territory Hitler would certainly never have entertained, would nevertheless have undoubtedly convinced the British Government to seek a negotiated peace settlement with Germany.

It is in the light of this line of reasoning that the strategic nature of the radiation bomb can be seen. It was this weapon, and not the atomic bomb, which should have been the decisive weapon in the world conflict, and ought to have brought Hitler victory.

The United States did not achieve criticality in a nuclear reactor until December, 1942, and the atomic bomb did not appear on the world stage until after Hitler was finished.

Thus for three whole years of the Second World War, from 1940 until the end of 1942, the United States left the way clear for Hitler's atomic physicists to design and develop the radiation weapon which should have obtained for Hitler the final triumph, the Nazi domination of the world.

The impotence of the United States and Britain at this most dangerous juncture of world history illustrates how vast was Heisenberg's contribution to the resistance to Hitler.

He had taken upon himself the thankless task of denying Hitler nuclear power; for so long as the Third Reich endured, Heisenberg's success had to be measured in terms of his own failure to build a working reactor.

Equally important was the prevention of evidence tending to show that a particular effort in one direction or another would lead quickly to a successful chain reaction.

The first test arrived within a matter of weeks, when Professor Paul Harteck, who had thoughtfully studied Heisenberg's early thesis, was suddenly inspired by a notion of brilliant simplicity.

Dry ice sublimates relatively slowly at a temperature of -78°C and is as pure as one part in a million. In addition, the oxygen atoms do not absorb neutrons in significant quantities at very low temperatures.

Concluding that carbon dioxide ice was an ideal moderator for his proposed pile, Professor Harteck suggested to the Heereswaffenamt that consideration be given to the planned arrangement and went ahead with it at once.

On 8 April, 1940, availing himself of his useful contacts with the firm of I.G.Farben, he induced the firm's research director, Dr Herold, to make him a gift of a 15 ton block of dry ice to be delivered in the period immediately preceding the end of May when commercial demand for the product was poor.

The War Office agreed to supply a railway wagon at short notice to expedite the consignment from Merseburg to Hamburg, where the pilot experiment was to take place, and Harteck approached Diebner in a letter unwisely putting the low figure of 300 kilos of uranium required because he thought that that 'was all that was available'.

It will probably never be know what machinations were practised on Diebner by Heisenberg and his accomplices to wreck Harteck's experiment. It must have been perfectly obvious to all concerned that in preparing to take possession of a 15 ton block of dry ice, a substance of which he could not obtain a resupply until after the summer, Harteck would implicitly perform his experiment within a week of its receipt.

Diebner had only 150 kilos of uranium oxide at the Berlin Dahlem Institute, but Heisenberg was waiting for the execution of a large order with the War Office and may have been holding a hoard as well; Diebner promised him that his indent would be met in June and asked him to settle the matter privately with Harteck.

Heisenberg suggested to Harteck in a letter that he was overstating the urgency of the Hamburg experiment, since there were a number of preparations to make first:

> 'Of course, if there is for any reason any urgency in your experiments, you can go first by all means. But I should like to suggest that for the time being you content yourself with just 100 kilograms.'[25]

He concluded by indicating in the most reasonable vein that he was quite prepared to let Diebner make the final decision.

Harteck replied by return, reciting all the compelling reasons for his obvious urgency, and begged Heisenberg to let him have on loan from 20 May, for three weeks at the most, as much of the Leipzig stock as he could see his way clear to releasing.

In the expectation that Heisenberg would relent, Harteck implored Dr Herold in Merseburg to delay shipping the ice until the last possible moment and contacted Diebner on two occasions to emphasize his need for a minimum supply of 600 kilos of the oxide for a meaningful experiment and to ask for an estimate of what he could expect to receive.

Towards the end of May Berlin Dahlem let him have 50 kilos on loan and a few days later Dr Riehl of the Auer Company personally brought him 135 kilos more. Neither Heisenberg nor anybody else sent him any.

Thus, when the block of dry ice moderator arrived in the first week of June, the experiment was already doomed and the only useful information it yielded was the first criteria for the distribution of neutron density in certain arrangements of uranium and moderator.

The importance of this sabotage was that it prevented Harteck obtaining definite proof of neutron multiplication enabling the critical size of a low temperature CO_2 reactor to be determined. Armed with this information, Harteck would have been able to approach weapons designers directly, allowing the SS to take over the entire programme to its successful conclusion later in 1940.

Wirtz[26] has confirmed that if Harteck had received what he wanted by way of uranium oxide, he would have obtained positive neutron multiplication and the necessary coefficient to calculate the critical size for his reactor, a point subsequently reiterated by Harteck himself.[27]

That Heisenberg deliberately obstructed Harteck's experiment becomes more obvious when his activities from May to December, 1940, are examined. The only pile attempted in 1940 was the Berlin Dahlem model built by Wirtz, Fischer and Bopp; Heisenberg rendered only two scientific papers on the uranium project to the Heereswaffenamt respecting his work.

In *Determination of the Diffusion Length of Thermal Neutrons in Heavy Water*[28] dated 7 August, 1940, he described his findings in which he had employed 9 litres of heavy water and 480 mg of a radium-beryllium source in which no uranium oxide had been employed at all.

In *Determination of the Diffusion Length of Thermal Neutrons in Preparation 38 (Uranium Oxide)*[29] published in December, 1940, he reported on his investigations into small samples of uranium oxide confined in a sphere of 12 cm radius. What use, therefore, Heisenberg had at Leipzig in 1940 for the ton of uranium oxide he ordered remains a mystery.

Shortly before the miscarriage of Harteck's pilot experiment in early June, German forces invaded Holland, Luxembourg, Belgium and

France in their successful western offensive and on the way captured the Belgian town of Oolen. At the warehouses of the Union Minière Company they duly found a quantity of uranium oxide totalling over 1200 tons and 1000 tons of sodium uranate, ferro-uranium and other refined materials which M. Sengier had most thoughtfully arranged to be there for them.

This was a most auspicious acquisition, because the Germans now held virtually all the uranium in Europe, and far more than they would ever need for weapons purposes.

There was in fact so much uranium available that Professor Harteck proceeded to plan his ambitious second experiment, a heterogeneous design consisting of 20 tons of uranium oxide in a lattice of shafts embedded throughout a 30-ton block of dry ice.

Upon announcing it, he began to encounter almost immediately the determined opposition of Heisenberg and presumably von Weizsäcker and others.

Heisenberg's critique was directed at the size of the experiment, informing Harteck that all he would learn from his project would be a great deal about 20 tons of dirty uranium oxide and perhaps something about 30 tons of pure dry ice, but whether Harteck thought that was something worthwhile he didn't know.

He expected that it would not work, however, because the uranium oxide would have to go to the chemical factory for purification first.

Harteck then came under growing pressure from other quarters, most probably orchestrated by Heisenberg, who argued that it was 'too extravagant' for a first experiment to use 50 tons of materials to do the whole programme at once, and Heisenberg returned to the attack by remonstrating about the unprofessional approach to the experiment.

Harteck bitterly conceded defeat, refusing to accept their opinion. He resented Heisenberg's attitude in particular, commenting that, to his knowledge, Heisenberg had never contributed a single basic idea leading towards the solution of the uranium fission problem; the decision to appoint a theoretical physicist who had never been involved in a large experimental venture before as the leader of a technological enterprise was not merely poor judgement, it was simply unbelievable. After all, the physics involved was not so complicated; the major problems concerned physical chemistry and technology.

Harteck attributed Germany's failure to produce a nuclear weapon to the antagonistic attitude existing between the theoretical physicists and the experimentalists; the former considered the latter as beneath them: 'a few egotists pushed the others aside'.

It is interesting to note, in connection with the alleged grounds of his objection to Harteck's second proposed experiment, the conclusions Heisenberg drew as regards the qualities of the respective oxides examined and reported on in his December, 1940, paper:

> 'Part of the purpose of this experiment was to compare the purity of the Belgian oxide with the product from the Auer Company in Berlin. The results summarized showed that from the measured values there was no detectable difference in the neutron scatter and absorption as between the two oxides.... even the slight contamination of the Belgian oxide with molybdenum would be unlikely to affect the neutron absorption level by about one per cent, and such a small difference as was detected fell within the set tolerances.'

In conclusion, Harteck considered how the dry ice low-temperature reactor would have placed Germany's nuclear programme on an entirely different footing, remarking to his interviewer:

> 'You must be thankful this didn't occur. Not that an atomic bomb would have been made. But if you have a carbon dioxide reactor and you let it run for a certain time, the cubes or rods of uranium would have become highly radioactive. Much radioactive material could have been made which could have been thrown about. That would have been very bad.'[30]

In the summer of 1940, measurements of the effective capture cross-sections of possible moderators were carried out, and in the most important of these, Heisenberg and Döpel worked on heavy water, and the Heidelberg experimentalists, Bothe and Peter Jensen, examined the carbonaceous substance electro-graphite.

In a paper reporting their results under the title *The Absorption of Thermal Neutrons in Electro-Graphite* dated 20 January, 1941,[31] Bothe stated that experiments on the purest carbon commercially available, electro-graphite from the Siemens Company, showed the rate of neutron capture to be so high as to preclude its use as a moderator.

Professors Joos and Hanle, who were back in circulation at the University of Göttingen following their release from conscription, submitted research bulletins to the Heereswaffenamt even though they were not affiliated to the official programme. Their treatise *Concerning the Existence of Boron and Cadmium in Carbon*[32] submitted to the Heereswaffenamt on 18 April, 1941, contradicted Bothe's erroneous opinion and highlighted his failure to detect the neutron absorbers boron and cadmium in the Siemens sample. The reduction of the graphite to ash for purpose of measuring its impurities had destroyed them, whereas Bothe had assumed that the impurities would survive the combustion.

Joos and Hanle had concluded by describing a method of producing moderator graphite of acceptable purity.

The Heereswaffenamt admitted the contradictory report and accepted that graphite was suitable as a moderator[33] and now found itself bound to decide between the two proposed substances, graphite and heavy water, on economic grounds.

A probable configuration for a reactor moderated by deuterium oxide had been estimated as 5 tons each of uranium and heavy water.

The production of 5 tons of heavy water by electrolysis required half a million tons of coal, but the important consideration in the equation was the fact that Germany now exercised control over the world's only major heavy-water-producing plant at Rjukan in Norway, which would relieve German industry of the burden of meeting the coal requirement.

As an alternative to the use of heavy water, Heisenberg had presumably calculated by now that a reactor moderated by electro-graphite required up to 40 tons of uranium and about ten times that quantity of the purest graphite. Production of such a quantity of graphite consumed 3,240 tons of steel electrode material leading in turn to a shortfall of 432,000 tons of steel. A bottleneck in the supply of graphite already existed and was being exacerbated by the demands of the rocket project. The V-2 rocket was fitted with a jet rudder assembly of graphite in order that the fins could withstand the extreme temperatures of the burning gases which engulfed them for the duration of the rocket's flight. The rocket programme had a higher priority rating that the atomic programme.

The production of a special graphite with enhanced purity to fulfil a recurrent demand at a prohibitive cost could, therefore, not be entertained. A moderator of graphite blocks would need regular replacement owing to radioactive contamination. Heavy water cannot be contaminated and can be used indefinitely.

It was on these grounds that the Heereswaffenamt decided that heavy water was to be the preferred moderator.

It is just barely conceivable that, in order to suppress any further investigation, they decided not to circulate the report of Joos and Hanle and copies of their own decision, which would justify Heisenberg's dubious assertion after the war that he did not come to know of it. Bothe's purported error in the estimation of impurities in German electro-graphite was, therefore, not an error of any consequence, but the question of whether it actually was an error remains open.

As an opponent of the Nazi régime, Bothe had been roughly deposed from the directorship of the Physics Institute at the University of Heidelberg in 1933 upon the accession to power of the Nazis and had been so harshly treated that he retired for a long period to a Badenweiler sanatorium. On his recovery, Professor Planck appointed him to the Kaiser Wilhem Institute of Physics at Heidelberg in 1937. Bothe had been frequently accused of scientific fraud by the Nazis in the pre-war period and, as will shortly be seen, it is more likely than not that his 'error' was deliberate and occurred at the instigation of Heisenberg.

Professors Bothe and Jensen, who had conducted the faulty absorption cross-section measurements of carbon at Heidelberg, had predicted in an extension to their report, subsequently confirmed later in an experiment with Professor Fünfer, that not only was graphite suitable for use as the reflecting material enclosing the core of the reactor, the purpose of which was to scatter back into the reaction those neutrons escaping at the perimeter, but that it was almost certainly the best reflector.

This was a most important conclusion and it is highly significant that not until January, 1945, did Heisenberg first use graphite as a reflector in any of his experiments, even though he had clearly arrived at the same conclusion himself by virtue of theoretical calculations in December, 1939.

In order to obtain a self-sustaining chain reaction, the obvious alternative to heat machines moderated by heavy water or graphite was the construction of a nuclear pile moderated by a liquid carbon compound at a very low temperature. The fission products would have produced benefits for the services in the form of luminous paints for cockpit dials and radioisotopes for various applications in medical research and as tracers in other branches of science and industry. Nowadays it might be widely argued that the latter uses of nuclear energy have been its greatest benefits to mankind.

Whereas the possibility of producing the artificial element, plutonium, and other fiercely radioactive isotopes in a simple, very cold reactor was naïvely indicated for the first time in a publication by the physicist, Houtermans, in August, 1941, it is clear that until that point, Heisenberg had successfully steered reactor designs into the orthodox channel and away from the refrigerated-moderator concept. Any mention of the subject was ruthlessly avoided or suppressed.

Hitler's opportunity for world conquest was thwarted by Heisenberg in the years 1940 and 1941, at which time the enemies of Nazi Germany were vulnerable to defeat by radiological weaponry in the form of nuclear waste.

By the time when the critical decision was taken by Hitler to build the radiation bomb in the autumn of 1941, following the publication of Houtermans' paper, Heisenberg had bought for the world just enough time to ensure that the weapon could no longer bring Hitler victory.

The Heisenberg-Döpel paper published from the University of Leipzig on 7 August, 1940, had concluded that the reactor moderated by heavy water would definitely come to the boil, and the irrepressible Harteck, who had studied heavy water in England under Lord Rutherford, now turned his attention to a consideration of how it could be mass-produced economically.

Water has excellent braking properties on neutrons, but neutrons are absorbed by the hydrogen atoms in ordinary water (H_2O). In heavy water (D_2O), the hydrogen atoms have been removed so that the liquid which is left consists only of its deuterium atoms. For this reason, heavy water is an exceptionally efficient moderator when used with natural uranium because neutrons collide with deuterium molecules in the water, but are not absorbed by them.

There is only one deuterium atom to every 6,760 atoms of hydrogen. When ordinary water is electrolyzed, the gas produced at the cathode is mostly hydrogen; if this is drawn off, the water remaining will have a slightly enriched deuterium content. The electrolysis, when repeated continually, will ultimately result in pure deuterium oxide.

Such a proceeding is extremely expensive; at Rjukan, 1000 kwh of electricity was required to turn out a single gramme of heavy water. In 1940 the world's only large production facility for heavy water was at Vemork near Rjukan in Norway, about 200 kilometres west of Oslo, where the firm Norsk Hydro operated a factory manufacturing ammonium nitrate for the fertilizer industry. Their hydrogen-electrolysis process was powered by generators installed at the foot of the Rjukan Foss Waterfall, and heavy water was a by-product of this operation.

In 1939 the plant was producing 10 kilos of heavy water per month, but when the Germans inspected the complex, soon after the occupation of Norway by their forces in 1940, they saw that, by using a catalytic exchange process, they could increase the output of heavy water tenfold without unduly compromising the primary purpose of the plant, which was the production of nitrogen. However, by the end of October, 1941, no useful quantity had yet found its way to Germany.

The suggestion has been made on more than one occasion that since

Professor von Weizsäcker reported in July, 1940, on the theoretical formation of a new nuclear explosive, now known as plutonium, in the fission products of an operating pile, then both he and Heisenberg must have wanted to build a plutonium bomb for Hitler.

Before considering the evidence as to whether that allegation is true or not, two useful by-products of such a report must be mentioned. In volunteering the information in advance of the field, the authorities were supplied with concrete evidence that the Heisenberg group was intent on working in the national interest, a most important consideration for saboteurs of Nazi science, and a factor which tended to strengthen their moral position within the national project with a view to influencing the direction of research. One of the policy purposes of Heisenberg's clique was to bestow upon the uranium project an aura of significance to the war effort so as to enable a claim to be made for the release and return of conscripted young physicists serving at the various battle fronts.

In the American scientific periodical *Physical Review* published on 1 September, 1939, Niels Bohr and John Wheeler, of Princeton University, expounded a theory under the title *The Mechanics of Nuclear Fission* which stated that if during the fission process the U^{238} nucleus (Element 92) absorbed two successive neutrons, then the binding energies in the new compound structure should be so high as to render it even more fissionable then U^{235}.

Professor von Weizsäcker obtained a copy of the June, 1940, issue of the same journal, the last available internationally, in the following month. In a letter submitted by two American physicists, proof was offered of the existence of neptunium ^{239}Np (Element 93) in research on the Berkeley cyclotron. This tended to validate the Bohr-Wheeler hypothesis and led to the assumption that the transformation series was probably fissionable in the same way that U^{235} was fissionable.

The decay series is actually:

$$U^{238} + 1 \text{ neutron} \dashrightarrow U^{239} \xrightarrow[\text{23.5 minutes}]{\text{beta ray}} {}^{239}\text{Np (Neptunium)}$$

and then

$$^{239}\text{Np} \xrightarrow[\text{2.33 days}]{\text{beta ray}} {}^{239}\text{Pu (Element 94 Plutonium)}$$

In his report *G59-Concerning the Possibility of Extracting Energy from U^{238}* to the Heereswaffenamt, Professor von Weizsäcker left the question open as to whether atomic decay proceeded further beyond ^{239}Np; if it did, it would possibly be fissionable, he suggested, but since there was no cyclotron in Germany, the elements could not be prepared in a sufficient quantity for their nuclear properties and chemical composition to be examined.

This lame excuse is further evidence of the way in which Heisenberg and von Weizsäcker held back research into the development of nuclear weapons and reactors. The radioisotopes of plutonium are created abundantly in any reactor irrespective of whether it is a heat machine or a very-low-temperature model, and both men were very well aware that the simplest method of attempting to get a reactor critical and obtaining plutonium for laboratory work was a low-temperature assembly such as Harteck's proposed dry-ice reactor. Had it been the intention of either Professor von Weizsäcker or Professor Heisenberg to provide Hitler with nuclear weapons, then this would have been the obvious starting point.

The Viennese experimenters Hernegger and Schintlmeister had both reached virtually the same conclusions about plutonium as von Weizsäcker at about the same time, but did not lodge their paper in Berlin until December.

In rebuttal of Heisenberg's repeated claims that the purpose of his group (consisting of himself and Professors von Weizsäcker and Peter Jensen of Heidelberg) was to function as a passive resistance to Hitler, the question is frequently put demanding to know why it was necessary to draw the attention of the Heereswaffenamt to the possibility of a second type of nuclear explosive which was possibly simpler to produce than enriched U^{235}.

However, it must always be recalled that the group's contemporary appreciation of the mathematics of nuclear reactions had as its basis a belief in two sets of theoretical calculations, both of which were false: that the amount of U^{235} required for a bomb was a matter of only a few kilos, and that a power reactor, in which plutonium might be bred, was incapable of control.

Their policy was therefore intended to deflect attention from the U^{235} bomb to the plutonium bomb. The emphasis on the latter, intended to influence the authorities prejudicially, was particularly noticeable early in 1942 when the newly appointed Armaments Minister, Speer, was agitating for the abandonment of the V-Weapons programme, which he rightly considered to be a white elephant, in favour of the atomic bomb.

Heisenberg saw that the building of formidable underground separation plants for the enrichment of quantities of the order of several kilos of U^{235} was an engineering operation which would have required a tremendous industrial effort, but with the help of the large electrical combines and almost unlimited slave labour it would not have been beyond Germany's capabilities, particularly if the 5 billion Reichsmarks invested in the V-1 and V-2 development programmes had been applied instead to isotope enrichment. This was undoubtedly why a blueprint in 1940 for the excellent von Ardenne electro-magnetic isotope separator (see Glossary), which in practice was a better version of the American design used at Oak Ridge, was treated by Heisenberg so pejoratively.

Professor Heisenberg was under the impression that two major barriers existed to the creation of plutonium, of which the principal one was his false belief in the explosive instability of power reactors.

A certain premeditation can be discerned in the handling of the second problem, concerning the reactor moderator.

Plutonium (Pu^{239}) is present in irradiated uranium in the reactor in the proportion of 250 parts per million. Since the critical mass of the plutonium bomb is about 5 kilos, the minimum quantity of uranium required from which that amount of plutonium may be extracted is at the very least 20 tons.

A heavy water reactor uses uranium fuel and heavy water in roughly equal quantities, and the cycle of a plutonium breeding reactor may exceed a year. By 1944 Germany's best efforts had provided her with a total of 2½ tons of heavy water in all, and this production problem was certainly foreseeable in 1940. Even after Harteck's chemists had managed to supply this miserable amount in full, it was obvious that the minimum of 5 kilos required for a single bomb would still have taken perhaps another seven or eight years to amass. Heisenberg recalled [34] anticipating that the achievement of a working reactor could be delayed for about three years until sufficient heavy water was available (conveniently forgetting to mention that at the time he also thought that he would be additionally hampered by the destruction of the reactor at criticality), after which a further number of years would have been needed to accumulate enough plutonium for a bomb. By then, he considered that Nazi Germany would have been defeated.

Despite his belief in the explosive instability of power reactors, Heisenberg was always obliged to proceed on the assumption that his theory might be incorrect. His great fear was the moderator carbon as an alternative to heavy water, but not essentially because of the explosive plutonium; to postpone criticality indefinitely was vital to the primary objective, the prevention of radiological weapons using fission products from the reactor.

A large power reactor could be built using graphite in which the uranium fuel would vastly exceed 30 tons. Accordingly, what neither Heisenberg's inner circle, nor their anti-Nazi colleague, Professor Bothe, wanted was a report proving that graphite was suitable as a moderator. It so happened that Bothe was to work shortly on this very subject, and the results of measurements reported by Professors Bothe and Peter Jensen came to the curious conclusion, as previously remarked, that although graphite was an excellent reflector, it was impracticable as a moderator.

This outcome was so convenient that there must have been collusion between Heisenberg and Bothe, who were on the best of terms, to have graphite condemned. It should not be overlooked that Professor Peter Jensen, who was co-author of the report *G-71 The Absorption of Thermal Neutrons in Electro-Graphite* (January, 1941), was the third member of Heisenberg's circle of three conspirators.

Once graphite had been eliminated, it was then safe for Heisenberg to speak preferentially for plutonium, since its prospects were hopeless. But this happy state of affairs was not to endure for very long, as will shortly be seen.

In the period from June, 1940, to December, 1941, scientific groups working at laboratories scattered across Germany, Austria and occupied France submitted over 100 reports on aspects of the uranium research ranging from materials measurement to isotope separation, heavy water production and experiments with various sub-critical uranium/moderator assemblies. The latter were conducted at three principal centres: the Kaiser Wilhelm Institute at Berlin Dahlem, the laboratory at Gottow and at Heisenberg's Leipzig Institute.

Owing to the shortage of uranium metal and heavy water, it was frequently necessary to substitute uranium oxide and paraffin wax for these in the experiments. This was a somewhat ponderous method of obtaining useful information and the important advance of observing a positive neutron multiplication was not to be achieved until the unexpected success of Heisenberg's L-IV test at Leipzig using the best materials in May, 1942.

The really crucial work of the 1941 period was not performed by the official project at all, but by the Post Office Research Institute under Baron Manfred von Ardenne at his Lichterfelde-Ost laboratory in Berlin. Early in September, 1941, Heisenberg had been horrified to receive a copy of the relevant technical treatise in which Professor Fritz Houtermans explained how, from a practical standpoint, a chain reaction could be simply and effectively brought about by the use of a liquid carbon-based moderator in a very low-temperature reactor.

The Post Office research was independently funded and Heisenberg was virtually powerless to interfere; he could also be certain that in the likely event that the Nazi Postmaster-General, Dr Wilhelm Ohnesorge, had read the paper, the possibilities for radiological and plutonium weapons production would already have been elucidated to the Führer.

With the greatest respect to Heisenberg, it may not be unfair to suggest that Houtermans was possibly the most brilliant physicist in the field of chain reaction theory in the Third Reich. He was hopelessly compromised by his Jewish lineage and known communist sympathies, and may have produced the work against his better judgement. His thesis was immediately recognized as an extraordinarily dangerous development by Heisenberg, who subsequently recorded in his autobiography that a faction comprising himself, von Weizsäcker, Wirtz, Paul Jensen and Houtermans met on several occasions to discuss the implications of the report and what could be done to counteract it. It was the appearance of the grisly spectre of fission weaponry for Hitler that ultimately motivated Heisenberg's celebrated mission to his former tutor, Niels Bohr, in Copenhagen that autumn in the forlorn hope that Bohr might agree to act as intermediary between Heisenberg and Allied atomic physicists in a combination aimed at preventing the general development of nuclear arsenals. This episode is more closely treated at a later stage (infra, pp. 109-111).

In contrasting the simplicity of the postulated cold reactor against the nuclear heat machine, Houtermans' paper drew renewed attention to the problem of temperature increase in the latter and specifically referred to the articles by Dr Siegfried Flügge (*Naturwissenschaften 27, 1939*) and the Frenchmen Halban et al (*Nature 143, 1939*) in which they had warned that the timely failure to collapse the chain reaction in the heat machine at criticality would lead to an immediate explosion with radiation release and melt-down. It will be recalled that this so-called problem was an error of theory resulting from the Germans' failure to appreciate the stabilizing effects of delayed neutrons emitted by the split nucleus after the initial fission process. Heisenberg, who correspondingly believed that it was going to be impossible to control a chain reaction in a heat reactor and who had deliberately neglected to give warning of this fact in his two pioneering papers in 1939, probably as a device to string out the research until the war's end, had thus been informed for the second time; but it would be some considerable time yet before he considered it to be propitious to put the card face up on the table.

On 3 December, 1941, the Armaments Minister, Dr Fritz Todt, notified Hitler of the faltering state of the military economy and bluntly advised him that any unplanned future expansion would have to be financed from the budgets of other departments. Consequently, Professor Erich Schumann, the Director of Military Research at the Heereswaffenamt, ordered a reappraisal of the uranium project and warned leading scientists that the continued financial support of the War Office for the nuclear project was dependent on the promise of a definite military application being made for the short term.

On 16 December, following a conference of the Directors of the various Physics Institutes at the Heereswaffenamt Headquarters, the preparation of a detailed report on the progress of the uranium research was embarked upon for the information of the Head of Army Ordnance, General Leeb. Whereas this report was positive in recommending that the industrial exploitation of nuclear power would work to the benefit of both the general economy and the Wehrmacht, Professor Schumann was not convinced and all the signs were clearly visible that the military would relinquish the project even before the review had been completed.

In January, 1942, it was agreed at a meeting of Professor Schumann, General Leeb and Dr Vögler, the President of the Kaiser Wilhelm Foundation, that the latter organization would take over the research in harness with the Reich Research Council, an agency of the Ministry of Education and Science.

Professor Abraham Esau, who had been ordered to desist from competing against the War Office in uranium research in 1939, was appointed scientific head of the new arrangement while the Education Minister, Rust, would be its President.

It was also confirmed that the Army research team under Dr Diebner was to retain a measure of independence under the restructuring and would continue to be subject to War Office control. As if to underline the insignificance which the Heereswaffenamt now attached to the uranium project, Professors von Weizsäcker and Harteck were served conscription papers in that month for military service on the Russian Front, and Heisenberg was obliged to exert all his influence to persuade Professor Schumann to rescind the orders and restore the two physicists to their reserved occupations.

The first convention of the Reich Research Council was held at its Berlin Steglitz Headquarters on 26 February, 1942, under the chairmanship of Reichsminister Rust. There was an agenda of eight ten-minute lectures by senior atomic physicists and chemists including Hahn, Bothe, Esau, Harteck and Schumann.

It had been expected that Nazi Party leaders, Himmler, Goering, Speer, Keitel and Bormann among others, would attend the assembly, but an agenda couched in highly scientific language had unfortunately been enclosed in error together with the invitations, and all had excused themselves from attending.

Heisenberg spoke on *The Theoretical Principles of Obtaining Energy from the Fissioning of Uranium*, and after explaining to his audience the simple mechanics of neutron increase and mortality, and its significance to chain reactions, he commented briefly on the enormous difficulties involved in enriching the U^{235} isotope to weapons grade. Moreover, there was an apparently impossible technical problem yet to be overcome beyond that, for he indicated that if only:

> 'one could assemble a lump of U^{235} of a size *such that the loss of neutrons at the surface were small in comparison with the multiplication in the core*, then there would be a sudden, enormous inflation in the number of neutrons and the combined fission energies of 15 billion calories per ton would be released in a fraction of a second.'

This statement was obviously intended to convince those Nazi military and political leaders for whose consumption the discourse had been prepared that atomic bombs were technically unfeasible.

The scientific reasoning behind the statement has already been examined, (pp. 31-2), and the description of the technical problem is couched in such negative language that one sees the problem as insurmountable.

Various historians (notably Margaret Gowing, *Britain and Atomic Energy 1939-1945*, pp.30, 42) have stated that the Germans appear not to have considered the question of fast fission chain reactions. This is clearly incorrect. The principle was appreciated, but the attitude of Heisenberg's dominant group was negative. After the war, in surprisingly acrimonious reflections on the subject (Ermenc, op.cit.), Harteck attributed Germany's failure to go for the atomic bomb to poor organization and to the attitude of Heisenberg's group.

Gowing also stated that the critical size of a U^{235} bomb appeared not to have been investigated, but Heisenberg would hardly have bothered to expound the principle of neutron surface loss in a sphere of critical mass if he had not first informed himself, albeit inaccurately, of the critical mass involved.

On the other hand, David Irving's assertion (*The German Atomic Bomb* p.92) that Professor Houtermans in his 1941 paper *G94 On the Question of Initiating Nuclear Chain Reactions* had made 'explicit calculations as to the critical mass of U^{235}' and 'had pondered the importance of fast neutron chain reactions' is not correct. Houtermans made no mention of the former and considered fast neutrons only in connection with the question of determining whether a chain reaction was possible with fast neutrons in natural uranium, i.e. in a reactor.

Heisenberg certainly knew the critical mass of the U^{235} bomb by 1945: at a physics colloquium in captivity in England in the week following Hiroshima he was surprised with a question as to the size of the American device and gave his estimate as 14 kilos, which was correct.

Piecemeal transcripts of the German physicists' secretly tape-recorded private conversations at Farm Hall, England, were included by General Leslie Groves in his book (pp.336-340).

Following the release of the full documentation by the London Public Records Office in February, 1992, it became apparent that General Groves had not been entirely honest in reporting what was supposed to have been said in these top secret conversations. For example he had stated (p.336) that the transcripts proved that Heisenberg 'had not thought of using the bomb designs we had used: ours took advantage of fast neutrons... the Germans thought they would have to drop a whole reactor.'

This was his understanding of Heisenberg's remark to his colleagues that:

> 'I knew it could be done with U^{235} using fast neutrons. That's why U^{235} alone can be used as an explosive. They can never make an explosive with slow neutrons, not even with the heavy water reactor.'

Concluding his Berlin Steglitz address with a mention of plutonium, Heisenberg spoke of it as an explosive with the same characteristics as U^{235}. That it was presumably endowed with the same physical disadvantages as U^{235} was not a matter discussed, Heisenberg emphasizing merely that it was easier to obtain, since it could be separated from the irradiated fuel in a nuclear reactor by chemical processes.

Possibly Heisenberg considered it to be inopportune to inform his audience that he thought a nuclear reactor would blow up within one second of going critical, since he made no mention of this aspect of the research.

Heisenberg was to remark later that, following this Reich Research Council conference in February, 1942, substantial funds became available to the project for the first time once Rust had been persuaded that the nuclear power reactor was definitely possible of construction.

On 8 February, 1942, the Armaments Minister, Dr Fritz Todt, was killed in mysterious circumstances in an air crash, and the following day Albert Speer was appointed to succeed him.

Speer reported[35] that he soon found his efforts to promote atomic physics research, by which he presumably meant the development of the atom bomb, were met by a 'rubber wall'.

On one such occasion he was astonished to encounter strident opposition in the party organ *Völkischer Beobachter*, which railed against him in an editorial captioned: 'JEWISH PHYSICS STIRS AGAIN!'

Speer also found it easy to incur the displeasure of the Führer in even mentioning the atom bomb, which Hitler privately described to him as the 'spawn of Jewish pseudo-science'.

In another of his postwar publications[36], the Armaments Minister recalled that although Hitler did speak to him occasionally of the possibilities of the atom bomb, the strategic benefits of having the weapon appeared to Speer to be beyond Hitler's mental grasp.

However, what Speer says about atomic affairs is best treated with a great deal of caution. It was clear to him that there was in existence some sort of secret arrangement involving the Post Office respecting which he was being left completely in the dark, and this appeared to be a matter on which, as Armaments Minister, he really ought to have been consulted. This was a source of irritation to Speer.

Explaining that there were 2200 recorded points of reference in his conferences with Hitler, and that there was only a single occasion when the subject of nuclear research appeared on the agenda, being passed over 'with laconic brevity', Speer noted Hitler's strengthening resolve not to pursue the matter.

The second of Hitler's objections to the atom bomb, and much more deeply entrenched, was his reservation that the atomic explosion might proceed to ignite the hydrogen in the atmosphere.

This was a point on which his physicists were unable to offer him any reassurance; even at Los Alamos on 15 July, 1945, the Italian-American physicist, Fermi, had wondered aloud whether the test bomb he was about to ignite might trigger the heavens, destroying every living thing on earth. Nobody really knew, and Speer confirmed this to be a major source of concern to Hitler, who saw no advantage in destroying the world.

Early in August, 1944, the German TranSozean Innendienst news agency reported the following extract from the Swedish newspaper, *Stockholms Tidningen*:

'In the United States, scientific experiments are being carried out on a new bomb. Its explosive substance is uranium, and when the elements within its structure are liberated, a force of hitherto undreamed-of violence is generated.

A 5 kilo bomb could create a crater one kilometre deep and of 40 kilometres radius.'

In his long discussion with Marshall Antonescu of Rumania on 5 August, 1944[37], a date by when he certainly would have had the news agency report drawn to his attention, Hitler enlarged upon his fears.

Touching upon the subject of a certain new explosive substance whose development had now been brought to the experimental stage, the German leader remarked upon having gained the impression that the leap from explosives currently in use to the new material under discussion was greater than that from gunpowder to the stage of explosives development at the outbreak of war.

When Marshall Antonescu replied that he personally hoped not to be alive when this new substance came into use, which might perhaps bring about the end of the world, Hitler recalled reading a German writer who had predicted just that; ultimately it would lead to a point where matter as such would disintegrate, bringing about the final catastrophe.

Hitler expressed the hope that the scientists and weapons designers working on this new explosive would not attempt to use it until they were quite sure that they understood what they were dealing with.

It will, therefore, be seen that a threefold combination of Nazi scientific racism, fear for the environmental consequences and the daunting industrial investment was the basis for Hitler's rejection of a German atom bomb.

This was not a matter communicated to Germany's atomic physicists or to the military chiefs of staff and, in ignorance of the decision at the highest level, the physicists and military leaders continued to act in the belief that the matter was still open. Heisenberg, for instance, had never denied that an atomic bomb was possible, although he considered the plutonium bomb to be unfeasible, and accordingly he sought to lay stress on the stupendous industrial effort and cost inherent in isotope enrichment for the U^{235} bomb, thus diverting interest towards the plutonium bomb.

Perhaps the most significant example of his repertoire in this respect with his performance at the meeting held on or about 4 June, 1942, at the Berlin Dahlem Headquarters of the Kaiser Wilhelm Institute when Hahn, Wirtz, Heisenberg, Diebner, Harteck and Thiessen met with

Armaments Minister Speer, Saur, his technical chief, Field-Marshal Milch and various representatives of ordnance production from the three services. Dr Albert Vögler and Dr Ernst Telschow attended on behalf of the Direction of the Kaiser Wilhelm Foundation.

While the purpose of the conference was to determine priorities for future nuclear policy with a military emphasis, Heisenberg identified this as merely another purse to be tapped for money towards research. He vacillated about how much he should request for fear that if he gave the impression that the atom bomb might be built before the war's end, then he might be asked to make one.[38]

In his address, Heisenberg went immediately onto the offensive and described how atomic bombs could be made, information much to the surprise of Vögler and Telschow, who had only thought of the reactor in terms of its industrial applications.

At the end of his lecture, when Field-Marshal Milch enquired how big such a bomb might be, Heisenberg replied that the explosive core would be, 'about as large as a pineapple', but then hastened to damp down the stirrings of excitement amongst service chiefs by pointing out that on economic grounds no such development was foreseeable in Germany.

When asked by Milch how long he estimated it would be before the United States had such a weapon, Heisenberg told him that once the Americans had a uranium pile running, it would be about two years after that, so possibly at the earliest by the summer of 1944; Heisenberg and von Weizsäcker had agreed earlier that it seemed prudent to go on record as having given advance warning just in case the Americans actually did drop a nuclear bomb on Germany. It will be noticed that the bomb under consideration here was the plutonium device which Heisenberg considered to be possible in theory, but not in practice.

After the conclusion of the day's business, Speer drew Heisenberg aside and asked him whether nuclear physics could be used to make an atomic bomb and received a discouraging lecture on the almost insurmountable technical problems and formidable expense likely to be involved.

Speer stated[39] that Heisenberg also drew attention to the lack of cyclotrons in Germany which he maintained was seriously hampering research, but Heisenberg asserted later[40] that not having cyclotrons was not a critical factor at all; he had requested them because then it would be possible to have better-trained physicists who could do more interesting experiments.

Speer was further misled on this subject when Heisenberg told him that Europe only had one cyclotron, a small machine which was installed at the College de France and which could not be used openly for military work. Speer was obviously unaware of the two Post Office cyclotrons at Miersdorf and Lichterfelde-Ost, the latter of which was stored at von Ardenne's house where it remained gathering dust throughout the war, and as to the existence of which Heisenberg did not enlighten him.

Heisenberg then rose to his theme and presented a long catalogue of complaints concerning Rust's neglect of nuclear research, about shortage of funds and equipment, and the conscription of scientific assistants.

For Heisenberg, the conference was a complete success. General Fromm released several hundred scientific assistants from the armed forces, and Speer was able to satisfy Heisenberg's request for a few hundred thousand marks, some priority metals and for a number of construction projects including a modern underground reactor bunker at Berlin Dahlem. Moreover, the project was relieved of any military objective.

When Speer received Heisenberg's miserable requisition, he concluded that the appropriations requested were so ludicrous that the physicists' work could not possibly be of any importance. Milch was likewise unimpressed.

Even when Speer asked them to reconsider and accept ten times as much, they advised him that they could find no use for the cash at the present time.

The economic base of Nazi Germany was neither broad nor stable and the military budget was tight. Speer saw the investment quandary as a straight choice between the rocket programme and the atom bomb, and, as a bomber, considered Peenemünde to be Germany's most misguided project. But he sadly concluded that:[41]

'even if Hitler had not been against nuclear research on doctrinal grounds: even if the stage we had reached in investigating the principles in June, 1942, had provided the atomic physicists with an objective for the investment of thousands of millions of marks towards producing the A-bomb, it would have been impossible for our strained war economy to have brought together the technicians, *materiel* and priorities for the project.'

Speer admitted that Germany could not have competed against the vastly superior productive capacity of the United States, which had the additional advantages of great wealth and freedom from the incessant air bombardment of its industry.

Germany's atomic scientists had been very vague about promising anything before 1947, whereas the war could not be continued beyond 31 December, 1945, the date when Germany's chrome ore reserves would be finally exhausted.

A month prior to his disappointment at the hands of Heisenberg on 4 June, 1942, Speer had arranged for Goering to be appointed head of the Reich Research Council which now replaced the body of the same name previously subordinate to the Ministry of Education.

The purpose of the restructuring had been to emphasize the importance of the new committee which Speer had resolved should superintend a progressive research programme for military purposes.

Goering's presidential council was comprised of twenty-one members who were either Cabinet Ministers, Chiefs of Staff or NSDAP (National Sozialistische Deutsche Arbeiter Partei) dignitaries.

Within a few weeks of assuming office on 9 June, 1942, Goering had delegated the management of the council's business to Professor Rudolf Mentzel, so that Professor Esau, the controller of the Physics section, was once again accountable to his former departmental head.

Although Esau was an old Nazi, he had no wish to build an atomic bomb for Hitler, and is even on record[42] as having advised Professor Otto Haxel of the German Admiralty research establishment to place stress always on the 'uranium engine' aspect of nuclear research.

On 1 October, 1942, Heisenberg, who had been attached to the Kaiser Wilhelm Institute for Physics at Berlin Dahlem since early 1940, was finally appointed to the Directorship at the Institute, following persistent pressure by von Weizsäcker and Wirtz, the latter being in charge of experimental work there.

The former occupant, Diebner, whose contribution at the Institute had been highly valued by Vögler, the President of the Kaiser Wilhelm Society, was obliged to surrender possession and he now returned to his nuclear physics laboratory at the Army's Gottow explosives test site. He soon noticed that a gulf was developing between himself and the Heisenberg administration.

It has been suggested that this was some sort of feud, but commenting on the alleged rivalry between the two groups[43], Heisenberg described Diebner as a good but not first-rate physicist who had come up from a lower class level into high office through his Nazi Party affiliation. This was undoubtedly the origin of the schism. Heisenberg went on to say that Diebner was not a convinced Nazi, and nor would he have betrayed them to the Gestapo, but he was well connected in that respect and 'extreme caution' was advisable in all dealings with the group which later included Harteck.

An accretion of factors, both personal and political, ensured that the unpleasantness had a permanent aura.

This was a significant rift historically since Wirtz[44] has stated categorically that, if the opposing groups had combined their heavy water resources in a single experiment, there would have been sufficient to moderate an energy-producing reactor in 1944.

During the latter part of 1942 Heisenberg began to devote an increasing amount of his time to problems in cosmic ray physics, and two papers published in the *Zeitschrift für Physik* in September and October, 1942, espoused a fresh approach to the theory of elementary particles based on a new concept known as the Scattering or S-Matrix, which laid the groundwork for the description of hadrons and their interactions.

In addition, he gave regular lectures at the Universities of Leipzig and Berlin on topics in theoretical physics.

In the autumn of 1942, a Swiss colleague, the physics lecturer Professor Scherrer, and a group of undergraduates wrote inviting him to visit Switzerland to address an audience of physicists and students at the University of Zurich. To his surprise, his application to travel was approved by the German Ministry of Education and Science. It was a condition of the arrangement that he would give a number of lectures in Berne and Basle as well, and that he should discuss only theory and avoid specific reference to any aspect of current German nuclear research.

In October information respecting his planned visit was passed to a physicist in the United States, Victor Weisskopf, who at once wrote to the atomic scientist Robert Oppenheimer suggesting that Heisenberg should be kidnapped while in Switzerland. Weisskopf volunteered to take part in the proposed mission, adding that he had discussed the matter with the senior physicist, Hans Bethe, who had given his consent, considering that it was well worth any risk involved.

Oppenheimer replied to Weisskopf in a negative vein, and it appeared that the matter had been dropped.

Heisenberg duly arrived in Switzerland and embarked upon his lecture tour. During his Zurich address, he noticed that one particular young man appeared to hang on his every word. Heisenberg had never seen him before and wondered if he was a Gestapo agent.

Heisenberg had been invited to dine that evening with Professor Scherrer, the head of the Swiss Institute, and had gladly accepted, stipulating only that political discussion should be taboo, and that no more than a small circle of Institute members should be present. This would eliminate the need for him to weigh every word carefully before speaking.

Scherrer accepted these conditions, and the evening passed off agreeably, Heisenberg being pleasantly surprised to find the intent young undergraduate seated close to him at table from where he inundated the physicist with the most intelligent and interesting questions. He had introduced himself as a Swiss student of physics who greatly admired Heisenberg's work. Although flattered, Heisenberg was careful to understate his achievement, made no mention of the nuclear project in Germany and sidestepped those questions which seemed to have a slant towards the destructive possibilities of atomic power.

At the end of the evening the young man insisted on escorting Heisenberg back to the German's hotel, and the two men talked animatedly as they strolled through the narrow, dim-lit streets of the Swiss city.

It was only after the war that Heisenberg discovered the identity and purpose of the engaging student, when he received a copy of Louis Kaufman's book *Moe Berg: Athlete, Scholar, Spy* (Little, Brown: Boston, 1975) and recognized in the face of its subject the 'Swiss undergraduate'. His companion that night had been a CIA assassin and a former American baseball star who had been carrying a loaded pistol in his coat pocket, with orders to shoot Heisenberg if he should give the slightest indication that he was working on a German atom bomb project. Moe Berg reflected that, for all his psychological training and experience, he had failed to detect the slightest flicker of Heisenberg's eyes, or the least defensive gesture, when he put to him the most loaded, insidious questions; nothing which might have given him the slightest excuse to execute his mission.

It is well to consider that if Heisenberg had been murdered then Harteck would have been the obvious candidate to succeed him, with all the ominous significance that such an appointment would have had for the German conduct of the war.

The economical pace of what passed for progress in the official German uranium project was dictated by the supply of heavy water required to moderate the prospective nuclear pile. Accepting Wirtz' statement that 2,500 litres would have been sufficient for success, the Germans had possession of a third of what they needed by the time of Heisenberg's appointment at Berlin Dahlem in October, 1942.

On 14 September, two weeks previously, an exchange process modification designed by Harteck and Süss had been introduced at the

Norwegian plant, and as a result, production was expected to rise shortly to 400 kilos per month, a fourfold increase in supply.

Within the British War Cabinet there had been mounting concern at Germany's interest in the heavy water facility at Vemork, and in July, 1942, a plan was drawn up to land up to forty airborne sappers close to the lake feeding the plant's turbines, from where an assault would be made on the factory itself. The mission was codenamed 'Operation Freshman'.

On 20 November, 1942, two Halifax bombers, each towing a Horsa glider, took off from Wick airfield in the north of Scotland and headed for Norway. The weather conditions were appalling and the target area could not be found. Low on fuel and with the wings icing up, the pilots took the decision to abort the mission. Close to the Norwegian coast on the return, one glider parted from its bomber when the towrope snapped. The wreck was found by Norwegian police about 100 miles from the intended landing site at Rjukan. The other paired unit came to grief in mountainous terrain about ten miles inland from Egersund in southern Norway.

The commandos in the gliders were found to be wearing khaki battledress from which all forms of insignia had been removed, and khaki woollen cap comforters instead of berets. Beneath the battledress was worn a blue ski-suit. They were interrogated briefly upon capture and then shot as spies without trial. The reason given by the Germans for this action was the irregularity of the uniforms and the inferred intention on the part of the commandos to be at large behind the German lines without uniforms after the sabotage had been completed. In fact, a secret instruction was in force that all commandos found abroad in German-held territories were to be executed, regardless of the circumstances, as a reprisal for the alleged suspicious deaths of German coastal infantrymen at the hands of Lord Lovat's commando force at Dieppe.

As a result of the information gained during the interrogations, together with documents and equipment retrieved from the wreckage of the gliders, the Germans were quickly able to establish what the objective of the operation had been. This information indicated to them for the first time that the Allied Governments understood enough about the Nazi atomic research project to risk the lives of nearly forty highly trained airborne engineers and the organization of the Norwegian underground with whom it had been arranged that the commandos were to liaise, in order to destroy the heavy water plant. Vemork was now clearly at risk.

Professor Diebner at least had not been ready to subordinate himself to a project increasingly dominated by Heisenberg. He was highly displeased with the poor progress of the research and must have considered Heisenberg's attitude towards it to be somewhat ambiguous. Feeling it imperative to take an initiative in the matter, he set up a number of uranium experiments at Gottow which he kept secret from Heisenberg, while using as a theoretical basis Döpel and Heisenberg's recent L-iv Leipzig paper *G-136 The Proof by Experiment of Effective Neutron Multiplication in a Layered Arrangement of Heavy Water and Uranium Metal in a Sphere*, given in April, 1942.

Diebner was able to report in November, 1942, in respect of his resulting G3b experiment, an aluminium sphere of 51 cm radius containing an arrangement of 240 5cm-sided uranium cubes totalling 540 kilos, in 525 litres of heavy water in a surround of paraffin, that the mathematics proved the use of the uranium cubes to be superior to Heisenberg's plates. It was an interesting advance, but can have done little to endear Diebner to Heisenberg.

After the war Heisenberg consistently maintained, in the face of widespread disbelief, that his purpose in remaining in Nazi Germany was to retain control of the uranium project in the hands of those opposed to Hitler, to frustrate the development of nuclear weapons, and to save German physics from utter ruin. The failing of historians who have examined his activities has arisen because they have been unable to imagine themselves psychologically into the mind of a saboteur of science in a murderous dictatorship. His sabotage consisted principally of acts of omission and the preparation of a plausible but incorrect theory which eventually led the project into a blind alley of Heisenberg's own making, and the key to understanding his work is to always bear in mind the fact that he was dedicated to never achieving a critical reactor in Nazi Germany.

Possibly one of the classic examples of this premeditated indolence is enshrined in his paper of 31 July, 1942 entitled *G161 − Observations on the Planned Half-Technical Experiment with 1½ tons of Heavy Water and 3 tons of Uranium Metal*. This experiment was to be undertaken using a magnesium alloy cylindrical vessel with a volume of 1.5 cubic metres corresponding to a sphere of 71 cms radius; it was admitted that a cylinder was less effective as a reactor vessel than a sphere.

Using Professor Bothe's 1940 report[31], in which it had been proved that the best reflector material with which to surround the reactor core was pure graphite blocks, Heinsenberg forecast:

'One can make the graphite reflector so thick that the loss

of stray neutrons to the exterior is excluded entirely. That is not to say that the next experimental pile will go critical, but it may mean that the graphite reflector is probably a *decisive improvement* on the ordinary water jacket and that we may perhaps get close to the critical point.'

It is interesting to record that this 'decisive improvement' was not incorporated into any of Heisenberg's future experiments until B7 in January, 1945, no less than two and a half years later.

'The fact that we may actually approach the critical point in the next large experiment, however, gives rise to the need to make a fresh and more precise investigation into the stability of the uranium reactor. In earlier reports, we [Heisenberg and von Weizsäcker] mentioned changes in the physical properties of layers upon the uniform warming of the whole reactor core. Once a reactor reaches criticality, if we find that the fissioning occurs with great intensity, it is obvious that the uranium metal will suddenly heat up whereas the moderator (heavy water) will scarcely do so at all.

150-200 MeV of energy is released at fission, and in general only a small proportion of that, say, 5-10 MeV, will be transferred to the ejected neutrons, and then passed on to the moderator.

Approximately twenty to forty times as much energy will be imparted to the uranium as to the heavy water, so the metal will heat by 500°C while the heavy water will heat up by only ½-1°C. The heat can be transferred from the uranium to the heavy water, but this takes time.'

Heisenberg remarked that there were two factors to be borne in mind. The warmth of the heavy water contributed materially to the stability of the pile; the U^{238} isotope was efficient at capturing neutrons only within certain energy ranges, and the width of these bands was very important for stabilizing the reactor. But little was known about the width of energy bands at very high temperatures in uranium.

'We need to understand about reactor stability. Our foremost fear is that the entire fission process at criticality will occur explosively in a fraction of a second while the heavy water is still practically cold.

Whether the reactor stabilizes or explodes rests solely on the behaviour of the energy bands. If the width of the energy bands is insufficient for stability, then it would seem that there is no other factor which can prevent the chain reaction cascade. This event would take place in a large reactor in -400 secs^{-1} and the neutron count would suddenly reach 10^{28}, enough for instantaneous energization of the fuel.... the investigation of reactor stability with respect to a rise in the temperature of the uranium only is one of the *most urgent* problems in uranium research.'

Concluding this horrendous scenario of a nuclear-type explosion in his laboratory, Heisenberg stated:

'Before we undertake any experiment which has as its object the achievement of criticality or super-criticality, we must first determine the question of stability in reactors through examining the temperature coefficient in heated uranium.'

Up to this time the theory and experimental work had been concentrated on the question of reactor geometry and materials. Only now that the project had arrived at the stage where it appeared physically possible to achieve a critical condition in a reactor was attention given to the question of whether that chain reaction could actually be controlled.

The *stability* of a reactor is its ability to hold a steady power level without action by the control system. The essential component of stability was seen to be a factor known as the Period of the Reactor.

The obvious way in which control is exercised is to regulate the reactor by the operation of neutron-absorbers, such as boron and cadmium rods, inside the reactor core through channels provided for the purpose. Full insertion of the rods causes the absorption of so many neutrons that the chain reaction is extinguished. As the rods are gradually withdrawn, neutron multiplication revives and a point is eventually reached at which the chain reaction just maintains itself. If the withdrawal continues further, the neutrons multiply and the reactor operates with increasing power. In the working reactor the time factor is sufficiently long to allow operators to maintain control by this method Since the use of control rods was a principle naturally appreciated by German physicists, it ought to have solved Heisenberg's 'most urgent' problem.

But the fact that no such research as recommended subsequently took place, confirms that the real problem was inherent in the theory of Stability itself, a matter of such fundamental importance to the project that Heisenberg was not prepared to commit it to paper. Such a problem could be related only to the Period of the Reactor.

The result with which Heisenberg was vitally preoccupied was a series of events culminating in an explosion. The worst possible credible accident involving a nuclear reactor is an explosion caused by the neutron multiplication factor becoming so large under the influence of temperature rise in the metal and fission products that a great multiplication takes place within a fraction of a second.

The indications are that such an explosion would approximate to an amount of TNT equivalent to the mass of fissionable material present in the core. Roughly speaking, if the critical mass of natural uranium there were 1½ tons, then the explosion would be the equivalent of 10½ kilos of TNT accompanied by a serious radiation release. Even if the reaction occurred relatively slowly, the reactor would be destroyed in a melt-down if the neutron multiplication continued long enough.

In investigating the Period of the Reactor, Heisenberg had calculated that the short-time interval between each generation of neutrons (10^{-3} secs or less) implied an ungovernably rapid power excursion. As the Period of the Reactor was less than a second, the time factor did not allow control of the chain reaction and consequently he had now at last tacitly admitted that it was impossible to harness energy in any reactor producing heat.

This was the critical moment in the official German uranium project, the dead-end.

At the instigation of Professor Abraham Esau in a letter dated 24 November, 1942, Professor Mentzel proposed to Goering's deputy, Doctor Fritz Görnnert, that a Nuclear Physics Research Group be established with Esau as its Plenipotentiary. Goering agreed, and signed the necessary decree to take effect on 8 December, 1942.

Esau was now endowed with far-reaching powers, including control of the budget; moreover, he now had power to direct the work of Diebner and his Army scientists who had been subordinated to the Reich Bureau of Standards, a body of which Esau was President.

Out of concern for the prestige and influence of the Kaiser Wilhelm Society, a meeting was held on 4 February, 1943, between Mentzel and the new Plenipotentiary on the one hand, and Vögler and Telschow, President and Secretary-General respectively of the Society, on the other. They agreed that the Kaiser Wilhelm

Foundation would continue to fund its own research programme and enjoy the patronage of the Armaments Minister, Speer, who held Esau in low regard.

If nothing else, this new arrangement ensured the continuation of the antagonism between the Heisenberg administration at the KWI, Berlin Dahlem and Diebner's Army faction, which rumbled on with fresh disagreements over the sharing out and borrowing of materials.

During 1942 Heisenberg had devoted an increasing amount of his time to fundamental problems of cosmic ray physics, which had no connection with the German war effort, and at the end of the year he decided to consolidate the reputation he had earned for himself as an ambassador for German science through his recent tour of Swiss universities. It is probably true that Heisenberg was a cultural imperialist, and even in politics he believed that European unity could only be successfully brought about by German hegemony. Therefore, whilst he certainly had neither the desire nor the intention to promote German culture on behalf of the National Socialists, he saw no impropriety in presenting his scientific manifesto on a platform provided by the Nazi Government. Max Planck and von Weizsäcker were other physicists who, whilst being acknowledged anti-Nazis, were mentally able to justify such a position.

The express consent of the Ministry of Education was required before a lecturer could participate in a speaking tour outside the Reich, and stringent regulations prescribed, among other things, the submission of all documents and texts, including those of the proposed lectures themselves, prior to travel.

Handling the arrangements in the country visited was the German Cultural Institute, to which the lecturer and his party were obliged to report immediately upon arrival. The Institutes were primarily concerned with propagating Nazi culture and ideology and were well used to organizing speakers to the best political advantage.

Planck, von Weizsäcker and Heisenberg visited Budapest in November, 1942, and in March, 1943, Heisenberg accepted an invitation to lecture at the University of Bratislava.

Also in early 1943, the Dutch physicist Dirk Coster approached both Heisenberg and Max von Laue with a request for them to intercede on behalf of the American scientist, Samuel Goudsmit, whose elderly parents were among many Dutch Jews who had been deported to Auschwitz. In response, Heisenberg drafted a letter for Coster's use in which he argued the great affection which Goudsmit had for Germany and the Germans, and suggested that the disappearance of the American's parents might cause political embarrassment abroad for

Germany. He ended by declaring the sorrow he would feel if 'for reasons unbeknown to me' 'difficulties' were suddenly to confront the elderly couple. In the circumstances, it is hard to imagine what else he could have done; the very act of signing such a letter in 1943 was highly dangerous. Max von Laue also drafted a plea, but forgot to sign it. Goudsmit's parents were murdered at Auschwitz.

Heisenberg's surreptitious campaign to discredit the Aryan physics of Lenard and Stark by preaching relativity and quantum theories as the basis of modern physics was gradually beginning to take effect, and his own rehabilitation since the *Schwarze Korps* affair in 1937 was underlined when the SS-Mannschafthaus, at Leiden in Holland, an Institute providing a Germanic education for Dutch students, proposed that he should lecture there on theoretical physics. He excused himself on the grounds of a full diary of engagements and suggested that he would be free in the autumn, but the SS did not renew their offer.

The expected attack on the heavy water production plant at Vemork, foreshadowed by the commando disaster in the previous October, was carried out in the early hours of Sunday 28 February, 1943, by a team of Norwegian saboteurs flown in from England. When plastic explosives placed under the containing vessels in the high concentration room of the electrolysis building detonated, approximately 350 kilos of pure heavy water were lost. There were no casualties and the hydroelectric power station itself, which provided power for the Norwegian civilian population, was undamaged. Production of heavy water was brought to a standstill for three full months; since output had been expected to top 200 kilos in March, the actual loss was very nearly a full ton for the quarter, a very critical setback for those who wished to see the success of the programme.

On 5 May, 1943, Heisenberg was one of several physicists who addressed the august German Academy of Aeronautical Research and delivered a lecture admitting his belief that it was neither as the propulsion unit for warships nor even as a generator of electricity in large power stations that nuclear fission would be of the greatest benefit to humanity:

'Once we have succeeded in establishing a working reactor, *the first and most important technical application* will be in the creation of artificial radioisotopes, for a reactor would radiate a thousand times more powerfully than the greatest cyclotrons yet built and make possible the production of large quantities of radioactive substances. The possible technical applications of such fission products have already been mentioned in his address by Herr Hahn.'[45]

It may be asked why, if Heisenberg believed the production of radioisotopes for medicine and industry to be the most important function of a nuclear reactor, he resolutely set his face against building a simple very-low-temperature reactor for that purpose on the lines suggested by Harteck and Houtermans. There is only one possible answer. No matter how great the benefits to humanity might be, the overriding factor for Heisenberg was his determination that Nazi Germany should never be given the opportunity to abuse nuclear power, for the military would seize upon radioisotopes as a weapon.

Although it is by no means certain that Houtermans had risked his life to tell Heisenberg exactly what was going on at von Ardenne's Post Office-funded laboratory, he may have known or guessed the purpose of the project, the facts of which will be enlarged upon later. In addition, he can scarcely have been ignorant of the interest being shown in the idea of particle weapons and radiological bombs by the Heereswaffenamt and the Luftwaffe from this time onwards.

In February, 1943, Professor Boris Rajewsky, Director at the Kaiser Wilhelm Institute for Biophysics, Frankfurt am Main, had been awarded Heereswaffenamt contract SS 4891-0194 (1642/11)-II43 to investigate *inter alia* 'the biological effects of corpuscular radiation[46] (including neutrons) with regard to the possibility of their being used as a weapon'.[47] A number of other contracts were placed with the Genetics Department of the Kaiser Wilhelm Institute at Berlin Buch for the determination of necessary levels of radiation protection and to study the effects of radiation on the body.

Professor Walther Bothe, the senior experimentalist at the Heidelberg Institute, reported to Professor Esau in June, 1943, that the German group at the College de France in Paris was considering a programme to investigate the possibilities of using radioactinides with a short half-life in gas warfare.

A French commission consisting of the atomic physicists, Professors Joliot and Moureu, and Dr Chovin inspected the Watten rocket silo at St Omer in the company of Mr Duncan Sandys, the appointee at the Ministry of Supply with special responsibility for weapons research, development and production, on 10 September, 1944, four days after its capture by Canadian forces. The party inspected all levels of the installation down to about 260 feet below ground. Access to even deeper galleries was prevented by flooding. Later, a denial was made that the factory might have been concerned in the production of a

German atomic bomb. What it was that drew the commission to investigate the bunker was not disclosed.

One of the disadvantages of using short-lived radioactinides is that the material has to be made up at a point close to where it is proposed to despatch the rocket or flying bomb. It is, therefore, possible that the Germans may have installed a cyclotron or other particle accelerator in the lower reaches at Watten. This might account for the fact that when Bothe was taken into custody by American forces at Heidelberg in April, 1945, he admitted to his captors after repeated questioning[48] that the cyclotron was considered by the Germans as a source of radioactive material for use in bombs. The term 'repeated questioning' implies that the interviewing officers had grounds for suspecting that the Germans intended using a cyclotron for the purpose of manufacturing radioactive corpuscles for military purposes. The Americans did not obtain that information from Joliot, since he had stated to them at the time of the liberation of Paris that the German group had given him their word that the Paris cyclotron was not going to be used for any military purpose, and neither was he aware of any such purpose which the Germans might have had in mind for it.

On 20 May, 1943, Field-Marshal Milch[49] spoke to Professor E. Schiebold of the Luftwaffe laboratory at Gross-Ostheim and asked him to prepare a feasibility study for the possible deployment of X-rays and gamma radiation as weapons against enemy aircraft. Schiebold told him that he believed it to be theoretically possible, and promised a full report by the new year.

In June, 1943, Heisenberg accepted an offer to visit the Dutch Universities, and in October he lectured at Delft, Utrecht, Amsterdam and Leiden, completing the tour by frankly discussing his experiences with the Commissioner for Holland, Seyss-Inquart, and advising him that, though scientific cooperation was clearly possible, the German viewpoint on almost every subject of political consequence was universally rejected by Dutch students.

The sabotage against the high concentration plant at Vemork in February, 1943, was repaired by the middle of April and production resumed in June with an output of 199 kilos, the largest amount supplied for any month during the war. This was a result of the successful introduction of Harteck's exchange process to one of the stages. However, on 24 July, 1943, the USAAF bombed Heröya, where there was a fertilizer factory, and caused substantial damage. Heröya was the principal user of Rjukan's synthetic ammonia, the hydrogen for which was drawn by pipeline from the hydrogen electrolysis plant at Vemork and, as a consequence of the fall in demand, Vemork was obliged to cut production.

The Reich Commissioner overrode the management and ordered Vemork to resume full output. The surplus hydrogen was to be released into the atmosphere.

German scientists added a second exchange process to further increase supply during August, and when Eriksen, the Director General at Norsk Hydro, rescinded the German instruction to allow the escape of the hydrogen and announced his intention to recommend to the board of directors the cessation of heavy water production at the plant ostensibly on the grounds that not to do so would be to invite the Allied air forces to destroy it, he was arrested and spent the rest of the war in a German prison camp. Nevertheless, the Germans found it politically desirable to limit their requirements of heavy water from Vemork to what was normally produced by the factory as a by-product of its ammonia enterprise.

On 16 November, 1943, the USAAF attacked Vemork and caused loss of life among Norwegians and damage to property in the town and at the power station, but the high concentration plant was not affected. The plant was nevertheless shut down owing to the disruption to the electricity supply and the Germans were forced to conclude that it had become a liability, Harteck finding support for his plans to build a manufacturing facility in Germany. A quantity of heavy water remained in the electrolytic cells for later retrieval.

The Germans had already completed a small pilot factory at the premises of the chemicals giant, I G Farben, at Leuna and had tested it using the Harteck-Süss dual-temperature exchange principle. They had reasoned that a full-scale plant would involve enormous financial investment. A new process developed by Harteck's pupil Geib proposed as an alternative the use of the dual-temperature exchange with hydrogen sulphide, which would have been a satisfactory method of production, but was dropped because of design problems which could not be resolved in the shorter term.

The rival groups under Diebner at Gottow and Heisenberg and Wirtz at Berlin Dahlem had continued with experiments into reactor geometry and fuel arrangement throughout 1943, culminating in a secret conference at the Bureau of Standards in Berlin summoned by Professor Esau during the middle of October.

The Heidelberg Professors, Bothe and Fünfer, reported that the eventual critical reactor would be fuelled and moderated by approximately equal amounts of uranium and heavy water, and that where 1 cm thick uranium plates were used, the best results would be obtained where there was a 20 cm thick layer of heavy water between them.

Professors Pose and Rexer offered conclusive proof that uranium metal cubes were superior to both rods and plates, while plates were the least favourable shape of all.

Understandably, Professor Harteck was extremely perturbed to learn from Heisenberg that he nevertheless intended to persevere with uranium plates during 1944 simply because plates were preferable to cubes for theoretical purposes.[50]

The cutting of the heavy water supply had pre-empted Diebner's analogous model pile, from which he had expected to obtain conclusive data for calculating the size of his critical reactor.

Diebner was further irritated at receiving instructions from Esau to pass his reserve of heavy water to Heisenberg for the unpromising uranium plate experiments at Berlin Dahlem. The actual date for the commencement of the tests had been delayed because of a shortage of uranium plate caused by casting problems at the manufacturers, and late in 1943 the supply of new metal was severely curtailed after the DEGUSSA factory at Frankfurt had been destroyed during a bombing raid.

At the end of 1940 the Heereswaffenamt had decided that uranium experiments were to involve the use of cast metal instead of uranium oxide powder. The Auer Company of Berlin had been awarded the contract for refining the uranium oxide seized by the Army at Oolen in Belgium, and a small plant had been set up at Oranienburg which, under the direction of Dr Nikolaus Riehl, turned out about a ton of refined uranium oxide each month. The product was free of rare-earth impurities, but retained a high content of boron which was a neutron absorber and was, therefore, unsatisfactory.

The Auer Company was not itself geared for reducing the uranium oxide to metal, and so sub-contracted the process to its subsidiary, the Deutsche Gold und Silber Scheideanstalt (DEGUSSA), which operated a plant at Frankfurt and later constructed a second at Grünau in Berlin.

Whereas the usual method employed abroad for the reduction was an electrometallurgical process, DEGUSSA opted instead for thermic reduction on the grounds of economy and in the belief that the resulting product was still of an acceptable standard of purity. In fact, their metal was contaminated by calcium imparted by the reduction process in addition to the existing impurities and was not particularly satisfactory. The DEGUSSA plant had a production capacity of one ton of metal per month, but whereas a labour force of only six was required to operate the factory, output never reached a maximum.

All the uranium metal produced in Germany during the war appears to have been cast at one or other of the DEGUSSA plants, and totalled about 14 tons, of which 9 tons was powder and the rest plates or cubes.

In October, 1943, after less than a year as Plenipotentiary for Nuclear Physics, Professor Esau was called for by his superior, Professor Mentzel, and informed that an unfavourable view was being taken of his continuation in office; Esau had accordingly little option but to resign, which he did after a brief furore.

He had made a number of influential enemies including Vögler and Speer, and Professor von Ardenne even accuses him in his autobiography[51] of scientific fraud by withholding a manuscript on the subject of radioisotopes in medicine submitted to Esau for security clearance and subsequently used by Esau as the basis for a lecture at Strasbourg.

An agreement had been worked out at the time of the creation of the office of Plenipotentiary in November, 1942, that the Reich Research Council would exercise independent control over the nuclear programme to the exclusion of Speer, the Armaments Minister, and it appears that there was some justification for Esau to complain that Speer, as the instigator of his removal, had acted beyond his authority. A reshuffle was approved by Speer which sent Esau to High Frequency Research as controller, while Professor Walther Gerlach succeeded him as Plenipotentiary on 1 January, 1944.

In December, 1943, Heisenberg lectured at the highly dubious Institute for German Eastern Work (*Institut für Deutsche Ost-Arbeit*) at Cracow in the General Gouvernement, formerly known as Poland, where he had been invited to speak by a former schoolmate, Hans Frank.

The subsequent award to him of the Copernicus Prize for Excellence in Physics by Frank was seen by Heisenberg as a further advance towards the overthrow of the Aryan physics of Lenard and Stark, a matter which he considered to be of the greatest importance. In mitigation of this particular lecture all that can be said is that Heisenberg may have been unaware of the exact details of the scientific research carried out by the Institute.

Heisenberg's prestige was now higher than at any previous time in the Nazi era and few would now wish to question whether his uranium work was as valuable as it might be.

The new Plenipotentiary, Gerlach, took up occupation in the Kaiser Wilhelm Institute for Physics at Berlin Dahlem early in January, 1944, and appointed Diebner as his administrative assistant.

Harteck made a prompt attempt to ingratiate his Hamburg group with the new occupant, reciting a list of complaints respecting the patronizing treatment he had received in the past from a certain quarter, and suggesting that Gerlach might profitably elect to rely on Harteck himself to carry out the most important projects remaining to the programme.

What Harteck said was true; if he had been the guiding light of the nuclear programme from the start, the war would have finished in Germany's favour by 1941. But Harteck had not initially had the utter confidence in himself to appreciate the fact that he was without doubt Germany's most gifted experimentalist and inventive thinker; now that he realized it, it was too late.

The unhalting aerial bombardment of the German cities brought about the dispersal of most of the major institutes to the provinces during the first few months of 1944. At Berlin Dahlem the large underground laboratory complex made removal unnecessary, but Harteck's Hamburg institute was evacuated to Freiburg and then to Kandern near the Swiss border; Heisenberg removed to Hechingen near Stuttgart, while Hahn took up residence at nearby Tailfingen.

In London, it was still considered very urgent that the remaining heavy water at Vemork should be destroyed, and when information was received that 39 drums containing the equivalent of 613 litres in 14 tons of water was to be shipped to Germany under special guard, it was decided that the rail-ferry *Hydro* should be sunk whilst transporting the consignment across the deep waters of Lake Tinnsjö.

Accordingly, saboteurs managed to place a quantity of plastic explosives against the interior bow plating of the vessel, and at about 10.45 am on the morning of 20 February, 1944, the device exploded and the ferry sank, taking with her all but four of the drums and twenty-six people aboard the ferry.

The loss of the balance of the heavy water left a total of just over 2500 kilos available to the nuclear project which, as has been mentioned, was just enough to moderate a successful experiment had it been assembled for a single attempt. It was the division of the materials between the various uncooperating groups rather than the shortfall of the optimum amount to moderate a pile which condemned the project to fail, and this was due largely to the unpleasant atmosphere fostered by Heisenberg, von Weizsäcker and probably Wirtz. What is extraordinary is that no effort was ever made to coordinate forcibly a single project using all the available materials in order to determine exactly how short of them they were, if at all.

Instead of a unified approach, it was increasingly left to Harteck to pursue the various avenues of possible production to resume the flow of heavy water. As an alternative, Harteck appreciated that if the U^{235} isotope could be enriched from 0.7 to 1.5 per cent in several thousand kilos of uranium, then a reactor could be made critical using ordinary water only, and it was Harteck's group which engineered the ultracentrifuge and saw the prototypes brought to the operational state. The centrifuge is today the favoured method of large-scale isotope separation in Europe; with a few hundred machines in an underground factory, Harteck might have enabled the Germans to build the first reactor using enriched uranium and ordinary water.

Following the request by Field-Marshal Milch in the previous May for a feasibility study into the possibilities of exploiting radiological physics for weapons purposes, the radiologist Schiebold submitted a thesis dated 19 July, 1944, in confirmation of an earlier oral report.[52]

Arising out of theoretical work at the Luftwaffe research institute, Gross Ostheim, the long dissertation reports on the possible use of specially designed X-ray machines to inflict death and radiation injury on enemy aircrews during air combat.

X-rays are simply electro-magnetic radiations produced when electrons moving at a very high speed strike a target. Dr Schiebold had designed a 25 MeV, 2-metre surface-radius anode tube from which positive ions were emitted with such acceleration that a beam was formed. This device was, therefore, in principle a rudimentary electron-beam weapon.

A second projected gun, a 200 MeV X-ray transformer designed by Dr Wideroe was unfortunately not described in the text of the report.

Schiebold stated that the scatter effect of focusing the beam on the metal parts of the aircraft's fuselage actually enhanced the deleterious effects of the ray in comparison with aiming the beam directly at the occupants.

He had not been able to establish for certain the dosage of X-rays required to inflict permanent injury to humans, although he was using a theoretical figure of 200 roentgens, which was known to cause permanent damage to the non-regenerative gonad cells.

Expressing the opinion that even a 100 roentgen dose would probably achieve a satisfactory result, he indicated that the transformer could be used for heights up to 1 kilometre, while in favourable conditions his own anode-tube invention would perform well up to about 5 kilometres of altitude; death appeared to be inevitable for the recipient of 600 roentgens.

Schiebold emphasized that the weapon installation would need to be manoeuvrable. At 5 kilometres height, the anode tube produced 7 roentgens per second, and the beam would have to be played over the enemy aircraft during a chase for about thirty seconds in order to deliver a dangerous dose of X-ray radiation.

Sometime in the summer of 1944 the President of the Post Office Research Institute, Gerwig, notified the radiologist Professor von Ardenne, whose laboratory was partly funded by the German Post Office, that he was about to receive a visit from Field-Marshal Milch and the Reichspostminister, Ohnesorge.

The purpose of the conference was to ascertain means by which enemy aircraft could be brought down by the use of atomic rays. Von Ardenne told Gerwig that he had never heard of such a thing. Owing to this discouraging sentiment, the visit was subsequently cancelled, but the Luftwaffe leadership nevertheless retained the most serious interest in the possibilities, as Dr Baer of the Planning Office of the Reich Research Council explained to von Ardenne when he called on him in January, 1945, in order to discuss the technicalities. A few days previously, Dr Baer had been instructed by Goering to investigate 'nuclear methods of defence against enemy bombers'.[53]

The X-ray gun proposed by Schiebold and Wideroe would have been particularly heavy and unwieldy and its installation into an aircraft of special design would have presented a large number of problems. X-ray apparatus is expensive and the machine is a comparatively complex device involving the generation of high voltages to energize the X-ray tube. Although asked to do so, Schiebold had not reported on the uses of gamma radiation since an appropriate quantity could not be obtained without a nuclear reactor.

Gamma radiation is a penetrating, high-energy electromagnetic radiation consisting of high-energy protons emitted at the speed of light by the nuclei of certain radioisotopes. Unlike alpha and beta radiation, gamma radiation does not consist of rapidly moving corpuscles, but of a radiation similar to visible light and moving at the same velocity. In physical nature gamma radiation is identical to X-radiation, although its quanta may have even higher energy. The effects of gamma and X-radiation are similar and the two types of rays cannot be distinguished once they have been emitted.

If the Reich Research Council project under Goering had been successful, enormous quantities of radioisotopes would have become available for use in gamma 'radiation guns' which would have been light enough to fit into the nose of a fighter. In principle, the device would have been a simple lead or concrete case containing the radioactive material which would be exposed to the target by remotely removing a lead cap from the muzzle and merely aiming the barrel.

It was out of their desperation at the inexorable disintegration of the

Nazi Reich that the concept of drastic terror weapons emerged and became widespread among the Luftwaffe hierarchy. Even the phlegmatic Professor Gerlach became infected by the possibilities inherent in radiological warfare and saw the programme of which he was the controller as the last great opportunity for Germany to obtain acceptable terms in a negotiated peace settlement.

During the first half of 1944 Heisenberg's team of physicists, led by Karl Wirtz, proceeded with experiments in the modern underground bunker complex at Berlin Dahlem using uranium plates and heavy water. They eventually announced that the ideal spacing between the plates was 18 cm. This finding merely confirmed what Bothe and Fünfer had reported at Esau's secret conference in October, 1943, and Vögler, the President of the Kaiser Wilhelm Foundation, considered the progress made by the group to be so unsatisfactory that he wrote complaining to Gerlach about it.

Heisenberg had been concentrating his mental energies for some time on the Theory of the Scattering Matrix, a collection of probabilities for all possible reactions involving hadrons in particle physics, a concept he had originally proposed early in 1942. His third paper on the subject was published in 1944 in *Zeitschrift für Physik*.

Heisenberg frequented a social group known as the *Mittwochgesellschaft* (Wednesday Club) which was an intellectual forum of conservative opposition to Hitler composed of academics, civil servants and industrialists. Its members included the diplomat Ulrich von Hassell; General Ludwig Beck, the nominal military head of the conspiracy against Hitler; the philosopher Spranger; the Prussian Finance Minister, Popitz; Ferdinand Sauerbruch, the Chief Surgeon of the German Army and Rudolf Diels, the founder of the Gestapo. Heisenberg undoubtedly knew of the conspiracy but had preferred not to become involved. Meetings were held at the Harnack House in Berlin, the headquarters of the Kaiser Wilhelm Institute at Dahlem, and Heisenberg was present at the last gathering of the circle on the evening of 18 July, 1944. At the time of the attempt on Hitler's life, Heisenberg was at his home at Urfeld, Bavaria.

On 7 June, 1944, at Harnack House, Heisenberg had received a visit from a slight acquaintance from his student days, Adolf Reichwein, a Professor of History and schoolteacher. Reichwein had come straight to the point and asked Heisenberg outright if he was willing to participate in a plot against Hitler.

Heisenberg was appalled by Reichwein's loud voice and incautious manner, and told him that if the plotters were going to 'underestimate the enemy like this', then the entire adventure was doomed to fail. He advised Reichwein to act with the greatest circumspection in future if he wished the plot to succeed.

The physicist would never have involved himself in a matter over which he had no personal control. He was not a revolutionary and considered that the time for revolutionary action was long past. Before the war, he had had high hopes for a military coup against Hitler, believing that only a coup attempted by those with access to the military means of enforcing their will could hope to succeed.

Towards the end of 1944 Diebner's group left Berlin for the south and set up at Stadtilm, near Erfurt, in the cellar of a school. Here they set about designing an experiment in collaboration with Harteck to produce radiosotopes from a reactor moderated by Pentene (C_5H_{10}) at a very low temperature. This was a very sinister development, for as Heisenberg guardedly recorded in *Nature* (edition 160; 1947):

> 'Gerlach had taken over the physics section of the Reichsforschungsrat and he strove to promote more particularly the scientific side of the uranium problem; and at that, not only the physical, but also the medical aspect.'

In connection with these medical applications, the construction of a low-temperature pile had been promulgated at the suggestion of Harteck. Heisenberg continued:

> 'Such a pile, even of small dimensions, could be expected to yield profitable amounts of radioactive elements for tracer research.'

Harteck's true purpose has been made only too clear by his later admission, and Heisenberg undoubtedly knew what he was up to. Gerlach had been informed of the interest of the Wehrmacht in the use of radioactive materials as a weapon in the course of his duties, and had corresponded on that subject in connection with a Wehrmacht contract with Professor Boris Rajewsky, the Director of the KWI for Biophysics. Useful as tracer research might be, it is inconceivable that the uses of reactor waste to intimidate enemy governments would have escaped Gerlach's notice. Indeed, what else can account for the optimism of the Plenipotentiary in his letter of 16 December, 1944, to Reichsleiter Martin Bormann, informing him:

'You undoubtedly know that we are dealing here with a project which may unexpectedly be of decisive importance for the war'?

Unaware of America's progress in atomic science, it had at last dawned on Gerlach that if Germany could obtain the world monopoly in nuclear power, radiological weapons would reverse her evil fortunes. He was confident that the atom bomb was not feasible for technical reasons, a fact of which he had appraised Goering's private office[54]. Speer wrote to Gerlach at about the same time, just before Christmas, 1944, speaking of the 'exceptional significance' of nuclear research, which he was following up with 'great expectations'.

The proposed reactor fortunately remained in the planning stages, probably because of a shortage of the uranium metal spheres which Diebner had calculated would be the most efficient fuel element shape, while difficulties with the acquisition of a suitable container vessel and refrigerating equipment for the great coldness required may also have contributed to the abandonment of the experiment.

It had been as early as July, 1942, that Heisenberg had brought out a paper announcing a Planned Semi-Technical Experiment using 1½ tons of heavy water and 3 tons of natural uranium metal. He expressed confidence that this experiment:

> 'will result in a 60 per cent neutron increase if the assembly is surrounded by ordinary water. But if, as is planned, a jacket of pure graphite blocks is substituted for the ordinary water, then the neutron increment will be greater; it is possible, therefore, that, with this arrangement, we will get close to the critical point.'

Heisenberg had first mentioned graphite as the ideal reflector in his pioneering paper of December, 1939, which Bothe and Fünfer had unequivocally confirmed in early 1941, but this was the first suggestion that Heisenberg actually intended to use graphite in a planned experiment.

However, there was the inevitable drawback, for:

> 'Before the experiment can be set with a view to achieving criticality, we must first determine the stability of the reactor through an investigation of the temperature coefficient of the heated metal.'

No further mention was made of the Planned Semi-Technical Experiment until the conference at the German Academy of Aeronautical Research on 5 May, 1943, when he informed his audience, during the part of his address concerning progress towards the construction of a reactor that:

> 'The next step is to build a reactor using about 1½ tons of heavy water and 3 tons of uranium metal in layers of metal plates,'

which he expected might come about in the summer of 1943 and which would supply definite conclusions as to the ultimate proportions of the working reactor.

In fact the most favourable layer arrangement turned out to be Bothe and Fünfer's B6c 'Layer Experiment with Variations on the Thicknesses of Uranium and Heavy Water' reported on in December, 1943, which gave a neutron multiplication factor of 2.35 using seven 1cm thick uranium plates weighing a total of 1.25 tons, together with 1½ tons of heavy water within an ordinary water reflector.

This was to form the basis for all the remaining theory, which continued to exclude experiments with graphite as a reflector until much later, while the halving of the uranium from 3 tons to 1½ tons in a proposed pile using 1½ tons of heavy water reduced the planned reactor significantly from a critical one to one which was strictly sub-critical.

As was expected, when Wirtz's experiment in December, 1944, at Berlin Dahlem, a full year later, faithfully repeated Bothe and Fünfer's effort while using a reflector of graphite blocks in place of ordinary water, it was discovered that there had been an increase in the neutron multiplication statistic from 2.35 to 3.37 which naturally could only be accounted for by the change in the reflector, consistent with Bothe and Fünfer's 1940 report, and finally embraced by Heisenberg in his paper of July, 1942.

The revised calculations now showed that the size of a self-sustaining pile had been overestimated. Moreover Diebner's Gottow experiments had proved that a lattice of uranium cubes was more efficient than uranium plates for the same amount of heavy water. Heisenberg recorded:

> 'The earlier experiments had shown, in accordance with theory, that the best configuration for a heavy water reactor is to have the uranium in cubes. The most favourable cube size in theory is sides of 6-7 cm in length.

A large number of cubes with 5 cm sides had become available after the Gottow experiments. Since it was not possible to produce a sufficient quantity of the optimum-sized cubes quickly, it was decided that we would have to complete our requirement with 5 cm cubes instead.'

It has been seriously suggested by the historian David Irving that the final B8 technical experiment was 'a last dramatic effort to build a chain reacting uranium pile before the war ended', but this romantic conclusion is not supported by the evidence. Thus Heisenberg:

'In order to be able to compare the next experiment with B6 and B7, it will have to be performed using the same magnesium cylinder with the graphite jacket as with the B7.'

Wirtz confirmed that the characteristics of the final B8 experiments were entirely determined by the exigencies of the comparison with the two previous experiments. They would therefore use 1½ tons of heavy water, 1½ tons of uranium metal in the form of 680 cubes with 5cm sides, and 10 tons of graphite reflector. The theory did not suggest that the B8 might go critical, but as Heisenberg could obviously calculate the improved neutron multiplication factor he was likely to obtain by using cubes instead of plates in experiment B8, he undoubtedly knew at this stage the quantity of materials which would be required for a heavy water reactor to go critical.

Professor Gerlach had now insisted that the final experiment pile B8 should be attempted at Berlin Dahlem where there were adequate bunker facilities to pursue the reactor project safely to its successful conclusion, but the intolerable situation in the capital from the incessant air raids eventually convinced him, late in January, 1945, that Stadtilm, near Erfurt, to where Diebner had removed, was the better venue.

Shortly before departure, Gerlach spoke to a close friend, Dr Paul Rosbaud, who was a consultant to the scientific periodical *Die Naturwissenschaften*, a man with pro-Allied sympathies. There was some conversation about the intended purpose of the heavy water. When interviewed later by American Intelligence officers of the *Alsos* Mission, Rosbaud stated that the heavy water had been produced in Norway, 'under false pretext, to be used in a most dreadful war machine against the civilized world'.

Gerlach, Diebner and Wirtz set off ahead of a convoy of lorries loaded with materials and equipment for Stadtilm, where Gerlach had decided that the culminating experiment was to be performed by Dr Diebner's team.

A pit had been excavated in the cellar of an old schoolhouse in the town, and an experimental assembly had been set up consisting of about 2400 kilos of heavy water inside a graphite jacket. In addition to most of the uranium metal, there were 10 tons of uranium oxide blocks and there was enough of all materials at Stadtilm for a critical reactor.

Upon arrival, Wirtz telephoned Heisenberg at Hechingen in Württemberg and warned him of Gerlach's intention, and on 5 February Heisenberg and von Weizsäcker turned up at Stadtilm after a harrowing 200 mile cross-country journey and persuaded Gerlach to allow them to perform the B8 experiments at Haigerloch, even though all the necessary materials were in place at Stadtilm and Gerlach considered that Diebner's preparations were much more advanced than those at Haigerloch.

Wirtz remained behind at the schoolhouse guarding the nuclear materials while Heisenberg's group scoured Baden-Württemberg looking for transport and finally succeeded in arranging for a convoy at Stuttgart. Dr Erich Bagge supervised the lorries, and after an involuntary stay of three weeks at Stadtilm, Wirtz and the nuclear materials were collected on 23 February and the convoy set off for Haigerloch travelling mainly under cover of darkness. After being regularly strafed by night fighters on the way, they eventually made it to Haigerloch on the third day.

But what was the point of such an unnecessary and dangerous proceeding?

There can be only one possible explanation.

1. Heisenberg's calculations had proved to him that there was enough heavy water and uranium at Stadtilm to assemble the critical reactor.
2. Heisenberg falsely believed as a result of theoretical error respecting the stability of a critical power reactor that it would become rapidly divergent at criticality and explode within a second, accompanied by radiation release.
3. Gerlach, Diebner and Harteck were not party to this belief, for, if they had been, Diebner and Harteck would have insisted that the resources of the project should be diverted at once to the very-low-temperature liquid carbon reactor which was safe in theory. This was the reason why Heisenberg had not enlightened them.

4. Heisenberg's motive in depleting the stock of heavy water at Stadtilm was to prevent an attempt by Diebner's group to build a critical power reactor, thereby believing he was saving the lives of Diebner's scientific team and those of the inhabitants of Stadtilm.
5. Heisenberg had no need to take an excess over the 1500 kilos of heavy water and the same weight of uranium cubes, since his aim was to perform only the B8 sub-critical experiment.

Heisenberg's laboratory had been built in a large cave within a massive rock in the Württemberg village of Haigerloch. A generator was installed at a nearby inn to supply the power for pumps and lighting, and a watertight concrete pit had been excavated in the floor of the cave to receive the outer alloy cylinder lined with the graphite reflector. The main reactor vessel slotted into its interior. Suspended from its graphite lid was a lattice of seventy-eight chains supporting 680 uranium metal cubes weighing a total of 1½ tons. Once the lid was secured in place, a radium-beryllium source was introduced through a chimney into the centre of the pile and the heavy water was gradually pumped in, also through the chimney, amid frequent pauses for measurements. The experiments began at the end of February, 1945.

Wirtz[55] states that Gerlach put in an appearance during the experiments and made a remark which Wirtz did not understand to the effect that if the experiment succeeded, that is, if the reactor went critical, then Germany would have a bomb of great destructive potential.

The experiments were concluded on 1 March, 1945, Wirtz announcing a neutron multiplication factor of 6.7, which is to say, 670 neutrons were measured at the surface for every 100 injected by the radium-beryllium source at the centre of the core.

It was calculated that the radius of the core was 71 cm and that the critical size was a radius of 80 cm, which would have been achieved by an increase of just under a further half of its dimension. This meant that the total of the uranium and heavy water held at Stadtilm and Haigerloch combined was sufficient for the construction of a critical reactor, but it could not possibly have been Heisenberg's intention that the B8 experiment should have proceeded to criticality.

In his first wartime paper in December, 1939, on the subject of the nuclear reactor, he had said:

'An extraordinarily intensive neutron and gamma radiation goes hand in hand with the energy production.... The radiation is, therefore, 100,000 times greater than that produced in a large cyclotron.... even if a substantial amount of this radiation is absorbed in the core of the pile. Nevertheless the working reactor would obviously require the provision of the most comprehensive biological shielding against radiation. This applies *especially* at the "switching-on" of the machine, that is, at the initiation of criticality.'

There was no biological shielding above the pit at Haigerloch, which was covered by an alloy lid with a lining of graphite.

Whereas the action of a graphite reflector is to repel most escaping neutrons back into the reactor core, graphite is not in the least effective against gamma radiation.

If we are to assume that there was any intention whatever to induce the Haigerloch reactor to become critical, then we must also believe that it was intended to shut the reactor down by the use of the neutron absorber cadmium in the fraction of a second between the onset of criticality and the rise in the core temperature beyond 320°C, the melting point of the cadmium. Moreover, the introduction of the cadmium into the core would have required the attendance of one of the physicists on the lid of the unshielded radiating pile in order to gain access to the chimney of the reactor for the purpose of inserting the rod.

Heisenberg's senior experimentalist, Dr Karl Wirtz, stated that if the heavy water reactor had gone critical, the expected output at the critical moment would have been only a few watts. One watt of power is produced for every 3×10^{16} fissions per second. The power output of the reactor is directly related proportionally to the number of fissions occurring in the core. If there were to be a change of reactivity of only 0.003 neutrons per cubic centimetre, the power level would soar to 8,000 times the original level in less than three seconds.

As has been previously explained, Professor Heisenberg was convinced that the Period of the Reactor, which was calculated on the prompt neutron lifetime and the increase in the number of neutrons of one generation over the preceding generation, was less than one second in length. Believing, in consequence, that the reactor power continuously increased exponentially with time, Heisenberg would have been inevitably forced to conclude that the reactor was impossibly dangerous in practice.

Only after the war, in his reproduction report respecting the Haigerloch B8 experiment, published in the *FIAT Review of German Science 1939-1945*, did Heisenberg acknowledge that his theory had been at fault, admitting:

'American work shows that the Period of the Reactor is substantially extended by the delayed emergence of a number of those neutrons liberated during the fission process.'

These delayed neutrons were first reported on by Joliot, von Halban and Kowarski in the periodical *Nature* on 22 April, 1939. This was the crucial fact of reaction chemistry that Heisenberg had omitted to include in his mathematical calculations since then and which had misled him into believing that a chain reaction in a reactor could not be controlled.

A small fraction of neutrons created in fission, approximately 0.75 per cent, are given off at discrete amounts of time after the fission process occurs, and these have a very large mean lifetime of from 0.2 to 80 seconds as compared with the mean lifetime of prompt neutrons ($5 \times 10^{+14}$ seconds). The effect, however, of a mere 0.75 per cent of delayed neutrons is such as to make the entire problem of reactor control a simple feasible one rather than an impossible one. Heisenberg had failed to appreciate that the generation time is a weighted average of the slowing down and diffusion time of the prompt neutron lifetime added to the mean lifetime of the delayed neutrons. This would have shown him that, while neutron density increases exponentially with time, the stable Period of the Reactor is 'not less than one second', but is about 54 seconds, and is almost entirely independent of the prompt neutron lifetime.

Similarly ignorant of the effect of the delayed neutrons, both the French physicist, von Halban in *Nature*, edition 143, p.793 (1939) and Dr Siegfried Flügge in *Naturwissenschaften*, edition 27, p.402 (1939) had stressed that if the chain reaction was not inhibited at the very instant of its onset, then it would swiftly lead to an explosion and melt-down with radiation leakage. They had tentatively suggested that, by placing in the reactor core beforehand a small unspecified concentration of cadmium, a very good absorber of neutrons in the thermal range below 0.625 eV, it might be possible to check the neutron avalanche and so bring the reactor to stability. Professor Houtermans had also made a pointed reference to the stability problem in a paper which definitely came to Heisenberg's attention in September, 1941, but not until July of the following year, into the third year of the German uranium project, did Heisenberg summon up a wary mention of the subject. Not that he intended to do anything about it. In his report on the final B8 experiment he explained:

'The cadmium rods were to have been inserted through the

chimney of the reactor for the purpose of stabilizing the reaction if it seemed that the critical size could be achieved.'

But this optimistic remark obscures the fact later confirmed in the same report that he had neglected to inform himself as to what quantities of cadmium might be required, for:

'the size of the cadmium rods required to impart a reliable stability to the reactor still needs close study.'

This was as far as he had got towards solving the problem of reactor stability in the six years since von Halban and Flügge had first mentioned it: if a means did exist to stabilize Nazi Germany's power reactor, then he did not wish to be the one to find it.

In captivity at Farm Hall, Huntingdon, after the capitulation, the German physicists were secretly tape-recorded in conversation immediately following the announcement of the dropping of the atomic bomb on Hiroshima. It was assumed that the bomb must have been a plutonium device.

Hahn:	'For 93 [the neptunium-plutonium decay series] they must have a machine that will run for a very long time. If the Americans have a uranium bomb, then you're all second-raters. Poor old Heisenberg.
Heisenberg:	Did they use the word "uranium" in connection with this atomic bomb?
Hahn:	No.
Heisenberg:	Then it's got nothing to do with atoms, but the equivalent of 20,000 tons of high explosive.... I am willing to believe that it is a high pressure bomb and I don't believe that it has anything to do with uranium, but that it is a chemical thing where they have enormously increased the whole explosion.'

Hahn's contemptuous dismissal of Heisenberg arose not because either scientist had wanted to build the Nazi atom bomb but purely on account of the exposure of Heisenberg's defective reactor theory. This is confirmed by Hahn's immediate impression that 'the Americans have a machine that will run for a long time'.

Heisenberg's disbelief in the feasibility of the atomic bomb was entrenched in his erroneous estimate of the fast fission critical mass, from which he had calculated that the U^{235} bomb could not be exploded beyond a fizzle by virtue of the physical law that a sphere small for its weight loses too great a proportion of neutrons at its surface to sustain a chain reaction.

Heisenberg had reiterated what he considered to be the insurmountable nature of this problem in his address to the Reich Research Council on 26 February, 1942. There are indications that Gerlach's Kummersdorf group under Diebner may have experimented with ordinary explosives in an attempt to cause a chain reaction in uranium by means of an implosion.

In a letter from Professor Gerlach, the Plenipotentiary for Nuclear Physics, dated 18 November, 1944, and addressed to Professor Mentzel, Gerlach had stated:

> 'According to all experimental and theoretical investigations undertaken to date... it is not possible to sustain an explosive chain reaction with small quantities of the substance. I can assure you that we have gone into this problem from more than just one avenue of approach.'

There is talk in the Farm Hall transcripts of a bomb with a critical size of between 400 kilos and 40 tons, but this must have been an idea created for the benefit of the eavesdroppers, whose presence must surely have been suspected. The 200 pages of conversations, notable for what was not said rather than for that which was, are in the main so trivial that one wonders why they remained secret for so long.

For reasons including Heisenberg's error as to the critical size, there was never any such thing as a German atomic bomb project. The very concept was an irrelevancy.

The only nuclear weapons projects in Nazi Germany which presented any danger of achievement were the attempts to construct a critical reactor for its fission products to be used in radiation weapons. This aspect of the State-controlled research, which had been sabotaged by Heisenberg, came to its unsuccessful conclusion at Haigerloch.

That Heisenberg had managed to divert attention away from the simple cold reactor for the entire war was his most extraordinary accomplishment. If ever he had confirmed his belief that the heat-reactor was impossible, the alternative low-temperature reactor would have been seized upon by Goering with the direst consequences for all.

When Gerlach was informed that the Haigerloch results had

confirmed the prognosis, he misinterpreted that ambiguous statement to mean that criticality had been achieved.

Celebrating the news with Dr Rosbaud, Gerlach talked of evacuating the research to the Führer's Alpine Redoubt for the six months he needed in which to carry out the 'chemical reactions'; the German Government could now use this triumph to obtain terms, he said.

By implication, 'chemical reactions' probably referred to a substantial fissioning of the uranium fuel in the reactor, which would require approximately a 180-day cycle to yield sufficient quantities of radioisotopes for weapons purposes. It was a cruel misunderstanding; months later in internment, Gerlach was still completely grief-stricken at the failure of the project.

A forward party of the 114-strong Allied Intelligence Mission, codenamed *Alsos*, under the overall control of General Leslie R. Groves arrived in France on 9 August, 1944, and established its Headquarters at Neuilly. The military head was Colonel Boris T. Pash, who had been charged with a mission that was to 'cover all principal scientific developments and to gain knowledge of enemy progress without disclosing our interest in any particular field'.

The scientific head was the physicist Samuel A. Goudsmit. Whereas the scope of the intended intelligence activity extended beyond the uranium project, Goudsmit's group of scientists were specifically concentrating their investigations into all aspects of German uranium research. From the outset Goudsmit had concluded that 'no one but Professor Heisenberg could be the brains of a German uranium project and every physicist throughout the world knew that'.[56]

For the six months following its arrival, the *Alsos* mission operated from Paris. Following the fall of Brussels on 9 September, 1944, Goudsmit went to the offices of the Union Minière Company and inspected their papers; a perusal of the stock ledgers showed that purchases of over 1000 tons of uranium materials had been imported into Germany during the four years of occupation.

Groves[57] records that information from a Dutch source indicated that in May, 1940, nine rail waggons containing 72 tons of uranium ore had been sent to Le Havre ahead of the German advance and that two waggons had been intercepted there by the Germans, while the remaining seven cars had been rerouted to Bordeaux. In late 1944 30 tons of these ores were recovered by the Americans at Toulouse but the remaining 42 tons could not be accounted for.

The *Alsos* mission entered Germany on 24 February, 1945. On 30 March they occupied the Kaiser Wilhelm Institute for Physics at

Heidelberg where they found Professor Bothe. Bothe told Goudsmit the whereabouts of Hahn, Heisenberg and Max von Laue and the German uranium pile, which, he told them, had been evacuated to Haigerloch in Württemberg and was known not to have gone critical.

At Lindau the bulk of the files of the Reich Research Council were seized, and on 17 April, 1945, Harteck and Groth's ultracentrifuge laboratory was discovered in a parachute-silk mill at Celle.

Within the remaining three weeks of European war nearly all the important atomic physicists were rounded up and, upon the discovery and destruction of the cave laboratory at Haigerloch, the programme came to its conclusion.

On 2 May, 1945, Heisenberg was found in the company of his wife and children at Urfeld by Colonel Pash, and the Americans were now satisfied that they knew everything.

The *Alsos* mission has always been hailed as an outstanding intelligence success, a model of its kind. But the real truth of the matter is that *Alsos* was a disastrous failure, of which the principal cause was the selection of the physicist, Professor Samuel Goudsmit, to be its scientific head. From the time of his appointment, he had closed his mind to the possibility that any German physicist but Heisenberg might be the brain behind the German atomic development programme.

When American military realists dryly suggested that possibly other German scientists of whom Goudsmit had never heard might be secretly working on some form of uranium weapon, Goudsmit derided the idea as an impossibility; it had to be Heisenberg.

The upshot of this unscientific proceeding was that the German Post Office project remained uninvestigated, since it was held to be unnecessary to ascertain from the Russians, or anybody else, the possible extent of Postmaster-General Ohnesorge's research simply because it had no connection with Heisenberg's programme.

Neither was Goudsmit the only culprit. General Leslie R. Groves could not plead that its possible importance had not been drawn to his attention, for together with the British Chancellor of the Exchequer, he had been one of the two addressees of the Anglo-U.S. Report of 28 November, 1944, issued by the British Nuclear Physics Directorate, known under the cover name of Directorate of Tube Alloys (DTA). He was advised

'there seem to have been some very interesting publications from the private laboratory of Manfred von Ardenne (Berlin Lichterfelde-Ost) who made money from radio patents and has, for some years, been working on the technical applications of electronics.... At the end of 1941 F G Houtermans published, from his laboratory, a long paper discussing, from a theoretical point of view, the energy consumption in the separation of isotopes and comparing the advantages of different methods with a view to a "possible future isotope separation for technical purposes." Since the appearance of this paper he has published others on nuclear physics with particular reference to fission, and there are indications that von Ardenne has installed a high-voltage generator in his laboratory for use in connection with this work. Reports have also been received that the Reichspost have laboratories in which high-tension apparatus has been installed and that the work carried out there is under the direction of von Ardenne and Dr Siegfried Flügge.

The activity of the Reichspost research department may of course imply that this Government department has a connection with the official organization of Tube Alloys (i.e. nuclear physics) work, but there is no proof of this as yet.'

In a concluding paragraph headed *Investigation of Tube Alloys' Activities in Germany*, Groves was advised of the DTA recommendation to the effect that

'In the first instance, detailed investigation of the Tube Alloys project in Germany be concentrated in two areas, Berlin and Bisingen and the surrounding country.

In Berlin, it should be possible to find traces of any official Wehrmacht or Nazi Party organizations responsible for the project; to examine the various laboratories of the Reichspost, and the private laboratory of von Ardenne.... These two preliminary investigations are likely, if conditions are favourable, to provide an accurate picture of the position of Tube Alloy work in Germany.'

On 23 April, 1945, General Leslie Groves, the overall head of the *Alsos* Intelligence Mission, reported to General George C. Marshall in Washington that the following could be concluded about the German atomic research:

'In 1940, the German Army in Belgium confiscated and removed to Germany about 1200 tons of uranium ore. So long as this material remained hidden under the control of the enemy, we could not be sure but that he might be preparing to use atomic weapons. Yesterday I was notified by cable that personnel of my office had located this material near Stassfurt, Germany, and that it was being removed to a safe place outside Germany where it would be under the complete control of American and British authorities.

The capture of this material, which was the bulk of uranium supplies in Europe, would seem to remove definitely any possibility of the Germans making use of an atomic bomb in this war.'

It will be observed from this injudicious statement that the determination of the question as to whether or not Nazi Germany had developed atomic weapons of any type rested solely on the basis of the opening and closing figures for the stock of uranium oxide seized in 1940 at Oolen.

There is no mention of the fact that General Groves' staff had been unable to account for the mysterious disappearance of 42 tons of the material last seen on a train bound for Bordeaux in May, 1940.

Groves had also failed to make a precautionary observation regarding the very substantial shipments of uranium products, amounting to well over 1000 tons, which had been purchased from the Union Minière between 1940 and 1944 by German brokers, a matter as to which Goudsmit had acquainted him.

The United States Government would hear again about atomic weapons, but from another source; within a month, they would know just how far they could rely on the assurances of General Groves.

Professor Samuel Goudsmit, a Dutch émigré, was the highest-ranking scientific member of the *Alsos* Mission, his selection having been approved by the Office of Scientific Research and Development and by General Groves personally. Although a physicist, he was not connected with the nuclear weapons project in any way, having spent most of the war working on radar.

He may have had limited access to technical information, but this hardly qualified him for the position. From a reading of the exchange of correspondence between Goudsmit and Heisenberg (1946-48) in his collected papers at the Institute of Physics in New York, it is quite clear that Goudsmit had not bothered to brief himself properly on the content of the German wartime nuclear physics papers even though he spoke the language, and consequently he did not know that Heisenberg had reported on the fast fission chain reaction in 1939, and others on the potential of breeding plutonium in nuclear reactors in the following two years.

Unable to sift out the material parts of these reports relating to the possible production of nuclear explosives, Goudsmit stumbled across Heisenberg's July, 1942, paper belatedly drawing attention to the possibility that a nuclear power reactor would probably explode at criticality, and concluded that this must be the German atomic bomb.

Goudsmit informed Groves that the Germans did not know the principle of the fast fission uranium bomb, and that they thought that they would need to drop an entire nuclear reactor instead in order to achieve an explosion. As we have seen, Groves accepted this without question and even included it in his book, (Groves, op. cit. p336) after he had become aware that the assertion was not correct.

After the war Goudsmit wrote a Germanophobic popular book, *Alsos — The Failure in German Science* (Sigma Books, London, 1947) which ridiculed the German research effort, portraying Heisenberg as a Nazi collaborator and a tragic failure. German science had wilted, he said, in an atmosphere of complacency and political interference.

It has been something of a tradition among American historians to speculate on whether Heisenberg would have built Hitler's atom bomb if he had been asked to do so, and the latest book of this genre, Mark Walker's *The Quest for Nuclear Power in National Socialist Germany 1939-1945* (Cambridge University Press, 1989) is a typical example of the rush to judgement without having first read the wartime physics reports with a modicum of scientific discrimination.

What distinguishes the enemy within from the collaborator is sabotage. An act of sabotage intended to be prejudicial to the National Socialist State justifies the presence of a person in any particular place if one of his primary purposes in being there is to commit an act of sabotage.

This was Heisenberg's claim: 'Effective resistance can only come from those who pretend to collaborate.' That was how he wished to be judged, as a saboteur. It is for the reader to make his own judgement as to whether any one single act or omission, or the conduct of Heisenberg as a whole, was purposely prejudicial to the uranium research project in National Socialist Germany.

If Heisenberg was a saboteur, then we must let him take his honoured place in history at last.

The British physicist Professor R. V. Jones, said of the German nuclear programme that he was only 'thankful that we were not put to the fearful test that faced our German counterparts'. But yet the presence of the greatest of them all during the years of trial was purely voluntary.

Heisenberg wrote about the pre-war *Schwarze Korps* affair[58] in terms which suggest that it was a deeply traumatic experience for him, but even so, when invited by Fermi to remain in the United States during his visit there in 1939, he explained:

> 'History teaches us that sooner or later, every century is shaken by revolutions and wars, and whole populations obviously cannot migrate every time there is a threat of such upheavals. People must learn to prevent catastrophes, not to run away from them. I have decided to stay in Germany, even if my decision is wrong.'[59]

Heisenberg was a patriot and a cultural imperialist of the old school who was rooted in Germany and had no desire to be anywhere else. He saw his duty as helping to prevent the catastrophe, not run away from it. In an interview immediately after the war with Professor Goudsmit, he stated that in his opinion, physicists on the whole had done only the minimum work necessary to preserve their university positions and hold together what remained of the great German tradition in physics. His own small circle had dominated the uranium project and steered the research away from the production of nuclear weapons. To him, the war was an interlude, and this is a point which does much to explain his attitude in the war's aftermath, in which he was anxious to sweep aside the rubble of old Germany and rebuild.

Emphasising the fact that Germany had not constructed atomic weapons, he made a public ritual of contrasting the moral character of German scientists, who had deliberately obstructed the research, with that of Allied scientists and politicians, who had not only built those weapons, but also used them, an attitude which was highly irritating to the Americans. Nevertheless, of all people, he could make the allegation with moral justification.

Heisenberg sacrificed his place in history for the sake of humanity, forsaking his great personal ambitions, on which many of his detractors have commented, to ensure that he headed an atomic programme that failed. This was the German Pimpernel, and his opposition to the National Socialist regime was probably the most destructive continuous act of resistance to Hitler.

If only because he prevented Harteck from developing the dry-ice reactor in 1940, which would have enabled Hitler to have used the monopoly of the radiation bomb to obtain victory for Germany in 1941,

Heisenberg's contribution to the ultimate defeat of Hitler was greater than that from any person on either side.

Against the advice of all the world's great physicists, he remained behind so as to work against the Nazi regime from within, and thus prevented the unimaginable catastrophe of a Nazi victory.

As a means of correcting Press inaccuracies following the announcement of the American atomic attack on the city of Hiroshima, the contingent of German atom scientists confined at Farm Hall, England, issued a memorandum on 7 August, 1945, presenting an outline in brief of the official German uranium project.

The document was drafted by Heisenberg, Wirtz and Gerlach after consultation with Bagge, Diebner, Otto Hahn, Harteck, Korsching, von Laue and von Weizsäcker.

Only the second paragraph alluded to the idea of nuclear weapons development philosophy, asserting in a single sentence that 'it did not appear feasible at the time to produce a bomb with the technical possibilities available in Germany.'

There was an explanatory footnote:

'As to the question of the atom bomb, the undersigned confirm that they have no knowledge of any other group in Germany which had the production of the bomb as an immediate goal. However, if such an attempt was in fact undertaken, then it was made by dilettantes, and should not be taken seriously.'

This will be an appropriate point to leave the official programme of uranium research and to look at a group of dilettantes.

CHAPTER 2

The Private Uranium Project Of The National Socialist Post Office Ministry

'Ohnesorge, the Postmaster-General, probably believed that he would rise enormously in his Führer's estimation if he of all people, though in charge of a civilian department, were to present Hitler one day with a "miracle weapon". But when the long yearned-for moment at last arrived and Ohnesorge, at a meeting of the Cabinet, started to hold forth about the present position of his studies in connection with the provision of a uranium bomb, Hitler interrupted him with the contemptuous observation, "Look here, gentlemen! You are all racking your brains to discover how we are going to win the war and, lo and behold, here comes our Postmaster, of all people, with a solution of the problem!"'

> Robert Jungk,
> *Brighter Than a Thousand Suns*

'Nevertheless, I, of all people, did in fact lead the way for the great advance of atomic development in the German Reich.'

> Wilhelm Ohnesorge (1872-1962) Postmaster-General in Nazi Germany from 1937-1945; attributed to him in an obituary, *Soldatenzeitung*, Berlin, 16 March, 1962.

THE EMINENCE BEHIND the independent German atomic research programme, Dr Wilhelm Ohnesorge, was born at Gräfenheinichen, Bitterfeld, on 8 June, 1872. He obtained a doctorate in mathematics and physics, but chose to pursue a career as an engineer in the new fields of telegraphy and telephony. He had an inventive mind, and one of his patents, the four wire trunking switchgear, found worldwide application.

During the First World War he served at the Kaiser's General Headquarters as the Chief of Telegraphy. After Germany's defeat in 1918, when he was 46 years of age, Ohnesorge continued his career in diverse areas of Post Office management, and by 1929 he had become President of the Reichspost Central Headquarters at Berlin Tempelhof.

Ohnesorge was an early convert to National Socialism, and was close to Hitler from the beginning of the movement. He merited his future Führer's favour for the distinction of having set up the first NSDAP district organization outside Bavaria, at Dortmund in 1920.

Following the seizure of power, Ohnesorge accepted the portfolio as Secretary of State for the Post Office on 2 February, 1933, and entered the Cabinet as Reichspostminister in 1937, a position he retained until the capitulation.

Ohnesorge was a disciple of Philipp Lenard, one of the proponents of the 'Aryan physics' dogma, having been converted at one of the physicist's Kiel lectures; Lenard states in his autobiography[1] that Ohnesorge delivered the keynote address during the celebration of the physicist's eightieth birthday in 1942.

He appears to have been a reserved, diligent individual much admired by Hitler[2] for his industry, in particular for his persistent search for practical applications for the inventions of his department's scientists and engineers. Hitler always observed Ohnesorge's birthday with a congratulatory telegram and often an invitation to an intimate table talk at the Reichskanzlei.

The German Post Office handled all telegraphic and telephone communications as well as the mails and had a large budget for research, part of which was allocated to an atomic development programme for which Ohnesorge had a particular interest.

Once again we see an odd pragmatism in the attitude of a confirmed Nazi who, while worshipping at the feet of Lenard, the guru of Aryan physics, which eschewed atomic physics as an alien pseudo-science, was at the same time an advocate of the atom bomb and would eventually make the Third Reich an atomic power.

The Post Office was almost completely divorced from the proceedings of the official physics community in Germany, with whom few relations were maintained, and it was in the atmosphere of secrecy which this self-containment engendered that the atomic weapons project was enabled to flourish.

Baron Manfred von Ardenne was born on 20 January, 1907, in Hamburg, the eldest of five children and the son of Egmont, Baron von Ardenne , an officer in the army of the Kaiser.

During the First World War his father served at the war ministry in Berlin, where he was engaged on the scientific evaluation of secret weapons. It was at this time that the first incidental acquaintanceship between the families of Ohnesorge and von Ardenne was made.

As for the young Manfred, a family photograph session during a summer holiday at Bayrischzell in 1912 awakened in the five year-old a burning curiosity to understand the optical laws that governed the operation of the camera; he was to remember in later life that it was from this moment that his early interest in all matters scientific stemmed.

At one time he aspired to be a professional photographer, but his interests soon crystallized into a desire to concentrate all his energies into radio technology.

Shortly after leaving High School, he obtained an indispensable training in a radio workshop laboratory; by the time his apprenticeship had been completed in 1924, he had even acquired a small income from technical treatises, from the royalties on his first books and from the proceeds of his inventions.

He was specializing in the investigation of High Frequency circuitry problems, but when a respected physicist advised him that his methods could lead only to partial solutions, and that he would begin to make real progress only with precision measurements and a thorough grounding in the theory, he took his advice and enrolled for four semesters at the University of Berlin studying the principles of physics, chemistry and mathematics.

During this period he was to fall under the spell of the great scientists who then distinguished that university: Einstein, Max Planck and Max von Laue among many others.

Completing his terms at university, he continued his work from a large laboratory installed in his parents' house. He was now frequently invited to speak publicly about his experimental work, and even made technical radio broadcasts; thus he was rapidly becoming a figure of note, and had besides numerous contacts with the leading scientists and engineers in the High Frequency discipline.

One of the significant discoveries he made in 1924 jointly with H. Heinert, that the sound volume of a receiver increased when the cathodes of the amplifying valves were very slightly heated, was reported in the *Yearbook of Wireless Telegraphy and Telephony* and was further evidence of the topical importance of his work. This was followed in 1926 by his development of the simple triple-valve receiver which, when marketed, sold several million units and led to the purchase price of domestic wireless receivers in Germany being cut by two-thirds.

By the end of 1927 von Ardenne was employing a number of scientific assistants, and the expansion of his activities, which involved the accumulation of large quantities of technical apparatus, dictated the establishment of a larger laboratory elsewhere.

In January, 1928, he rented a large house at Jungfernstieg 19, in the Berlin suburb of Lichterfelde-Ost. The contract, for which his father was guarantor, contained a loose option clause for the later purchase of the dwelling and the 5,000 square metres of ground in which it stood. Although he had concluded a long rental, within a year the lessor invoked the option and insisted that von Ardenne either buy the house and land or quit.

He had already installed much of his equipment and its removal would have meant a substantial financial loss to him. He was not rich and it was thus with a heavy heart that he decided to buy the house. It was to be his home and workplace for the next sixteen years.

Until then all his income had been directed into building up the laboratory facilities; now at the age of twenty-two, he had taken upon himself an enormous debt of 150,000 Reichsmarks.

A third of this sum he obtained as a short term loan secured on his laboratory from a previous employer, the radio firm David Loewe; von Ardenne had no alternative but to accept the possibility of the loss of his business in default. He suspected that the primary purpose of the loan was to obtain possession of the laboratory, and he developed an iron resolve that he would deny them.

The windfall of a very lucrative contract from the Post Office for the production of measuring instruments put von Ardenne into a position where he could repay the debt to David Loewe; the businessman never forgave him for settling in time.

The Secretary of State for the German Post Office in 1930 was Dr Kruckow; he was later to tell von Ardenne that, knowing of his financial plight, he had ensured that the contract was steered in his direction. Nevertheless, despite the cash injection from the Post Office and the revenues derived from the licensing of his inventions to manufacturers, his circumstances were so straitened that he slept for eighteen months in a bedroom which had neither wardrobe nor carpet.

His poverty was so evident that when he was confined to bed with a virus and David Loewe came to visit him with a gift of roses, tears of pity welled up in eyes that had always been cold. Had he looked in on the laboratory on his way out, he might not have been so sympathetic.

The contract with the Post Office brought von Ardenne to the attention of Wilhelm Ohnesorge; the two men met for the first time at the Berlin Technical High School in 1930 at a public meeting chaired by the Commissioner for the Reich Radio Service, Dr Hans Bredow. The subject under discussion was an enquiry into von Ardenne's far-reaching proposals relating to the installation of a chain of relay stations aimed at overcoming the problem of poor quality wireless reception in cities.

The system he had devised would have been of special appeal to lower income groups, because it brought with it a general fall in the purchase price of domestic radio receivers; its attraction became the rallying point for its opponents, the manufacturing concerns, and Dr Bredow ran into such opposition that he was unable to take any decision. von Ardenne made himself a host of enemies, and found consolation only from the scientists, Barkhausen and Möller, while Ohnesorge, then a Post Office functionary, offered him sympathy once the meeting had broken up.

An example of the way in which von Ardenne was always able further to diversify his technological genius was shown on Christmas Eve, 1930, when he demonstrated an elementary television to Post Office Secretary Dr Kruckow; four months later he repeated the exercise before the directors of Telefunken, Fernseh AG and scientists of the Post Office.

Experiments with the cathode ray tube occupied him for the next two years, and by 1933 he could be sure that his laboratory had a firm basis both as regards finance and reputation. He had been awarded a contract by C. Lorenz AG for the development of television and radar; in 1936 his laboratory, or 'Institute' as he now preferred that it should be called, supplied cathode ray oscillographs to experimental centres of the civilian airline and the German Navy for the study of radar technology.

Every year von Ardenne's 'Institute' was represented at the television exhibitions staged by the German Post Office. In 1933 at the Berlin Radio Exhibition, von Ardenne was presented to Adolf Hitler by Ohnesorge, who introduced him with the most generous references to his early work for the Post Office.

Early in 1934 Ohnesorge granted von Ardenne a private laboratory facility for radar research inside the Post Office Central Headquarters, and he seized the opportunity to perfect a transducer, the patent for which was applied for on 25 February that year. At this time he was subjected to increasing pressure to join the Nazi Party, but such was his status that he was able to decline, as his father had done before him.

At the instigation of Ohnesorge, now Reichspostminister, at the end of 1937 a permanent contract was signed between von Ardenne's Lichterfeld-Ost Institute and the Research Establishment of the German Post Office (*Forschungsanstalt der Deutschen Reichspost*) for the development of radar and television, supplemented in 1940 by the discipline of nuclear physics.

For the three years following 1937 von Ardenne devoted himself to the development and review of electron-microscopy, and his labours were rewarded in July, 1940, by Krupps with a contract for their entire research programme in that field.

In the 15 August, 1939, edition of the daily newspaper *Deutsche Allgemeine Zeitung* there appeared an article by the theoretical physicist Dr Siegfried Flügge under the headline 'The Use of Atomic Energy'. This was followed, after a short preamble, by a long paragraph headed:

Fantastic Energies

'Following the announcement by Professor Hahn at the end of the year of the splitting of the uranium nucleus, we asked ourselves the question. "Since the collision between a neutron and a nucleus produces the release of a number of fresh neutrons, what happens to these?"

The answer is that each will have the opportunity to split another uranium nucleus, and then those newly released neutrons will bring about the production of more fresh neutrons and so on, as long as there is enough uranium fuel available for them to work on.

All the available uranium fuel is therefore instantaneously split down in a rapidly inflating avalanche of neutrons. This is what is called in chemistry a chain reaction.

So now we can achieve something which has never been done before; with just a single neutron to set it off, we can transform any lump of uranium of critical size and release its nuclear energy.

It is possible to calculate fairly accurately just how much energy can be got from it. In nature, uranium comes in the form of uranium oxide, the purified form of the ore pitchblende, which is mined at Joachimstal in the Sudetenland.

One cubic metre of this oxide weighs 4.2 tonnes and contains 9,000 billion billion uranium atoms. When a uranium nucleus is fissioned, approximately a three-billionth part of a kilogram-metre is released; and 27,000 billion kilogram-metres for the entire cubic metre lump of the oxide.

Remembering that a cubic kilometre of water weighs a billion kilograms, this energy would be sufficient to lift one cubic kilometre of water to a height of 27 kilometres, and that means catapaulting the contents of Lake Wannsee into the stratosphere!

There had been a more scholarly exposition of the principle two months earlier in the periodical *Naturwissenschaften*, but von Ardenne recalls that it was Flügge's popular article which was the catalyst for his own interest in nuclear physics, as it also appears to have been for many figures in higher State and even scientific circles.

von Ardenne inferred that the enormous significance of atomic physics had not been appreciated by the science heads of Germany's great electrical concerns, since there was no evidence to show that they were interested in developing the larger types of particle accelerator essential to the expansion of the physics. He visited Professor Philipp, one of Professor Hahn's associates, and asked him if he would not try to set such a programme in motion, but Philipp replied that the moment was inopportune, as the matter had already been considered and passed over.

He found the attitude of Hahn's Institute disappointing, even apathetic; von Ardenne called on Ohnesorge towards the end of 1939 and lectured him on the enormity of Hahn's discovery, subsequently reiterating the main points in a letter.

In December of that year, Professor Max von Laue visited the Lichterfelde-Ost laboratory and viewed von Ardenne's electron microscope. On 2 February, 1940, the great physicist Max Planck called on him, ostensibly to see the instrument, but primarily on an errand at the instigation of Hahn[3] with a view to influencing von Ardenne to moderate his enthusiasm.

Max Planck was shown the highly magnified frames depicting for him for the first time a view of the microcosmos in stereo. Once the visit was over, von Ardenne drove the Professor home. As they motored through the Berlin streets to the house in the Grunewald district, the conversation centred on atomic physics, and von Ardenne asked Max Planck for his opinion of the consequences of Hahn's achievement in splitting the uranium nucleus.

It will be unimaginable. Think of the danger if the new power should get into the wrong hands.'

von Ardenne suggested that it was perhaps the most powerful energy source in nature.

'Indeed it is,'Professor Planck responded, 'and it ought to be devoted to the benefit of mankind. But that will turn out not to be the case.'

In his autobiography *Ein glückliches Leben für Forschung und Technik* (Verlag der Nation, East Berlin 1972), von Ardenne stated that it was this short conversation with Max Planck which fuelled his scepticism for Nazi politics, that it represented a turning point in his thinking, that it was precisely then that it struck him that the insane war which Hitler had initiated could only end in total disaster.

It is, however, difficult to reconcile this assertion with his subsequent activity, for his fascination with Hahn's discovery was inexplicably driving him ever deeper into the quest for the atom bomb.

In the course of an exchange of house calls at Berlin Dahlem and Lichterfelde-Ost, von Ardenne had shown an ominous interest in nuclear explosives: finally he came right out with it and put the question to Hahn and Heisenberg as to how many grams of the pure U^{235} isotope it would require 'to unleash a chain reaction running its course within a single moment', that is, a uranium atom bomb.

Glancing uneasily at each other, the two Professors told him, 'a few kilos'.[4]

It was not lost on either of them that von Ardenne had not been impressed by Max Planck and that he was still giving serious consideration to the possibility of physically constructing an atom bomb; with his dynamism and business acumen, he was quite capable of planning the entire operation and motivating the electrical concerns to support him.

As has been mentioned earlier, the explosive substance in a uranium atom bomb consists of two sub-critical lumps of the isotope U^{235} enriched from 0.7 per cent to about 70 per cent. When the two lumps, which in the aggregate exceed the critical mass, are fired together by conventional explosive within a gun assembly, the explosion occurs instantaneously.

In his conversations with Hahn and Heisenberg, and later with Ohnesorge, von Ardenne had stated that he considered it to be technically feasible, using highly sophisticated mass separators, to obtain kilogramme quantities of the enriched isotope U^{235}, provided one could obtain the co-operation of industry. He had in fact already designed a prototype based on the mass spectrometer, he informed them; a preliminary study had indicated that electro-magnetic techniques were probably the most efficient of all for separating the uranium isotopes. The isotopes could not be separated by chemical means. Because they were chemically identical, the separation had to be done by a physical method.

Whereas Heisenberg was alarmed at von Ardenne's interest in the atomic bomb, he was more probably concerned to swiftly stultify interest in the 'mass separator' because it was clearly the best possible means to enrich the U^{235} isotope from 0.75 per cent to 1.5 per cent, enabling the construction of a critical reactor using ordinary water instead of heavy water as a moderator.

Explaining his brainchild to Ohnesorge later, von Ardenne found the Nazi Postmaster-General enthusiastic: Ohnesorge promised to speak to the Führer about it.

According to Ohensorge himself[5], he saw Hitler alone and the interview lasted but a few seconds. When Ohnesorge said, 'Mein Führer, I can give you the atomic bomb!', Hitler replied dryly, 'Now wouldn't that be a fine thing, having my Postmaster-General invent the atom bomb!'[6]

The mystified Reichsminister departed from the Presence and sadly informed von Ardenne that the Führer appeared simply not interested in an atom bomb.

Ohnesorge's disappointment was shared only momentarily by von Ardenne , whose versatile mind had already seen other interesting avenues to explore within the atomic science discipline, in particular the application of radioactive isotopes for use as tracers in the analytical fields of medicine, biochemistry and biology.

Nowadays radioisotopes are an irreplaceable aid in scientific research. They are used as tracer atoms, differing essentially from the ordinarily used stable isotopes of the same element only by being radioactive. Even a minute addition of a radioactive substance is easily detectable, and thus, by adding the radioisotope to the stable isotopes of an element, it is possible by the use of sensitive instrumentation to investigate the properties and behaviour of that element a thousand times more efficiently than by weighing, or by chemical or spectographic methods.

Since nearly all the elements and nearly all their compounds can be tagged in this way, the radioactive indicator is now a universal means of research and has led to the most significant advances in biochemistry, metallurgy and metallography, and medical science.

This was the work which had now begun to fascinate von Ardenne, and which was to culminate in the widely acclaimed publication *The Physical Principles of the Application of Radioactive or Stable Isotopes as Indicators* which he published in 1944.

To assist him in producing radioisotopes in large quantities, he thought that it would be most helpful if he could build a nuclear reactor.

To von Ardenne's surprise, the representations he had made to Ohnesorge in December, 1939, now bore fruit and the Postmaster issued instructions for the building of a one-million volt Van De Graaf generator (subsequently completed in 1941) in the house at Lichterfelde-Ost, and he also ordered the setting-up of a second Post Office atomic research facility at Miersdorf-Zeuthen to the south-east of Berlin, which was to be equipped with a Phillips Cascade generator. Both centres received the component parts of a small 60 ton cyclotron for construction on site and finally von Ardenne took possession of the pilot plant for his electromagnetic isotope enrichment scheme.

In 1947, when the design of the equipment used by the Americans at their Oak Ridge, Tennessee, complex was published in *Physical Review*, the essential similarities of the two models were recognized, von Ardenne's invention having the better plasma ion source.

His paper, *Respecting A New Magnetic Isotope Separator for High Mass Transport* issued by the Forschungsanstalt der Deutschen Reichspost in April, 1942, was cold-shouldered by the official programme, probably as a result of lobbying by Heisenberg. In order to discourage further his unwelcome interest in the nuclear programme, Professor von Weizsäcker, Heisenberg's close friend, went along to see von Ardenne on 10 October, 1940, with a cock-and-bull story about atom-bombs not being feasible because the rising temperature in the mass would shut down the chain reaction prematurely.

In contrast to the State institutes and the State controlled or subsidized laboratories of industry, which were subject to the provisions of the law of 7 April, 1933, 'on the restoration of the professional civil service' which proscribed Jews, half-Jews, political offenders and various other categories from public office, it was open to von Ardenne to employ such persons and he had made it known that he was prepared to assist in suitable cases. Professor Max von Laue made representations to him in May, 1940, on behalf of the nuclear physicist Fritz Georg Houtermans.

As von Ardenne was hoping to expand the atomic physics section of the Institute at the time, and was himself preoccupied with his experiments into radioactive and stable isotopes for his Indicator method, he was especially pleased to be able to accede to von Laue's request.

An Austrian national, born on 22 January, 1903, of a Dutch father and a Viennese Jewess, Houtermans was also a Communist and, therefore, fell foul of the Civil Service law on two counts; his circumstances could hardly have been less favourable.

He had obtained his PhD at Göttingen in 1927 and was Assistant Professor at the University of Berlin by 1933. He was without doubt one of the foremost physicists of the twentieth century, his special field of interest being thermonuclear and chain reactions. On the latter subject he had delivered his inaugural address to the Technical Academy in Berlin in 1932, stating that he believed neutrons to be the key to the release of the most powerful forces dormant in matter. His paper expounded the idea that the neutron, which was electrically neutral, could penetrate to the atomic nucleus in spite of the latter's protection by electric barriers of millions of volts, dissipating its energy in the collision. This theory anticipated Hahn's discovery of the splitting of the nucleus in 1938, and the confirmation by the French team of Joliot and others in 1939 of the chain reaction, for he gave as his condition the single requirement that the collision should cause the release of more than one fresh neutron per fission by which the process would be continued repeatedly.

He spent two years in the United Kingdom in 1933 and 1934, where he worked as resident physicist with the firm EMI at Hayes in Middlesex. In 1935 he was drawn by his Communist convictions to accept a position in the Soviet Union at the Ukraine Institute of Physics in Kharkov, where he continued his studies towards the elucidation of the question of the chain reaction.

In 1937 he was lecturing on neutron absorption to the Soviet Academy of Science and it has been thought likely that he must then have been close to the discovery of nuclear fission himself.

In that year, however, together with other foreign Communists, he fell victim to Stalin's great purge, and was imprisoned and tortured in an unsuccessful attempt to extract from him a false confession of scientific espionage.

In 1939 he was offered rehabilitation and a full restoration of his former offices together with Soviet citizenship, but he declined on the grounds of their maltreatment of him.

In 1940 the Soviet secret police deported numerous foreign scientists, among them many, including Houtermans, who had originally been fugitive from Hitler's Germany, and delivered them into the hands of the Gestapo at an agreed exchange point at Brest-Litovsk on the German-Russian frontier in occupied Poland.

Paroled into the custody of Professor von Laue on the latter's intercession, and on the condition that he remained under Gestapo observation and did not engage in any State or university research project, Houtermans was thus placed with von Ardenne.

It is interesting to note that in August, 1944, Houtermans issued a report from the Reich Bureau of Standards which indicates that for the purposes of the Civil Service law he had ceased to be a proscribed person, since that was a State office. What follows may suggest the reason how this was accomplished.

On 1 January, 1941, Professor Houtermans was received into the family of laboratory workers at Lichterfelde-Ost where his imaginative genius soon thrust him into eminence. Earlier in his career, he had performed important calculations to lay the groundwork for the development of the hydrogen bomb in principle; now he was set the task of estimating the energy requirement for isotope separation, a matter which von Ardenne had recognized to be of importance not only for his own Indicator method using radioactive isotopes, but also for the realization of a working nuclear reactor in which uranium slightly rich in the isotope U^{235} could be moderated by ordinary water. On completion of the exercise, he compiled a table of cross-section measurements for slow neutrons.[7]

But the most significant results of his work were assembled in a Classified Report *On the Question of Initiating Nuclear Chain Reactions*,[8] a submission of 29 pages which he had proposed should not be published but which, as he remarked in a footnote to a reviewed version of it three years later, did enter limited circulation among the atomic physics community in August, 1941.

There can be no doubt but that this report was the decisive instrument of atomic weapons policy in Nazi Germany, but all major commentators have missed its significance. It was a magnificent piece of work. Houtermans had not had sight of any of the German classified wartime physics reports, as his table of reference papers proves, and his conclusions were based largely on his own experimental work, the results of which had not previously been published.

The primary purpose of the report was to show how a chain reaction in a nuclear pile could be brought about in the quickest and most effective manner; although he covered the production of plutonium, the fact that all working reactors produce plutonium had already been appreciated amongst German physicists since von Weizsäcker and the Austrians Schintlmeister and Hernegger had published their papers on the subject in the previous year.

Houtermans argued that if energy production was not required of the reactor, then the use of heavy water or graphite as a moderator was not necessary. If the reactor was required to produce fission products for the radioisotopes they contained, then a very low temperature reactor would suffice for the purpose.

Houtermans considered first the question of isotope enrichment. It will be recalled that the purpose of enriching the U^{235} isotope so that its proportion in the mass is increased from 0.7 per cent to about 2 per cent is to enable ordinary water to be used as a moderator instead of heavy water. This is then possible because the enrichment of the U^{235} compensates for weak absorption of neutrons by the impurity hydrogen present in ordinary water.

At first sight the work requirement necessary to enrich the isotope from 0.7 per cent to a mere 2 per cent might not appear a substantial task when compared to that of enriching it from 0.7 per cent to 70 per cent for an atom bomb. When using a percentage constant, however, it will be noted that the effort required is almost a quarter of that necessary for the weapons grade enrichment.

Houtermans had no doubts on the matter:

> 'The possibility of producing a chain reaction with thermal neutrons exists by enriching the U^{235} isotope... and it would seem that a two- or three-fold enrichment, that is to say a concentration of U^{235} at 1.5 per cent to 2 per cent, would be sufficient to achieve the critical value.
>
> But isotope separation of such substantial quantities would at the present time present such enormous difficulties and demand such enormous energies that under these circumstances the energy needed to enrich the isotope might actually exceed the energy gained from the reactor.'

Dismissing the question of isotope separation on these grounds, he considered it preferable to concentrate on achieving a working reactor without enriching the U^{235} isotope to do so. Throughout the report he emphasized the importance of using pure metallic uranium to reduce the absorption of transient neutrons by impurities in the fuel which might cause the collapse of the chain reaction.

Moving on to review the various moderators, Houtermans confirmed heavy water as a particularly efficient slowing medium for neutrons, but remarked on the enormous costs of producing it and the difficulty of assembling a large enough quantity for a working reactor.

He indicated the possible suitability of graphite, which appeared to have a favourable cross-section as regards neutron absorption, but expressed a reservation that what was gained by having no absorption losses might be offset by losses in neutron energies caused by graphite's high mass number. The same applied to carbon in compounds.

However, what had been observed in the course of his experiments with moderators was that the absorption of neutrons by the hydrogen molecules in carbon compounds appeared much reduced at extremely cold temperatures. Now this was of great significance, for it was very probably attributable to the nuclear Doppler Effect. If that were to be brought into the reckoning then it would also bring about:

1. an increase in the fission cross-section of the U^{235} atoms by virtue of the $T^{-\frac{1}{2}}$ temperature energy law, thus making fissions much more likely, and
2. a reduction in the width and level of the U^{238} neutron

absorption bands, thus increasing the probability that slow transient neutrons would avoid capture by U^{238} atoms.

Houtermans contended that it was quite probable that the nuclear Doppler Effect alone would enable a carbon compound to be used to moderate a nuclear pile effectively. He considered the most favourable such substance to be liquid methane, CH_4. Methane is a colourless, odourless, flammable gas of abundant occurrence, the first and simplest member of the alkane or paraffin series of hydrocarbons, which is liquid in the temperature range -164°C to -186°C.

In his formulae for a chain reaction using slow neutrons at very cold temperatures, Houtermans indicated that the most favourable container vessel for the reactor would be a sphere, the critical radius of which could be easily determined by reference to the calculated critical mass of the uranium, to which it was proportional. The sphere would be lined with a reflector of natural uranium, which had the best scatter cross-section for neutrons in comparison to all other non-absorbing substances.

The innumerable geometric experiments involving uranium lattices which had so occupied the physicists of the official programme were superfluous for Houtermans' design because the very low temperature of his moderator endowed the uranium fuel with the equivalent of many degrees of enrichment. This allowed for the homogeneous distribution of the critical mass of uranium in the solution of liquid methane.

In common with all other German atomic scientists of the time, Houtermans appears to have overlooked the stabilizing influence of the delayed neutrons of fission, the omission to account for which had effectively stultified Heisenberg's 'uranium burner' research from 1942 onwards.

Houtermans' postulated reactor, however, created no concerns as respects safety and stability. Since the machine could operate only by virtue of its very low temperature, it was obvious that the chain reaction would automatically collapse once the temperature began to rise substantially towards freezing point.

While in theory he would have planned to use regulating rods to control neutron multiplication, in practice Houtermans would have found his reactor to be unexpectedly stable due to the unsuspected effect of the delayed neutrons.

Such was the world's first critical nuclear reactor, a device of great simplicity, which was to make Nazi Germany the world's first atomic power in the autumn of 1942, in a bunker beneath the home and laboratory of Professor Manfred von Ardenne, at number 19, Jungfernstieg, Lichterfelde-Ost, Berlin.

Summarizing his paper in a section headed *The Significance of a Chain Reaction in a Low Temperature Environment as a Neutron Source and as an Apparatus for Transforming Isotopes*, Houtermans confirmed that because plutonium is a different element from uranium, and, therefore, chemically distinct, then concentrations of Pu^{239} should be obtainable relatively easily by chemical separation from the reactor fission products, and this would be an explosive, since it was also fissionable. This confirmed the opinions of the physicists Hernegger and Schintlmeister made the previous winter.

> 'We must now look at the question of what applications this reactor would provide for us, for a heat engine which can only produce at very low temperatures is, of course, of no practical use at all.
>
> But such a unit can be an apparatus which will yield us enormous quantities of neutrons and in amounts which no other instrument in atomic physics can possibly supply. For example, if we compare the neutron yield from such a neutron reactor with that of the best neutron source known hitherto, the cyclotron, we may calculate that the production of one tonne of radioisotopes from the reactor could not be achieved with less than between 10,000 and 100,000 cyclotrons.
>
> Once we actually abandon the idea of obtaining power from the reactor, there are energy sources which can be extracted from the radioactive substances, if they are sufficiently long-lived. Moreover, such a pile would be a macroscopic neutron source for all those purposes of great technical significance which arise from the application of neutrons and artificial radioactive substances in the fields of applied physics, chemistry, biology and, above all, physiology.'

At the foot of the report, Houtermans acknowledged his employer:

> 'For the invitation to do this work, and for making it possible, I thank the Baron Manfred von Ardenne.'

When Heisenberg saw the report he was aghast. It was not only the mention of the production of plutonium, for this was not new, as has been remarked upon; what horrified him more was that for the first time a scientific thesis had entered circulation which proposed a simple low-temperature nuclear reactor for the purpose of making radioisotopes in great quantities. Obviously if Ohnesorge saw the report he would be bound to bring it to the attention of Hitler. Heisenberg concluded that the situation was already beyond redemption; he could not now interfere.

> 'We were not absolutely sure, but we saw now that it was almost certain. Von Weizsäcker in particular and I were deeply disturbed. It now looked like it was definitely possible to make a reactor.
>
> We agreed that if we could make them, then the Americans could too. If they could make reactors then plutonium was probably possible too, and so on.
>
> It was from September, 1941, that we saw before us an open road leading to the atom bomb.[9]

The alarming thesis from the Post Office laboratory at Lichterfelde-Ost now provoked Heisenberg to make a celebrated but imprudent and ill-considered visit to his former mentor, Professor Niels Bohr, at the University of Copenhagen, in October, 1941.

Ernst von Weizsäcker (1882-1951), the father of Heisenberg's close colleague, was Under-Secretary of State at the German Foreign Office, where he was one of the opponents of the Nazi régime. In 1938 he had informed the British Foreign Office of the existence of a group of civilian and military leaders ready to overthrow the Nazi Government if Hitler should go to war over Czechoslovakia, and was himself a major conspirator in what appears to have been the best prepared coup ever planned against Hitler.

But Chamberlain and Lord Halifax, who had been asked to provide a strong demonstration of their determination not to tolerate the assimilation of the Czech state, disregarded the request, believing that an accord with Hitler was still possible. The German plotters were considered to be Jacobites.

The elder von Weizsäcker remained a focus of resistance in the Nazi State at war, and he had been instrumental in ensuring, through the offices of the German Ambassador to Denmark, that Niels Bohr's Institute at the University of Copenhagen remained a physics sanctuary after the German occupation. Not until after Bohr's emigration in 1943 did the German army of occupation take possession of the buildings.[10]

Professor Bohr himself was allowed to visit his summer house in Tisvilde, from where he occasionally sailed a small sloop in the waters between Denmark and Sweden, during which outings he customarily passed information to the underground network for onward transmission to London and the United States. In common with the *emigré* physicists in America with whom he retained tenuous links, Bohr had failed to understand Heisenberg's motives in remaining voluntarily in Nazi Germany and considered that a person choosing such a course was morally flawed.

Unaware of the Danish scientist's opinion, Heisenberg, von Weizsäcker junior and the Heidelberg professor, P. Jensen, held an unfounded confidence in Bohr, and it was probably at the suggestion of Jensen[11] that Heisenberg arranged a meeting with Bohr through the German Embassy in Copenhagen in the guise of a lecture at Bohr's Institute.

Heisenberg's purpose was to signal to Bohr that senior atom physicists in Germany would prevent the construction of atomic weapons in the hope that the Americans, with whom Germany was not yet at war, might abandon their own development, thus keeping the war non-nuclear.

Being engaged on highly secret military work, Heisenberg's scope for any sort of discussion was strictly limited; he was aware that a single indiscreet word could lead to a charge of high treason against the Nazi state. He made a conscious effort to steer the conversation in such a way that he did not put his life in immediate danger, and began by asking whether it was right or not for physicists to devote themselves in wartime to the uranium problem. It is fairly clear that Bohr thought that by 'physicists' Heisenberg meant 'German physicists', whereas Heisenberg meant physicists of all nations at war, or, as in the case of the United States, actively preparing for it.

In response, Bohr demanded to know whether Heisenberg believed that the fissioning of uranium could be used to construct weapons. When Heisenberg admitted the point in principle, Bohr concluded that the motive for the meeting was probably to enable Heisenberg to inform himself as to the Allied nuclear programme, and when he was asked to try to influence Allied atomic scientists to obstruct nuclear weapons research in their own countries, undertaking to do the same in Germany, Bohr became even more suspicious.

Thus all that Heisenberg achieved was the alienation of Bohr, who, by stating that it was not possible for scientists to unite in a cause against the will of their governments, was obliquely advising

Heisenberg that if he dissented from the German project, he should remove himself entirely from it.

But Heisenberg's dilemma was that he could see what Bohr could not; that any hope there was for mankind amongst German scientists was only ever to be found within the circle of physicists which had Heisenberg at its nucleus.

Upon the failure of his mission, Heisenberg returned to Germany where, on 28 November, 1941, he became the first of a succession of notable visitors to the Lichterfelde-Ost laboratory of Professor von Ardenne . According to the Swiss historian Robert Jungk, he had a further talk with Professor Houtermans in company with von Weizsäcker. This was a long, frank discussion as to the work Houtermans had been engaged in under von Ardenne, and in conclusion it was agreed that their overwhelming priority was to conceal from the Government departments involved 'the *imminent feasibility* of manufacturing atomic weapons'.[12]

But the knowledge that the explosive plutonium could definitely be bred in a reactor did not make an atomic bomb *imminently* feasible unless the reactor was capable of immediate construction to criticality and beyond. It was therefore Houtermans' statement in his paper that a chain reaction could undoubtedly be obtained in a cold reactor moderated by freezing methane that afforded his visitors the grounds for their very real fear that Nazi Germany was within reach of nuclear weapons. Whether these weapons would be plutonium bombs or large canisters of reactor waste for scattering by ordinary explosive means was immaterial. Heisenberg and von Weizsäcker took their leave, assuring Houtermans, who was the cause of all their troubles, that they would attempt to suppress his scientific thesis if it should come their way officially.

On 10 December Otto Hahn and three colleagues from the Kaiser Wilhelm Institute for Chemistry also called in, but what was discussed was not mentioned by Hahn in his autobiography, although it appears likely that Houtermans had already been notified of what Ohnesorge required of him by that date. Early in December, 1941, Houtermans had had a soul-searching talk with his protector, Professor Max von Laue, on the subject of a secret assignation he had been given. In connection with this task, Houtermans reportedly sent a cryptic telegram to his former colleague Eugene P. Wigner in the United States which read:

'Hurry! We're nearly there!'[13]

Precisely why Hitler chose the radiation canisters in preference to the plutonium bomb will forever remain a mystery. It is certain that

Ohnesorge would have offered him the choice of either weapon; possibly it was the earlier readiness of the radioactive poison which decided Hitler, or perhaps the arguments which have been presented previously. Other considerations may have been the fact that the radiation weapon was a poison or the negligible demand on the public purse to finance it, or its availability in substantial quantity. Whatever it was, Ohnesorge was given the responsibility of supervising the construction of the world's first critical reactor, the purpose of which was the production of reactor fission products for use in radiological weapons. The proposed weapon was the most dangerous that had ever been conceived in the history of the world.

The possibility that Harteck's group was involved in assisting Houtermans is very strong. A copy of Houtermans' thesis was sent to Harteck personally by von Ardenne, as the latter has confirmed.

In the 1944 revised version of the paper, Houtermans concludes with an explanatory page referring to certain assistance rendered to him in connection with the theory of low temperature work by Professor Johannes Jensen, who was one of the five leading physical-chemists in Harteck's group.

The possible use of radioactivity as a weapon by Hitler appears to have been only vaguely appreciated by Washington and London, the Americans believing that if it were to be used at all, then Britain would be the victim. Climatic factors, however, clearly dictated that the weapon should be deployed as far from German-held territory as possible in order to preclude the unhappy situation where the radiation might drift back with the elements to contaminate the homeland and the biological purity of the German race. After all, the purity of the race was at heart the ideology of National Socialism.

Although the use of the radiation weapon may have resulted as a German reprisal for a British chemical or biological attack against German civilians, or as a riposte for an atomic attack by American aircraft operating from British airfields, or as a means to seize victory at a stroke, the intended target of the radiation bomb always was the civilian population of the United States. And the fact that the development of the weapon had been approved in the last quarter of 1941 may go some way to explaining the mysterious strategy behind Hitler's policy towards the United States in December, 1941.

On 6 December the Russian armies began a surprise counter-offensive of major proportions against the German front line, which, although stemmed, allowed the subsequent relief of Moscow and marked the first great turning point in the fortunes of Nazi Germany. On the day following the beginning of the counter-offensive Japan attacked the United States fleet at Pearl Harbor, and although Hitler was not bound to assist Japan unless she were to be attacked by a third power, he nevertheless allied himself with his eastern treaty partner on 11 December, 1941, only four days later.

Up until then Hitler had acted with great caution in his dealings with the United States, most notably on the high seas, where the conduct of the United States amounted to an *ipso facto* act of war against Germany.

The regular supply of vast quantities of war materials and contraband to Britain by Washington exceeded the limitations imposed by neutrality conventions to which the United States and Germany were signatories.

Since Hitler may have felt that he was virtually at war with America already, he was gaining in the transaction by siding with Japan. It cannot be discounted, however, that the prospect of acquiring the radiological weapon by the end of 1942 for distribution across American population centres as an inducement to the United States to adopt strict neutrality in Europe may well have determined his decision.

He may have seen not only the sundering of the anti-Axis alliance by the departure of the United States from it, but also the priceless bonus of convincing Britain that she should join the Americans in an onerous neutrality. This would have left the way clear for the Axis partners to combine against the last serious opponent, the Soviet Union, which could then be simultaneously confronted from west and east.

It was a dangerous gamble, for nearly everything depended on Hitler retaining a monopoly of nuclear power; in the upshot, he may have decided that the risk should be accepted once he had glimpsed the ultimate defeat of Germany by conventional means during the winter campaign in Russia in 1941.

In his autobiography[14] Professor von Ardenne states that, because of his arrangement with Ohnesorge to instal the cyclotron, an apparatus which required the personnel using it to be shielded against radiation, he now had a pretext for asking for the construction of several large underground concrete bunkers at his Lichterfelde-Ost institute; the work was soon under way.

The main bunker had a floor area of 10 by 10 metres and was 10 metres down. The steel-reinforced concrete walls and ceiling were 1½ metres thick and, needless to say, this would have given enough radiation protection to the occupants of the house and the neighbours against whatever might have been going on in the bunker.

Adjacent to it was a smaller bunker which housed the 250 kW

transformer station, and next to that, but without a connecting door, an air-raid bunker measuring 2 by 3 metres.

This underground complex was ready by the late autumn of 1942, which was, as von Ardenne confirms, just before the step-up in bombing activity over German cities of which Berlin was the major target.

He says that he made up his mind to put all the most valuable instrumentation and the important installations into a small area of the bunker in a working condition, but according to the table of important events in his diary[15], the main evacuation of the laboratory did not take place until 1 August, 1943.

There is, therefore, a period of about nine months between the fall of 1942 and the end of July, 1943, when the use of the greater part of the main bunker has not been accounted for, and at a time when Berlin was being subjected to extremely severe air raids.

von Ardenne mentions that Professor Houtermans had been overjoyed at the possibility of access to a cyclotron, of which only one other model was available in all of Germany, at the Post Office laboratory at Miersdorf. Use of the machine had also been promised to Professor Hahn at the Kaiser Wilhelm Institute for Chemistry as a means of forging a closer relationship between Hahn's Dahlem circle and the Lichterfelde-Ost laboratory. The cyclotron, however, was never brought into operation 'because of the air war'.

So it came about that the cyclotron, the purported purpose for which the bunker complex had been constructed, an invaluable physics apparatus of which only one other model existed in the German Reich in 1942, and a source of envy to the external physics community, was never completed.

The construction of the bunker complex, and no doubt the theoretical work on the reactor geometry, and the arrangements for the appropriation of the necessary supplies of uranium metal powder and refrigerating plant, all of which we may be perfectly certain had approval at the highest level, lasted throughout 1942.

The Armaments Minister, Speer, wrote disapprovingly[16] about the unaccountable optimism in Hitler's demeanour whenever the subject of nuclear energy came under discussion in the early summer of 1942, and this hopeful disposition of the Führer appeared to him to have the closest possible connection with a clique consisting of the Postmaster-General, Ohnesorge, Goebbels and Hitler's personal photographer, Heinrich Hoffmann,[17] who all apparently knew something secret.

Speer concluded that since Hitler spurned responsible sources of information and preferred to rely instead on having knowledge peddled to him by these dilettantes, it all went to prove not only Hitler's partiality for dabbling, but also how little he understood of the scientific principles involved.

The full implication of this turn of events remained fortunately concealed from Speer, who, if he had been made party to the secret, would probably have had few scruples in coercing the official physicists to develop the same thing for the Wehrmacht.

It is an odd circumstance that Hitler should have appeared to shun atomic physics in the company of his Armaments and Munitions Minister whilst openly affirming his enthusiasm for its future prospects to his closer circle at table.

Martin Bormann's stenographer, Henry Picker, recorded[18] the fact that Hitler considered the splitting of the atom to be the most important of all scientific achievements for Germany's future to the extent that it was Hitler himself who was inspirational in having the short documentary film 'Gold', starring Hans Albers, repeatedly exhibited in cinemas in order to popularize the subject of nuclear science.

It is thus clear that by early 1942 Nazi physics had quietly broadened its perspectives to accommodate the atomic reactor, while the atom bomb remained Jewish physics. Whatever it was that now distinguished one from the other was not easy to determine.

Coinciding with the completion of the underground bunker complex at the Post Office-funded laboratory of Baron Manfred von Ardenne at Lichterfelde-Ost, on 15 October, 1942, the Weapons Testing and Development Section of the Heereswaffenamt at Peenemünde confirmed the placing of a contract with the Research Institute of the German Post Office at its Berlin Tempelhof headquarters. The document declared that the addressee was 'hereby contracted to investigate the possibility of the fullest use of radioactivity and chain reactions'. The usual euphemism *zum R-Antrieb* 'for rocket propulsion', which was used by the War Office to disguise atomic warfare projects, was tacked on to the end of the sentence.[19]

It was noted earlier that the Auer subsidiary company, DEGUSSA, apparently the only casting plant for uranium metal in all Germany, supposedly manufactured the entire quantity delivered throughout the war. At the end of hostilities in Europe, 14 tonnes of uranium cubes, plate and powder, virtually all of it, fell into the hands of one or other of the victorious powers.

This fact was probably one of the conclusive factors which persuaded officers of the *Alsos* mission that the Germans had not embarked upon an atomic weapons programme.

It is, of course, possible that the Auer Company and DEGUSSA may have jointly kept false ledgers for security purposes, but in the absence of evidence to support the assumption, it is highly probable that the source of the uranium metal for the Post Office reactor must have been some other reduction plant in Germany or abroad, and what evidence there is tends to support the second contention.

It was acknowledged that the metal produced by DEGUSSA contained substantial impurities which were highly disparaged by Houtermans who, in his August, 1941, report, stressed the necessity for pure uranium metal. Furthermore, the great secrecy surrounding the radiological weapon project would have rendered it desirable to conceal from the physics community the fact that large quantities of uranium metal were being delivered from the Auer Company to a suburban house in Berlin.

A bilateral agreement existed between Germany and Japan to the effect that the industrial resources of either were pledged to the use of the other without reference to the question of cost, a matter to be determined in the aftermath of the common victory. This arrangement was eventually confirmed in the Treaty between Germany and Japan respecting Economic Co-operation, signed by Matsushima, Economic Attaché at the Japanese Embassy in Berlin, and Emil Wiehl, Leader of the Economic and Political Department of the German Foreign Ministry.[20]

The reduction of uranium oxide to uranium metal powder in quantity and to a high specification was not an economical enterprise in Germany, but the problem may not have been insurmountable in Japan.

For the purpose of obtaining radioisotopes as the sole purpose of his reactor, Houtermans had emphasized uranium metal powder of the highest purity. This very fine grey powder is highly pyrophorous and tends to ignite spontaneously on contact with air. If shipped on board a merchant vessel, it would have to be stowed on deck as hazardous cargo and located where it could easily be jettisoned if necessary, since once afire it is extremely difficult to extinguish.

A consignment of an unidentified shipment of 70 to 80 sacks of a very fine grey powder, each sack being about 10 inches high with a diameter of about 12 inches and estimated to weigh 2 cwts (100 kilos), was reported to have been stowed on deck forward when the German blockade runner *Doggerbank* was loaded at Yokohama in December, 1942.

A crew member with many years' experience of cargo handling, Fritz Kürt,[21] stated that he had never seen a similar substance before. He also failed to establish the nature of the 'mysterious, heavy contents' of the sacks, despite his tactful enquiries.

The imprudent decision of her captain, Lieutenant Commander Paul Schneidewind, to arrive a fortnight early at position 29° 10'N, 34°10'W, 1,000 miles west of the Canary Islands, for a rendezvous with his escort led to a misunderstanding with regard to her identity and the *Doggerbank* was torpedoed and sunk in error by the German submarine U-43 (Lieutenant Commander Schwandtke) on 3 March, 1943.

The tragedy was a parallel of a similar disaster which took place on 31 January, 1942, north of the Azores when the 5083 GRT blockade runner *Spreewald* was sunk in error by U-333 while waiting for her escort outside her rendezvous area. On that occasion the U-boat commander had been court-martialled for manslaughter, but in the case of the *Doggerbank*, Admiral Doenitz was said to have been so concerned at the likely repercussions arising out of the sinking that he had the relevant pages of the U-boat's war diary elaborating the disaster expunged from the record.

Gibson (op. cit.) suggests that Goering appears to have had an unexplained especial interest in the safe arrival of the *Doggerbank*.

Crewman Fritz Kürt was the only survivor of the *Doggerbank* from a crew and passenger list containing over 300 names.

Up until late 1942 German merchant vessels enjoyed, on the whole, a reasonable degree of success in completing the trip from the Far East to Biscay ports carrying a variety of valuable commodities and raw materials.

From early 1943, their losses rapidly became intolerable and the transport of the most essential elements of these cargoes was undertaken by Japanese submarines and homecoming German U-boats, of which a number reached French ports from the Far East in the spring and summer of that year.

The incident of the *Doggerbank* suggests a possibility that for reasons of product quality, secrecy and continuity of supply (bearing in mind the increasing severity of air attacks against German industry), a technical co-operation existed between Japan and Nazi Germany for the economical conversion of uranium oxide concentrate into pure, powdered uranium metal, the most appropriate form of uranium for the purposes of radioisotope production. Whether the *Doggerbank* consignment was intended for Houtermans to continue his successful work under von Ardenne, or whether it was to be used by Diebner and Harteck in their proposed low temperature experiments, must remain a mystery.

What further evidence is there for the assertion that Nazi Germany became the world's first atomic power in the autumn of 1942 by virtue of Professor Houterman's methane reactor at von Ardenne's Lichterfelde-Ost Laboratory in Berlin?

The corroboration for the successful Post Office nuclear reactor programme is contained in Dr Henry Picker's substantial volume *Hitler's Tischgespräche im Führerhauptquartier 1941-1942* which has appeared in numerous reprints over the years including Gerhard Ritter (Athenäum Verlag, Bonn, 1951); Percy Ernst Schramm together with Andreas Hillgruber and Martin Vogt (Stuttgart, 1963, and Seewald Verlag, Stuttgart, 1976).

But until this present work, there has been no evidence for the existence of the 'uranium bombs' spoken of by Hitler, nor proof that the Germans knew how to achieve a chain reaction in a nuclear reactor, using an alternative to graphite or heavy water as a moderator. This has led to the assumption by default that the weapons development programme under the Postmaster General must have been imaginary, and an additional unhelpful complication supplied by commentators including Picker himself, who was just as much in the dark as anybody else, was the surmise that Hitler's uranium bombs must have been atom bombs.

The major part of Hitler's monologues were taken down by a National Socialist lawyer, Heinrich Heims, who had been a Nazi Party member since July, 1920. He shared an office with Dr Hans Frank who was the preferred attorney for the NSDAP and its leader. Heims was also engaged on legal matters for the Party and throughout the Nazi era was concerned in arranging the affairs of the NSDAP Relief Fund which Martin Bormann administered.

When Bormann was appointed Hitler's Chief of Staff in 1933, he set out to organize an efficient party HQ and recruited Heims into his entourage and empowered him to resolve all questions relating to State justice. By 1939 Heims was a senior civil servant at ministerial advisory level.

When at the outbreak of war Bormann, who was the liaison figure between Hitler and the Party leaders, joined Hitler in his Headquarters, he brought Heims along with him as his Adjutant. Heims remained in the office until the spring of 1942 and then returned to Munich where he spent the rest of the war laying the groundwork for the post-war reorganization of Europe.

Decisive for the appointment of Heims in the Führer HQ had been the wish of the Führer himself, for he desired to be surrounded only by people whom he knew. Heims had an additional advantage in being numbered amongst the earliest Party adherents.

As Bormann's Adjutant, Heims not only ate regularly at Hitler's table, but was frequently invited to the evening tea-hour in the Bunker, occasions reserved for the closest political intimates and female secretaries. Such a circle would seldom consist of more than eight people.

Following Heim's departure from the Führer HQ, Bormann asked a number of NSDAP Gauleiters for suggestions as to a substitute. Among the names supplied was that of a senior privy councillor, Dr Henry Picker. The Party Chancellors drew up a short list of candidates and it was left to the Führer to make his own decision.

Senator Daniel Picker had done sterling work to advance the cause of the NSDAP in Wilhelmshaven and in 1929 had arranged for Hitler to meet representatives of the Navy and naval dockyard. On his visits to the port, Hitler was made welcome on numerous occasions as a guest in the Picker household. Hitler's selection of Dr Henry Picker was, therefore, made partly out of respect towards the Senator.

Henry Picker differed from Heims in that he was not in the Führer's HQ as a Nazi official or lawyer, but was there to do duty as the Adjutant of Martin Bormann. One of his standing duties was to take a note of Hitler's conversations during the official meals, a task performed for the information of Bormann, who was thereby enabled to keep abreast of developments in the Führer's thinking more or less as it happened.

Dr Henry Picker's publication is based on his contemporaneous notes which have been authenticated by signed certificates testifying that they truly and accurately reflect the substance of Hitler's conversations at table.

The former adjutants on Hitler's Headquarters Staff subscribing their signatures were:

Rear Admiral Karl Jesko von Puttkamer
Naval Adjutant 1939-45
Oberst Nicolaus von Below
Luftwaffe Adjutant 1937-45
Generalleutnant Gerhard Engel
Army Adjutant 1939-45

As Adjutant and stenographer to Martin Bormann, Picker was in almost permanent contact with another inhabitant of the Bunker, Hitler's Chief ADC, SS-Obergruppenführer Julius Schaub (1898-1968), who had also been a member of the Nazi Party since its humblest beginnings.

Schaub had been wounded in both feet during the First World War, and later, when he joined the Party, he had followed Hitler around from place to place on his crutches. When Hitler learned that Schaub had lost his employment on account of his Party membership, he offered Schaub a job as his manservant. A willing and devoted worker, Schaub had soon made himself indispensable to Hitler and in 1933 became his ADC and later the chief of his personal adjutants in the rank of SS-Obergruppenführer.

He was also Hitler's personal chauffeur. Schaub was the only member of Hitler's entourage who belonged to the 'Old Guard' and he was the guardian of very nearly all of Hitler's secrets.

Towards the end he developed a deafness and was often to be seen limping along on his damaged feet with a hand perpetually cupped around his better ear. On 22 April, 1945, Hitler told Schaub to burn a number of documents in the Bunker, and then sent him off to Munich and Berchtesgaden to do the same, thus sparing him at the last.

There are numerous references to the 'uranium bombs' in Dr Picker's testimony. At the outset it should be pointed out that physicists and politicians in Nazi Germany knew the concept of the atomic bomb by the German word *Uranbombe*, 'Uran' being the word for uranium in the German language. Hitler's miracle weapon was, therefore, distinguished from the atom bomb by the use of the label *Uraniumbombe*.

To have called the weapon *Strahlungsbombe* or Radiation Bomb would have given the game away immediately; the term *Uraniumbombe* concealed its nature and function from everybody not in the know.

Firstly, Picker reports Schaub as saying that the uranium bombs are the weapons of frightfulness (*die fürchterlichen Waffen*) on which Hitler had based his strategy and pinned his hopes.

Secondly, in Hitler's *Tischgespräche im Führerhauptquartier* (Stuttgart 1976, p.148) Picker describes where the uranium bombs were developed and mentions the unprecedented security measures in force there:

'Dr Ohnesorge's "Reichspost-Forschungsanstalt" in Berlin Lichterfelde, where − in parallel with an unsuccessful professorial team − a prototype of the German uranium bomb was in fact developed up to the stage of construction, received visits from Hitler during his periods of residence in Berlin, during which Dr Ohnesorge never once permitted Hitler's military entourage to view the research establishment. Ohnesorge, born in 1872, insisted on the greatest secrecy. Amongst co-workers in the Reich Research Institute were such authorities as the atom physicist Baron Manfred von Ardenne.'

So secret was the laboratory work at Lichterfelde-Ost that even Hitler's personal bodyguard could not be permitted to see anything of what went on there.

Thirdly, according to Schaub, who had been told about the uranium bomb by SS-colleagues at the SS-Mittelwerk concentration camp where it was assembled, it was the 'size of a small pumpkin' (*in der Grösse eines kleinen Kürbis*) and when assembled in a warhead, the explosive would be set round 'with several small uranium bombs' (*mit mehreren kleinen Uranium bomben bestückt*).

Clearly, uranium bombs cannot be atom bombs, since one atom bomb is itself the explosive. One of the methods, however, of distributing the radioactive contents of a number of radiation bombs would be to pack them round a conventional explosive which would scatter them to all points of the compass at the time of detonation.

Fourthly, Schaub had told Picker that the uranium bombs were being produced in a 'subterranean SS-factory in the South Harz mountains with a force of 30,000 workers' (*werden in einem unterirdischen SS-Werk im Südharz mit einer Produktionskapazität von 30,000 Arbeitskräften hergestellt.*)

On the night of 17 August, 1943, the rocket research establishment at Peenemünde was visited by a large force of British aircraft. 520 bombers arriving in three waves, unloaded a total of 2000 tons of high explosive and incendiaries which killed 120 Germans, including the leading scientists Thiel and Walther, and 612 Russian and Polish slave labourers in a barracks at Trassenheide. The material damage was not extensive and more than 80 per cent of the bombs fell on open land and in the woods. The effective pattern had mostly damaged non-industrial or easily repairable facilities. An advance air-raid warning had been ignored since it was believed that the operations at Peenemünde were undetectable from the air.[22]

The commanding officer, Colonel Walter Dornberger, reviewed the damage at first light and concluded that the site would be operational again within six weeks at the most, but on the following day the head of the SS Security Police, Kaltenbrunner, arrived in order to initiate personally enquiries into a purported security leak.

Kaltenbrunner's intervention offered Himmler an excellent opportunity to raise the matter of having the entire V-weapons project transferred from the Army to the SS. The raid had clearly compromised

Peenemünde as a rocket-testing and assembly centre, and when Hitler now ordered the project relocated underground, Himmler hastened to East Prussia on 19 August and argued convincingly that Peenemünde must have been betrayed from within. The satisfactory continuation of the V-Weapons programme could be guaranteed, he suggested, only by placing it under the supervision of the SS, and ensuring secrecy by using concentration camp inmates for the work force.

It is highly unlikely that Himmler knew of the radiation weapon programme, but it is worth mentioning that the Peenemünde complex included the Danish island of Bornholm which was used for V-Weapons development and glider-bomb experimentation. Rumours persisted long after the war that there had been a uranium bomb factory on the island.[23]

A factory was necessary for the assembly of the weapon. There are severe difficulties involved in constructing a radiological weapon.

The waste products from the reactor are mixed in with quantities of extraneous material and, in order to obtain a high concentration of radioactivity, chemical separation is necessary, after which the extracted fission products have to be packed into lead containers for storage. All stages of preparation involve enormous problems in protecting handlers against radiation exposure.

The search for an underground factory for the SS had been in hand since 22 July, 1943, when the rocket component plant at Friedrichshafen had been destroyed by bombing, and a suitable location had been discovered at Niedersachswerfen near Nordhausen in the Harz Mountains. The extensive underground workings there were owned by the firm Wifo (*Wirtschaftliche Forschungsgesellschaft*), which was now dispossessed by Führer-edict.

The subterranean factory, the largest in the world, was burrowed into the chalky rock of the Kohnstein Mountain and comprised two parallel tunnels 2,600 metres long and wide enough for a double railway track in each, with 46 adjoining chambers, each 200 metres long, between them. A third tunnel at the level of the eighteenth chamber ran at right angles to the main corridors.

The entire floor area amounted to 125,000 square metres and the available space was ¾ million cubic metres. Twelve large ventilation shafts circulated the air and heating was maintained at 17°C with low humidity. All corridors and chambers were equipped with strong electric lighting.

The original purpose of the works had been the storage of strategic chemicals. The conversion began in September, 1943, with the assistance of 15,000 concentration camp inmates from Buchenwald and

Natzweiler and 2,000 engineers. The facility, known as the 'Nordhausen Central Works', and also 'SS-Mittelwerk' by reason of its geographical position at the centre of Germany, now took over from Peenemünde the responsibility for meeting all contracts placed there by the Heereswaffenamt.

The initial indent for labour had foreseen the employment of a work force of 30,000 concentration camp inmates, a figure based on an over-optimistic production estimate.

Needless to say, the conditions for the prisoners at SS-Mittelwerk were barbarous, and initially the mortality rate was 15 per cent compared with 84 per cent at Auschwitz (excluding persons murdered on arrival).

When the rocket engineer Wernher von Braun visited the tunnels in January, 1944, where he saw 10,000 inmates at labour, he walked the corridors in silence and left despondent. Following the intercession of Speer in the wake of a visit in December, 1943, food and living conditions improved beyond measure and the prisoners were not only permitted to see the light of day, but were even eventually lodged in barracks outside the caves.

Entrusted with the running of the enterprise from its inception was SS-Brigadeführer Dr Hans Kammler who, as engineer in charge of the building department of the WVHA, the SS-Chief Economic and Administration Office, had had responsibility earlier for the planning of some of the extermination camps and had personally supervised the construction of the Auschwitz satellite camp at Birkenau.

Somewhere in a dark recess in the SS-Mittelwerk underground concentration camp, in conjunction with the assembly of the V-2 rocket, the V-4s, Hitler's radiation bombs, were manufactured and stored. The radiation protection provided for the inmates handling the raw material from the reactor is best left to the imagination.

And finally, as Picker himself heard from the Führer's lips, the radiation bombs were principally intended for deployment against the civilian population of the United States. At first the means of delivery had been envisaged to be the A9/10 intercontinental rocket, and Hitler was confident that the arrival of the first few missiles on New York would quickly render the American Government 'ready for peace' (*friedensbereit zu schiessen*).

The exigencies of the V-2 rocket programme, however, had led to the suspension of all development work on the gigantic, two-stage missile in October, 1942, and only the top half of the joint projectile, the A-9 (a V-2 with wings) eventually completed a test flight. The entire project was scrapped in early 1945.

Philip Henshall, who had twenty years' experience of work on guided missiles, both air-launched and seaborne nuclear deterrents, suggested in his book *Hitler's Rocket Sites* (Robert Hale, London, 1985) that two monumental bunkers built in 1943 at Watten and Wizernes in northern France, lying 9½ miles apart and straddling the town of St Omer, were capable of launching not only the V-2 rockets but all projected developments, including the A9/10 long-range missile.

Measurements which he took showed that the working heights inside each silo could accommodate the projected A9/10 rocket minus its warhead. He also reported that Watten was completely self-contained and impregnable from the exterior by virtue of its massive armoured doors, while at both locations the 23-feet thick lid forming the dome to the structures could not be penetrated by any known bomb even hitting directly.

He concluded that since the greater part of the concrete constructions were devoted to bunkers and silos, none of which were necessary for launching V-2 rockets, the actual purpose of the bunkers must have been to store nuclear materials and to house the A9/10 'New Yorker'.

The A9/10 rocket, however, received such a low priority rating in the programme that Watten and Wizernes can realistically have been built only as a contingency for deterrence at some time in the remote future.

German scientists were additionally never able to solve the problem of designing a proximity fuse capable of detonating an explosive warhead 100 feet above the ground for a missile arriving from the heavens at Mach 3. While this matter remained unresolved, large rockets such as the V-2 were useless for carrying radiation bombs since, instead of broadcasting the radioactive material far and wide, they would deposit it into the 40 feet deep crater which the rocket created on impact with the ground.

In the summer of 1942 an unofficial experiment approved by Admiral Doenitz was carried out by a leading Peenemünde scientist, Dr Johannes Steinhoff, to launch a number of solid-fuel rockets from a submerged U-boat. The Type IXc submarine *U-511* commanded by his brother, Lieutenant Fritz Steinhoff, made a successful launching of twenty 21-cm calibre artillery rockets automatically triggered from a modified Nebelwerfer apparatus mounted on the after deck at a depth of 20 metres. All the rockets landed close to a target 3 km distant from the point of discharge.

According to Intelligence sources[24] these experiments were repeated and extended in 1944 from the U-boat *U-1063*. French agents reported that in the same year apparently similar experiments were conducted on Lake Toplitz in the Austrian Alps when manned midget submarines were seen to practise firing rockets which resembled 'small-scale V-2s'.

The highly successful forerunner to the V-2 was the A-5 rocket which was one-twelfth the size and had never experienced a failure in twenty-five launches.

The latter experiments from *U-1063* and at Lake Toplitz were stated to have been satisfactory and one must conclude that the ultimate object of these operations was to take east-coast cities of the United States under fire from submerged U-boats well offshore. The development of a launcher to fire a battery of rockets, each fitted with one or two radiation bombs around a warhead, for a spread across an American city would have been a far sounder proposition technically and financially than the grandiose A9/10 idea. The deceleration of the rocket on its descent to a speed enabling a proximity fuse to detonate the warhead for the purpose of scattering the radioactive material above the ground would have been achieved in these circumstances by the deployment of a parachute.

On 1 August, 1943, von Ardenne at last obtained vacant possession of the large bunker complex in the grounds of his property and proceeded to remove most of his laboratory into it. The association of the Post Office Research Institute at Lichterfeld-Ost with the nuclear weapons development programme in Nazi Germany was thus terminated.

In his autobiography Professor von Ardenne does not state how Professor Houtermans occupied his time at the laboratory between August, 1941, and August, 1944. Whilst von Ardenne and his co-workers produced a total of forty scientific papers and treatises in that period, Houtermans published only his August, 1941, report, amended in 1944, and a brief work on separation in ultracentrifuges in February, 1942.

Houtermans has told the Swiss scientific writer Robert Jungk[12] that he was averse to war work, but that he was in no position to refuse a task set him by Professor von Ardenne. He told his interviewer that although he knew that plutonium could definitely be generated in a nuclear pile, he 'did not report on that aspect of his work' since he had not wished to alert the authorities to the possibility of making atomic bombs. He also stated that his thesis had been placed in a safe at Post Office Central Headquarters by Dr Otterbein so that 'there should be no publication of his studies in the secret reports of the Heereswaffenamt', and there it had safely remained until 1944.

Is that true? Houtermans' memory was clearly at fault. An

explanatory passage introducing the 1944 amended version declares:

> 'The present work, which was completed in August, 1941, as a review of the uranium question, was not originally intended for publication. Copies need to be altered to reflect what follows.'

It is, furthermore, certainly untrue for him to have said that he had not reported on the formation of plutonium in a reactor, to which he devoted one and a half closely typed pages.

In May, 1940, as a half-Jewish communist sympathizer, Professor Houtermans was proscribed, under the Nazi racial and political laws, from working in any State enterprise, and was subject to Gestapo supervision. What can account then for the fact that by August, 1944, he was employed at the Reich Bureau of Standards, an institution of the German State, and was later to be entrusted with an intelligence-gathering mission to the Soviet Union?

Perhaps the answer is contained in the remainder of the explanatory extract introducing the 1944 Revision which:

> 'contains some points in respect of the application of low temperatures to a chain reaction for the purpose of producing neutrons which, to the author's belief, are made known for the first time, having been proved in another connection.'

Just as man should not speak the name of God, so man should not speak the name of the methane reactor. Houtermans never spoke of his brainchild. He was part of the eventual, unholy conspiracy of German scientists and American politicians against history, that the secret of the methane reactor and the radiation weapon should remain a secret for ever. The only person who ever subsequently confessed was Harteck.

At the end of hostilities in Europe, the Lichterfelde-Ost villa, together with all its valuable equipment, including the ruins of the 1-million volt Van de Graaf generator, the unused cyclotron and the prototype electro-magnetic isotope separator all went to the Russians, as did von Ardenne himself, as he had planned. For the next six years he worked on the USSR atomic weapons project on the Black Sea. Ohnesorge, too, preferred the eastern zone.

Professor Houtermans was the only scientist of any consequence attached to the Post Office programme to be interviewed by the American Intelligence Mission *Alsos*. When seen by them at Göttingen on 17 April, 1945, he gave the Americans the impression that he had only been on the fringe of German nuclear research and satisfied them that he was unable to contribute additional intelligence of any particular importance.

Houtermans said that his government had sent him to the Soviet Union to learn what nuclear research work was being undertaken there. He had discovered nothing much of note, but thought that the Russians were very interested in the subject and he had heard a rumour that Professor Kapitza was working on it, obtaining uranium ore from the Ferghana district of Turkestan.

The Americans let him go. He was not a physicist from whom anything useful might be obtained, they reasoned; he had merely worked on the independent Post Office research under the slightly ridiculous figure of the Postmaster, Ohnesorge, and, as Professor Goudsmit makes clear in his book *Alsos* [25], the Post Office nuclear project was treated as a joke by the Americans.

It was in these circumstances that they permitted the biggest fish to slip through their fingers.

Professor Houtermans remained at the University of Göttingen until 1952, when he accepted the Chair of Physics at the University of Berne in Switzerland.

Coinciding with the termination of von Ardenne's involvement in the project, the month of July, 1943, was marked by the first verbal salvoes opening the V-weapons campaign, and SS-inspired rumours soon began to circulate about new bombs 'built on the atomic principle' of which twelve would suffice to destroy one million inhabitants of a city.

On 23 February, 1944, at a confidential meeting of all Gauleiters, Reichsminister Goebbels may have had Hitler's radiological weapons in mind when he promised:

> 'Retribution is at hand. It will take a form hitherto unknown in warfare, a form the enemy, we hope, will find impossible to bear.'

And in visits to the Ruhr and Rhineland, his biographers, Viktor Reimann and Wilfred von Oven, report that Goebbels said a good deal more on the subject not only of rockets but also atomic-type weapons, than he ever allowed to appear in print.

Reports of these miracle weapons inspired new hope for a German victory, and revenge for the destruction of Germany's western cities, but when the actual offensive began in June, 1944, the new era was ushered in by the disappointing V-1 flying bomb and the V-2 rocket, and not with a weapon of mass destruction.

The use of rockets was not hitherto unknown in warfare, and the Propaganda Minister's dark references were echoed by Hitler himself in a speech to troops reported in the RMfVP (Reich Propaganda Ministry) circular *Tätigkeitsbericht* of 25 September, 1944, when he said,

> 'God forgive me if I have to turn to that terrible weapon in order to end the conflict.'

He could not have meant the V-1 and V-2, since by then both had already been deployed against Britain.

In a talk with Marshall Antonescu of Rumania in the Führerhauptquartier on 5 August, 1944,[26] probably one of the most historically useful of all his reported intimate conversations with a political ally, Hitler spoke specifically about the four V-weapons which Germany would soon employ.

The German noun *Vergeltung* has a dictionary meaning of 'retribution', 'retaliation' or 'reprisal', but in Nazi terminology it had an essentially broader interpretation, for the concept of retaliation as such merely contemplates the taking of revenge on the enemy.

In the case of the United Kingdom, for example, this would simply imply the taking of measures to inflict as much or more damage on British cities than the RAF and American air raids had inflicted on German cities, a militarily purposeless enterprise.

Nazi propaganda was at pains to emphasize that it was by no means the object of the V-Weapons programme to exchange 'rubble for rubble'; the concept of *Vergeltung*, as it applied in that case, meant the use of retaliation to terrorize the enemy's civilian population as a political tool to coerce their Government into seeking an armistice.'

The fact that the Nazi leadership derived some brutal satisfaction from the act of inflicting this terror on the people of London, for example, should be seen as merely incidental to the policy. What they really sought was not to punish Londoners *per se*, but from it to extract Britain's agreement to withdraw from the war and to expel from her soil the American presence there.

Hitler now informed Marshall Antonescu that Germany would soon introduce four V-weapons into the conflict. Two months previously the V-1 flying bomb had made its debut in the skies above London; in a month, the first V-2 rocket would be fired at the British capital from The Hague. These two weapons were indiscriminate and were designed to maintain a persistent light bombardment of southern England. The

V-3 was never specifically described by Hitler, but was almost certainly the 'England Gun' or 'High Pressure Pump'.[27]

The fourth V-Weapon was described to Antonescu as being one:

> 'of such potent effect that all human life is exterminated within a radius of three to four kilometres of the point of impact.'[28]

Some commentators have attempted to show[29] this weapon to be a putative atomic bomb, but it will be clear from Hitler's emphasis that the weapon is one for the mass destruction of people only.

Hitler now proceeded to expound the most important ground rules respecting the introduction and use of new weapons. In general, the Führer had ruled that a weapon should be brought into use immediately if it was guaranteed to bring the war to a victorious conclusion forthwith. This rule held good even if no counter-measure had yet been devised to the weapon.

This would appear to confirm that the radiation bomb would have been introduced at any time from the outbreak of war until early 1942, when Hitler could be sure that he alone possessed it.

In the majority of cases, however, the probability existed that the enemy would eventually obtain the same substance for himself, and the discovery of the counter-measure to it was thus obligatory as a precondition to its introduction in use.

Citing as a close parallel the poison gas diphenyl-arsin developed by German scientists in 1915, Hitler explained that not until 1918, when a cover was devised which could be snap-fastened to the standard German gas-mask and so protect the wearer against this particular type of gas, was it possible to introduce it finally to the battlefield. Thus a weapon of the second category was not 'complete' until the scientists showed that they had the counter to its use against Germany by her enemies.

Very possibly radiological warfare was classified by Hitler as analogous to gas warfare, the ground rules for which he had expounded in a table talk with Marshall Antonescu of Rumania on 24 March, 1944, at Salzburg in the presence of Keitel and others:

> 'Whether the enemy for their part will engage in gas warfare cannot be determined at present. In any case, Germany is well prepared here, being ultimately the country of the chemical industry and she certainly has better gases and explosives than the enemy.
>
> Germany for her part will not start a gas war, because

there is no sort of protection for the civilian population against the new types of gas'.

If it had been certain that no enemy power had succeeded in developing a critical reactor by the time that the radiation bombs were ready, Hitler would undoubtedly have used them at once, but his information at the turn of 1942 suggested that the United States was close to making an achievement in nuclear science. Accordingly it became necessary to discover the counter-measure to the weapon before deploying it.

As for the radiological weapon, what suspicions were held by the intelligence services of the United States and Great Britain as to its existence in the period from 1944 until the end of the war in Europe? In January, 1944, in conversation with Churchill, the American General Devers had suggested to the British Prime Minister the idea of a German bomb 'capable of causing radioactivity over an area of up to two square miles', dealing out sickness and death and leaving the area of contamination unapproachable for years. Devers admitted that the Americans had made their own experiments with such weapons.

The possibility of using fission products bred in a nuclear reactor as ingredients in a radiological device appears to have been contemplated in the United States originally by Arthur Compton's National Academy of Science Committee in 1941. It is possible that American physicists may have got wind of the successful German project during 1943, for a memorandum passed from the atom scientists Hans Bethe and Edward Teller to Robert Oppenheimer on 21 August of that year stating:

'Recent reports both through newspapers and the secret service have given indications that the Germans may be in possession of a powerful new weapon which is expected to be ready between November and January. There seems to be a considerable possibility that this new weapon is uranium.'

No further information, however, was received to support this suspicion and James Bryant Conant's sub-committee concluded that the possibility of attack by radioactive bombs was 'rather remote', Conant emphasizing that he thought it 'extremely unlikely that a radioactive weapon will be used against the United States, and unlikely that the weapon will be used at all.'

Later Lord Cherwell stated to Churchill that it was 'most improbable' that the Germans had conceived of such a weapon; British Intelligence was prepared to stake its reputation on the fact that no uranium weapons project had been undertaken by Berlin and that accordingly neither atomic bombs nor radioactive poisons need be feared from the Germans.[30]

Germany's atomic physicists failed in their hopeless task to discover the counter-measure to gamma radiation, which would have enabled Hitler to have introduced it into his V-Weapons programme. Since it was reasonably certain that the United States had now achieved a working reactor, Hitler's rules governing weapons deployment forbade him the opportunity to use the radiation bomb first in the conflict. Nevertheless, that would not have precluded the retaliatory use of radiation bombs to eradicate the population of London and other cities of southern England, had Churchill's intention to use the biological contaminant, anthrax, against German cities in the late summer of 1944 been put into effect.

The circumstances in which this nearly came to pass are now examined.

The first of Hitler's V-Weapons was the V-1. This was the Fieseler 103 unpiloted flying bomb launched from a short ramp under its own jet power and carrying a 1-ton explosive warhead. Its maximum speed was 650 km per hour and its range 370 km. At the nose was a small log consisting of a propellor connected to a revolutions counter, which was preset with the number of turns of the propellor imparted at a particular speed and height in reaching a known distance. As soon as the preset number of revolutions had been achieved, the counter cut out the engine, and the bomb then dropped. The weapon was grossly inaccurate and thus intrinsically indiscriminate.

On 13 June, 1944, the long-awaited bombardment of London with the unpiloted flying bomb began. Ten days later Goebbels was prompted to explain the intended effect of the campaign, which had his personal endorsement, in the following vein:

'Of course, a 1,000-ton raid has a different effect. But the effect of the German bombardment lies in its persistency.... I can imagine how, quite apart from any damage it might cause, it would gradually build up on your nerves. It's like toothache. The pain is of itself possibly not so bad. But when the tooth aches and throbs all day and all night, then you think it will drive you off your head; you can't think clearly, in fact all you *can* think about is this accursed pain, and finally you have to do what you should have done all along. You go to the dentist....

The V-weapons bombardment will be continued come what may and it will increase each month until England comes to her senses, that is to say, until the English inner circle sweeps away those responsible for this insane British policy and clears the way for an understanding with us.'[31]

This outlook summarizes the philosophy behind the V-weapons campaign. Rejecting any consideration of the deployment of the V-1 at the Front against armies in the East and West who had now begun the converging movement towards the borders of the Reich itself, the Nazi hierarchy resolved to rely entirely on the psychological effect of the terror bombardment on London and the Home Counties in the hope of forcing the United Kingdom to the negotiating table, and in the unspoken hope that, if that were not to be the case, then that the United Kingdom Government might in desperation resort to some act so escalating the slaughter of German civilians that Hitler could justifiably respond with the ultimate weapon of terror, the radiation bomb, against selected cities.

As the bombardment entered its third week, the intermittent attacks continued day and night, imposing a severe strain psychologically on the inhabitants of London. The flying bombs had already killed nearly 2,000 of them, and seriously injured persons numbered 5,000; over a quarter of a million houses had been damaged and 7,000 destroyed.

By 6 July, 1944, it had begun to succeed in its desired aim. In a Most Secret[32] minute to the Chiefs of Staff on that day, Churchill wrote:

'If the bombardment of London really becomes a serious nuisance and great rockets with far-reaching and devastating effect fall on many centres of Government and labour, I should be prepared to do *anything* that would hit the enemy in a murderous place.'

Churchill was particularly attracted to the idea of using poison gas against the civilian population:

'It may be several weeks or even months before I shall ask you to drench Germany with poison gas, and if we do it, let us do it 100 per cent.... Pray address yourselves to this. It is a big thing and can only be discarded for a big reason. I shall, of course, have to square Uncle Joe and the President, but you need not bring this into your calculations at the present time.'

At a meeting of the Chiefs of Staff two days later to discuss Churchill's

132

proposal, Sir Charles Portal, Chief of the Air Staff, stated that he was not convinced that the use of poison gas would produce the result suggested by the Prime Minister. It was, he said, 'very difficult to achieve a heavy concentration of gas over a large area.'[33]

Since June, 1944, the control of the biological warfare programme had also fallen within the ambit of the Chiefs of Staff and eventually the Joint Planning Staff were requested to undertake:

> 'a comprehensive examination of the points raised in the PM's Minute, and to include in that examination consideration of the possibilities of biological warfare and of the form which enemy reprisals might take.'

The terms of reference to the Joint Planning Staff were further elucidated:

> 'The Prime Minister has directed that a comprehensive examination should be undertaken of the military implications of our deciding on an all-out use of gas, principally mustard gas, or any other method of warfare which we have hitherto refrained from using against the Germans.
>
> (a) as a counter-offensive in the event of the use by the enemy of flying bombs and/or giant rockets developing into a serious threat to our ability to prosecute the war; or, alternatively,
>
> (b) as a means of shortening the war or of bringing to an end a situation in which there was a danger of stalemate.
>
> The Chiefs of Staff have instructed the JPS to carry out this examination, which should cover the possibilities of use of biological warfare by us. It should take the form of a thorough and practical examination of the military factors involved and should ignore ethical and political considerations.'[34]

The Joint Planning Staff were enjoined to consider 'an unrestrained use of chemical and biological weapons' and were not to consult the Americans.

On the evening of 27 July, 1944, a 14-page copy of the JPS report entitled '*Military Considerations Affecting the Initiation of Chemical and Other Special Forms of Warfare*' was handed to the Prime Minister.

The report stated that combined British and American stocks of gas in the United Kingdom were sufficient to produce 'a formidable scale of gas attack on Germany' and production levels were sufficient to enable a 'continuous effort of 20 per cent of Bomber Command', but the Joint Planning Staff were rather in favour of a single blow using the combined strength of the entire British and American bomber force. Twenty-five per cent of the payload would be high explosive to destroy buildings and create panic and then the main force would arrive to deliver the gas bombs.

One thousand tactical targets or twenty German cities would receive phosgene on the scale of 16 tons to the square mile. This would result in heavy casualties amounting to 5 per cent to 10 per cent deaths of civilians and civil defence personnel. Mustard gas would be used against 1,500 tactical targets or sixty cities:

> 'In the large scale gas attacks on cities, vapour burns would be caused on such a scale as to necessitate wholesale evacuation, thus paving the way to a subsequent incendiary attack. Speedy wholesale evacuation might well be a physical impossibility, in which case large casualties would follow.
>
> The initial effect of using chemical warfare agents against large centres of population in Germany would be to produce great confusion, probably amounting to panic in the areas immediately concerned.'

In an appendix, sixty cities were listed. The Joint Planning Staff also considered the likely effect of gas warfare in France and found that on the whole it might be against British interests.

They also thought that, 'if the Allies initiated chemical warfare, the Germans would immediately retaliate both in the field and against the United Kingdom. London would be the primary target and could expect to be attacked by flying bombs filled with gas and by up to 120 long-range bombers carrying chemical payloads.' In the circumstances, the JPS was not prepared to recommend the use of chemical weapons, but added:

> 'N (i.e. anthrax) is the only Allied biological agent which could probably make a material change in the war situation before the end of 1945. There are indications, which lack scientific proof, that the 4lb bomb charged with anthrax and used on a large scale from aircraft might have a major effect on the course of the war.'

These would be $106 \times 4lb$ bombs loaded into a 500 lb cluster bomb casing. 2,000 would contaminate a large town. Both the British and German civilian populations were defenceless against anthrax to which there was no known prophylactic measure.

Whilst advancing no arguments against anthrax bomb attacks on German citizens, the Joint Planning Staff cautioned that the stock level of the weapon was lower than forecasts had predicted.

On 28 September, 1944, when the Chiefs of Staff met, they reported that they did not support the use of chemical or biological weapons in the current arena for fear of the public response in the event of German retaliation.

The next day, in conceding the point whilst not being convinced by the report, Churchill noted that the matter should be kept under review and brought up again when things got worse.

There are reports that he received pressure from the American Commander-in-Chief, Eisenhower, not to proceed with the idea.

Hitler's dislike of poison gas, possibly derived from his personal experience of it at Ypres in 1918, is widely known. Karl Brandt, Hitler's former surgeon, stressed that the German leader was opposed to the use of poison gas except in retaliation.

If the Allied air forces had indeed used any of the proposed agents in raids on the civilian population of Germany, the temptation to exterminate the entire population of London as a reprisal might have been difficult for Hitler to resist. The British and American Governments would have been taken completely by surprise by the use of the radiological weapon and the measure could conceivably have utterly destroyed the political infrastructure of the United Kingdom. The long desired objective of ending the involvement of Great Britain in the conflict might also have resulted from the tactic.

The American Government would have been placed in a very difficult position if Hitler had then initiated diplomatic overtures coupled with an intimation that he would supply the radiation weaponry to Japan for a joint attack on American cities from both the Pacific and Atlantic coasts.

In this light, it will be apparent that the pressure applied by Eisenhower on Churchill, and the negative advice from Churchill's Chiefs of Staff based on their understanding that the British public might not be able to tolerate the German retaliatory measures, and demand an armistice, undoubtedly served to prevent the war taking a fresh course entirely unforeseen by Churchill.

There is a great deal of difference between the reaction of one's own public and allies to the first use of a particular vile weapon of mass terror by the enemy, and to the use of it by him in circumstances perceived as a justifiable response to one's own breach of international convention.

As has already been mentioned, President Roosevelt notified General Groves at the time of the Yalta Conference to be prepared to drop the first American atomic bomb on Germany if the weapon was ready before the Nazi Government had been defeated, but on 23 April, 1945, Groves assured the Secretary for War, Stimson, that 'the target is, and was always expected to be, Japan.'[35] The reasoning behind the selection of Japan to receive the first atomic attack rather than Nazi Germany is not clear. It may have been that the German war was not expected to survive the period of the bomb's development, or that the assembling of the atom bomb on a Pacific island was preferable on safety grounds to doing it in England. Two other possibilities mooted have been the idea that the Americans wished to retain the complete control and use of the weapon in their own Far Eastern theatre of war, or that there was a racial bias in the selection of the enemy to be attacked.

It was all very well for American war leaders to speak glibly of dropping an atom bomb on Germany, but whether the deployment of one or even two atom bombs against Nazi Germany would have brought about its unconditional surrender is an open question. It certainly does not appear that the atomic destruction of Hiroshima and Nagasaki was the primary cause occasioning the surrender of Japan. If in such circumstances Nazi Germany had sought an alternative to surrender, it is clearly probable that as soon as they had discovered the presence of radioactive fallout at the target, resulting from an atomic bomb delivered by an aircraft operating from a British airfield, the Nazi impulse would have been to deposit across England, as soon as possible, as much of their inventory of radioactive waste as could be spared in a last attempt to bring the war to stalemate.

This was the risk which the British military commanders ran. Their apprehension at the possible public reaction to the possible German retaliation would then, as in the case of the proposed use of chemical and biological weapons by Churchill, have been the determining factor in obliging the Americans to use the weapon elsewhere.[36]

His arsenal of radiation bombs presented Hitler with a crippling dilemma. Knowledge of their existence might invite the enemy to strike pre-emptively with his own radiological weapons if, as was suspected, the Americans also had them.

Since their existence could not be admitted, they could not be used either to intimidate the enemy nor to entice him to sue for peace.

By 1945, their usefulness as a weapon existed only if they could be introduced against the Americans on their own ground and even then only provided that Hitler was not implicated in their employment.

Alternatively, he could hope that his atomic scientists might yet discover the protection against radiation and so enable him to deploy the weapons immediately in Europe. Thus historians who have inveighed against Hitler in the final months of his rule as being given to fantasies about 'wonder-weapons' which existed only in his imagination are completely mistaken. The weapons of frightfulness certainly existed; they were incomplete only in the sense that no new weapon in his armoury was ready for deployment until the counter-measure to it had been discovered. He would not introduce them for that reason except in retaliation.

Ashen with the pallor of the Bunker, drained of energy, eyes lifeless above heavy bags, all that kept his spirit alive in the closing months was the desperate hope that, even at the last, circumstances might yet permit him to use his weapons of frightfulness in a final throw.

But the dilemma had made him indecisive; he distrusted his Japanese ally and her continuing overtures to the Soviet Union and so dallied too long before taking the decision he should have made as soon as he had enough of the venomous material to share with them.

Accordingly, when at Schloss Ferienwalde on the Oder on 11 March, 1945, he implored General Theodor Busse and officers of the 9th Army to stave off the Russians for as long as it might take for his new 'wonder-weapons' to be ready, he was honest in promising them that 'every day and every hour are precious for the completion of the weapons of frightfulness which will bring the turn in our fortune!', but far too late. He was asking the impossible in beseeching his troops to hold the line for the few extra months it would take to deploy the radiation bombs against the people of the United States, and so relieve him of the enemy at his western gates, for they were already giving everything they had; they knew what a Russian occupation would mean.

Nevertheless what he said was true; even as he spoke, a U-boat awaited orders to sail from what remained of Kiel; aboard her she carried the precious shipment which was to be used to punish the American people for the ruin inflicted on Germany's cities and perhaps to save the German Reich from annihilation.

But the perilous voyage would take a submarine at least four months to complete, and this would ultimately cost Japan her chance to achieve something worthwhile both for Nazi Germany and for herself in the war against the United States. General der Flieger Ulrich Kessler, appointed to be the new Luftwaffe attaché to the German Embassy in Tokyo, stated[37] that the original plan had been to fly the material the 8,500 miles from Berlin to Tokyo in a Focke-Wulf 200 Condor four-engined transport packed to its limits with extra tankage, refuelling in China. The decision not to proceed with the plan had been taken with great reluctance but the flight entailed crossing air space controlled by the Soviet Union, which gave the operation much less than an even chance of succeeding.

Even before the outbreak of war in Europe in 1939, an arrangement existed between the German and Japanese governments permitting German blockade runners, supply ships and oilers to use a small number of bases within Japan's sphere of influence. By 1940 German tankers and supply ships were based in the Japanese ports of Yokohama and Kobe, from where they sortied to replenish the raiders *Orion* and *Komet* operating against Allied merchant shipping in the Pacific. Following the entry of Japan and the United States into the war on 7 December, 1941, and the declaration of war on the United States by Germany four days later, the German Naval Command was soon to contact the Japanese authorities with a view to discussing the lease from them of U-boat facilities in the area. This prospect became particularly attractive after Japan had subjugated Burma, Thailand, Indonesia and most of the islands of strategic importance in the eastern Pacific.

The Germans established themselves at the ports of Singapore and Jakarta, the operational terminals for the exchange of raw materials, but typifying the mood of co-operation between the Axis partners at the time, it was not until early 1943, when the alliance had begun to come under pressure from the Anglo-American naval presence, that Japan agreed to the deployment of German U-boats in the Far East.

Correspondingly, in addition to the existing harbours, U-boat Command was awarded the base at Penang, Malaysia, in the summer of 1943, and at the beginning of 1944 a fourth at Surabaya (Java), where stranded German naval and mercantile crews were remustered as dockyard personnel.

In May, 1943, the first four boats *(U-177, U-178, U181* and *U-198)* sailed from France and, having refuelled at sea off Madagascar, arrived at Penang in August to become the *Monsoon* Group. A fifth boat, *U-511*, which, as has been mentioned, had been used in the Baltic in 1942 for the submerged test firing of artillery rockets, was presented to the Emperor as a gift.

During 1943 the transport of raw materials between German-occupied France and the Far East was assumed by Axis submarines once Allied naval superiority had begun to take a serious toll of merchant vessels running the blockade.

Although at the outset of planning the German Admiralty had intended to introduce purpose-built transport U-boats, they eventually settled for converting existing large minelayers.

By the summer of 1944, as the probability of defeat for Germany within the course of the following 12 months became ever more likely, the Axis partners, undoubtedly aware of the designs which the western Allies and the Soviet Union had on leading German scientists and technicians and their developments, began joint negotiations for their transfer to Japan by U-boat in order to remove them from reach.

Restricted by the carrying capacity of the transport, emphasis was placed on the carriage of patents, inventions and weapons of vital importance to the war effort, together with limited numbers of specialists.

In August, 1944, three converted U-boats of Type IXD/1, (*U-180, U-195* and *U-219*), were despatched to Japan from France with cargoes of optical instruments, mercury, dismantled V-weapons, torpedoes, radar equipment, blueprints and technical personnel.

One of the boats carried the prototype liquid-fuel plant for piloted jet-bombs which were based on the design of the German glider-bomb, a specimen of which had been shipped to Japan earlier that year. These kamikaze weapons, 6 metres long with a 5-metre wingspan, obtained a speed of 1000 km per hour from the thrust of the fuel unit. The supply U-boats would bring back to the Reich cargoes of wolfram, tin, molybdenum, raw rubber, quinine and opium.

U-180 was lost in the Bay of Biscay on the outward voyage, but *U-195* and *U-219* both succeeded in reaching Japanese bases by December, 1944.

Since the level of development and technical innovation of the Japanese war economy had persistently lagged behind that of the western Allies and Germany, it is incomprehensible that these arrangements for the exchange of technology had not been taken in hand three years earlier. In January, 1945, for example, the German chemicals firm I G Farben was compelled by the Reich Government to supply the Japanese with details of the process for the production of synthetic fuel spirit, which Foreign Minister Matsuoka had first requested in 1941.

Towards the end of 1944 Hitler's neglected ally had estimated that the defeat of Germany could be expected at the latest by the summer of 1945, and Japan's own position was clearly desperate.

Whilst the Japanese now sought any solution by which they might acquit themselves from the conflict with a modicum of honour and no loss of face, Hitler's primary aims included a desire to exact revenge upon the civilian population of the United States for the destruction wrought on Germany's cities, and, if possible, to force the Americans into neutrality. Undoubtedly he was willing and eager to use the radiation weapon against the Americans, but only without directly implicating Germany; and in this strategic weapon, the Japanese, who had far less compunction than Hitler about the scattering of blight and plague, would have seen a glimmer of hope for their salvation. But only after it had become certain to Hitler that Japanese diplomatic overtures to the Russians had found no response was it possible for him to play the last trump he held and offer his treaty partner the ghastly weapons.

Only after they had been forced hopelessly onto the defensive did the Axis partners begin to engage seriously in close political and technological association.

Only at the last was the decision taken at the highest level in Germany to supply the Japanese with a weapon 'hitherto unknown in warfare' as a means to bring about the disengagement of the United States from the conflict against the two Axis partners.

It was in December, 1944,[38] that the corresponding plan was finally drawn up for the evacuation of 27 German specialists from the jet fighter and V-weapons centres together with certain strategic weaponry.

They would sail in a U-boat directly to Tokyo, and even the newly appointed Luftwaffe attaché to Japan would be aboard.

The Voyage Of The German Submarine U-234

'The war was being brought home to Uncle Sam, carried to his front door step.... Here was one of the prime exploits of the war under the sea — a phase of it, at any rate, of by far the greatest interest to us Americans.'

Lowell Thomas,
Raiders of the Deep
(The Story of the Kaiser's U-boats)
William Heinemann Ltd, London, 1929

'I LEFT LORIENT AS Petty Officer Hirschfeld on 28 July, 1943, to begin training for promotion to the rank of Warrant Officer. The Personnel Office at Kiel confirmed to me during that October that on successful completion of the course, a posting to the Signals Office of the 2nd U-boat Flotilla at Lorient would follow.

There was talk of new, streamlined U-boats already nearing completion, with a phenomenal underwater speed of 18 knots. It was almost incredible. I wondered if this could be the turn in the fortunes of the U-boat fleet? With such boats as these, a convoy could be penetrated to its heart with impunity, leaving the escort vessels floundering. The only question was, how long would it be before these wonder-boats arrived at the Front in large numbers, and why should the current stock of old slow boats have to bear the merciless killing techniques of the Allied navies until they did arrive?

On 19 January, 1944, my Senior Officer handed me a telex.

"Your posting. You leave tomorrow."

I thanked him and tucked the paper into a pocket.

"Wouldn't you like to read it?"

"Thank you, lieutenant, but I already know where."

"I should have a look at it if I were you," the officer said with a grin. I unfolded the message and read:

"Oberfunkmeister Hirschfeld to report on 20 January, 1944, to the 1st Baulehrcompagnie, Kiel, Germania Werft, for *U-234*."

It was a hammer blow. Quickly I rang a contact in the U-boat Personnel Office in Kiel.

"I can't talk on the phone," he said. "You'll have to come to Kiel first."

"Just answer me this. This *U-234*, is it a streamlined boat?"

"No, it's a large Type Xb, a 2,000 tonner. It got a bomb hit on the slip in 1942 and has only just been finished. She's entitled to have a Warrant Officer in charge of the telecommunications and that is yourself."

I replaced the handset, my head sunk in gloom. So, after everything, I was still likely to find a watery grave.

I arrived in Kiel the next evening in the middle of a heavy air raid. Flak thundered from a thousand barrels. I sprinted to the great Hummelwiese bunker, but they wouldn't let me in. Only for women, children and civilians, said the watchman, and slammed the door in my face. So I took to my heels again through a rain of flak splinters in a desperate run to the Germania Werft.

"We don't have a bunker," said the man at the door, "only some slit trenches. They're in the shelter of the overhang of the aircraft carrier *Graf Zeppelin*. They seem to be pretty safe."

In the darkness, I stumbled into one of the trenches and found a place to sit next to an engineer lieutenant-commander. The ground was quaking, and the great hull of the aircraft carrier was trembling in the blast of the enormous explosions. In the pale light of a candle, I saw all the care-worn faces. They were nearly all of them U-boat men. It was just like a depth-charge attack under water, only here you couldn't be drowned by a near miss.

Once the bombers had gone, the engineer officer glanced at my shoulder-straps and asked my name. When I told him, he said, "Well, you're one of us then," and introduced himself as the Chief Engineer of *U-234*, Horst Ernst.

We went off together to the accommodation ship *Holstenau* where the officer arranged a cabin for me. Then he explained how my posting had been changed. Although the boat's telecommunications section was fully staffed, the captain had noticed upon reading the operating specifications that he was entitled to a Warrant Officer to take charge of the radio office, and he had gone to the Personnel Bureau in Kiel to find out if there was one available with U-boat experience. Only I was on the list and so I was volunteered. On the following day I reported to my new captain, Lieutenant-Commander Johann Heinrich Fehler.

Fehler was a Berliner like myself, born at Charlottenburg in 1910, the first of three children and the son of a judge. His mother died of an illness which should have been curable had the surgeons not been away at the Front. His brother died in similar circumstances the following year. Fehler's ambition from childhood onwards had been to become a Merchant Navy officer, but a boy had to be under the age of sixteen years to qualify for nautical school and his father compelled him to complete his education.

By his nineteenth birthday, he was, therefore, too old for sail training and found that in order to sit his mate's certificate, it would be necessary to serve fifty months at sea, of which at least twenty months had to be in sailing vessels. He signed on as deck boy with the small 140-ton oak-built galeasses which plied the ports of the Baltic, until, after twenty-seven months of this rough, cold, harsh life, he could finally become apprenticed aboard the motor ships and steamers of the great German shipping lines. Soon he was in the Far East aboard the 7,600-ton North German Lloyd motor ship *Havel*.

On one of his infrequent returns to Germany in November, 1933, he said that he found the country transformed and the common people imbued with an 'awakening spirit' and a fresh sense of purpose; he was sufficiently impressed to allow himself to be recruited into the Nazi Party during a membership drive. No deep political conviction lay behind his decision; he said it was merely the grandeur of the times.

On 2 April, 1936, Fehler entered the German Navy as an officer cadet, and by the outbreak of war had command of the minesweeper *M-145* operating out of Wilhelmshaven; by the turn of the year, he had been drafted aboard the commerce raider, *Atlantis*, as Mines and Explosives Officer. The *Atlantis* was the former cargo liner *Goldenfels* fitted out with concealed guns and torpedo-tubes and sent out to disrupt mercantile commerce on the high seas; between March, 1940, and November, 1941, Fehler spent a total of 622 days at sea aboard the *Atlantis* in a voyage which twice circumnavigated the globe sinking 22 Allied trading vessels.

Returned to Mürwik in 1942 as an instructor, his impatient importuning of the authorities for a command − a U-boat − eventually bore fruit and by September, 1943, he had qualified as a U-boat commander.

In a conversation with me, Lieutenant-Commander Fehler said that he was upset to have been assigned *U-234*, a minelaying submarine, when what he really wanted was a fighting U-boat. It upset me even more, however, to discover that Fehler had no previous operational U-boat experience. A commander who knew nothing of the treacherous North Atlantic, or of the deadly peril lurking in the clouds, was a definite liability, but I much appreciated his buoyant optimism and warm personality. Of the officers, only Ernst, the Chief Engineer, had even been on a training boat in the Baltic, although all the Senior NCOs were old U-boat hands and there was a highly experienced nucleus amongst the junior NCOs as well.

The seven U-boats of Type Xb were the largest in the German Navy, displacing 1,650 tons, 2,100 tons laden, and had been designed as minelayers, equipped with 18 mine shafts arranged laterally and in the foreship 66 mines could be carried.

90 metres in length and 9 metres broad, the class had diesel-electric propulsion providing maximum speeds of 17 knots surfaced and 7 knots for short periods submerged. The most economic cruising speed, 10 knots, gave them a range of 21,000 sea miles, ideal for long-distance cargo missions.

Armament was two stern torpedo tubes and a complement of seven torpedoes, which were stored one in each tube, two on the stern room floor plating, and three beneath.

The artillery consisted of two twin 20mm cannons on the upper gun platform abaft the bridge and one twin 37mm anti-aircraft cannon on the lower platform.

U-234 had been seriously damaged by a bomb hit in May, 1943, while still under construction and was not launched until 23 December, 1943. By the time of her commissioning on 3 March, 1944, four of the fleet of seven had already been sunk. Of the remainder, *U-219* was at Bordeaux waiting orders to sail for the Far East, and *U-233* and *U-234* were working up in the Baltic.

We spent two months in and out of the builders' before we fetched up at Rönne on the Baltic island of Bornholm on 27 April, confined in the harbour because of an uncleared minefield outside. It was a marvellous spring morning, and I sat with the Quartermaster, Paul Rische, and ERA Sandmüller in the winter garden in the warm sunshine.

"I like it here," Paul said. "I wouldn't mind staying a bit longer." Sandmüller agreed. "The minesweeper boys can take their time. Every day wasted brings the end of the war that much nearer."

We all lit up and puffed away contentedly.

"You know something about the subject Wolf," Paul Rische said, "so you can believe me when I say that the very thought of the Atlantic makes me sick inside."

"Yes," I replied, "it's a year and a half since I was out there. The other side have got themselves all sorts of new devices. It gives me the creeps when I hear of our losses." I paused.

"*U-233* is going out on her first mission soon."

"As a supply boat?"

"No, Atlantic refuelling is all over with. My counterpart, Rafalski, told me it was a minelaying sortie."

"Huh, sixty mines on Roosevelt's doorstep, fancy that," laughed Sandmüller, "what use will that be? You can see what good the mines are here. They just sweep them up and we carry on as normal."

"I don't understand why they keep on sending the old boats out," I said. "They're even still building the old Type VIIs."

"You wouldn't believe how mad I get about that, Wolf," Paul Rische remarked. "I think they send them out just to get them sunk. And when I think of the kindergarten we've got on this boat.... Sure, we've got experienced Senior NCOs, but why doesn't the captain get himself some experienced officers?"

"There aren't any left, Paul."

He shook his head. "I don't think that's true. All the old commanders they're forcing back to sea manage to get them."

"Maybe you're right. Possibly the captain doesn't know the right people. He's new to the U-boat Arm. That's the disadvantage of being at sea for two years in a raider."

The Quartermaster nodded grimly.

"But even so," I continued, "these new anti-U-boat devices caught out some of the best of the old aces. Think of Kuppisch, for example. Our only real chance of surviving is on these new Type XXI Walther boats with their very high underwater speed. Without that, we're lost."

We arrived at Hela for more working up exercises on 25 May, 1944; I was spared for a short posting to a course in Kiel at the beginning of June, where I learned that *U-233* had sailed on a minelaying mission on 27 May. Rafalski had said to me in April, when he knew where they were going, "Can you imagine what type of defence the Americans will have over there? U-boat Command thinks it's still Operation Paukenschlag."

On 6 June the course lecturer drew me quietly aside and told me that the Allies had landed that morning on the Cotentin Peninsula with an armada of ships.

"Well, we'll see," I said, for I fully expected our forces to throw them straight back into the Channel.

In beaming sunshine on the morning of 20 June, 1944, *U-234* set off for a position just seawards of the Hela mole for a practice dive. The depth was 60 metres. The alarm bells rang to start the exercise and we submerged with an extremely steep inclination of the bow, boring deeply into the mud on the sea bed within a few seconds. When we were stationary, the captain raised the periscope and calmly informed the Chief Engineer, Ernst, that the stern was still above water.

145

Paul Rische was raging in the control room. "We've been training for four weeks, and all the Chief has learned is this. I tell you, Wolf, this Ernst is a typical learner. Useless! Well, I've had enough of it. I'm getting off this boat."

"If only it was so easy," I said.

Our plight had been noticed from the shore and a launch had been despatched, her commander enquiring on arrival if there were any survivors. It seemed to be an age before the Chief got the boat trimmed, and the only comfort we drew was from the continued presence of the launch, slowly circling above us.

Seizing the opportunity at Memel to slip ashore for three hours with the captain on a private errand on 19 July, 1944, I found the place almost deserted. The remaining townspeople had aged noticeably since my last visit here, with lines of worry and anxiety in their faces. They were weary and nervous, for although they could not yet hear the artillery, they knew that the Soviets had reached nearby Mitau, and when the Red Army did eventually sweep into Memel there was no knowing how they might behave, particularly towards the women and girls.

Returning before time to the *U-234* aboard the commander's launch, Fehler said to me, "Take a good long look at it, Hirschfeld. You may not get another chance."

I looked at him in astonishment. "Don't you think the Army can hold the Russians?" I asked him.

He gazed across the harbour. "It was a long way from Stalingrad to Mitau. And now we have a European continental war on two fronts. Do you want me to spell it out?"

It was on the following day, 20 July, 1944, whilst pounding through the Baltic chop en route to Palmnicken for the tactical exercises with the U-boat depot ship *Waldemar Kophamel* that we heard of the attempt on the Führer's life. We were all most relieved to hear him speak to the nation in a radio communiqué later that same day, and we took an extremely dim view of the actions of the Army officers involved in the plot. Whereas they were undoubtedly acting from the best motives in seeking a just armistice, "unconditional surrender" remained Roosevelt's terms, and the Russians would almost certainly have grabbed the chance to roll on over our surrendering armies and not stop until they reached the Rhine.

Our watchword was Lenin's adage "If we have Germany, we have Europe", and so we preferred to fight on in the hope that Hitler's promised "miracle weapons" might yet bring the turn in our receding fortunes.

As soon as we clambered aboard the *Waldemar Kophamel*, I was summoned to the bridge of the depot ship with instructions to report to her commander. I had no idea who he was, but when the helmsman pointed to the bridge wing where an officer was standing with his back to me, silently observing the U-boat flotilla manoeuvring alongside the hull of his ship, I reported myself. He turned slowly, and I gasped as I recognised Lieutenant-Commander Wilhelm Wissmann, who had been the first lieutenant for the third and fourth voyages aboard *U-109*, and then had commanded *U-518*.

"Hirschfeld, how delightful to see you again," he exclaimed.

We shook hands, and he said, "I saw your name on the Instructor's list and could scarcely believe it. I thought you had drowned on *U-109*."

I grinned. "I thought I would never see you again either. There were some dreadful stories doing the rounds. They said you were in Landsberg prison."

With a laugh, Wissmann retorted, "Not quite as bad as that. Doenitz relieved me of command of *U-518* because I refused to sail with the ridiculous Biscay Cross aboard. I told him I wanted a proper radar."

"Is there such a thing for U-boats?"

Wissmann nodded bitterly. "Yes, the Hohentwiel, which we could have had from the Luftwaffe in 1943. That would have reduced many of our losses. But how did you manage to get off *U-109*?"

"I had a skin fungus which I caught from those damned French Navy hooped jerseys we used to wear. The Fleet Surgeon, Dr Lepel, considered it was likely to be fatal if it penetrated any further beneath my skin."

Our conversation lasted for many hours, and thus we spent a convivial evening before the commencement of the sea exercises. Wissmann was the only officer who had sailed aboard *U-109*, besides Bleichrodt, to survive the war, and speaking to Lieutenant-Commander Fehler later of the advantages of ship-borne radar, he promised me that he would ensure that we obtained a set, and later did so.

The next day the Senior Telegraphy Instructor began by bluntly describing to the radio-communications crews the deteriorating position in the eastern Baltic, where the Soviets were attempting to break out of Leningrad. The exit from the port had been sealed by an extensive mine and net barrier and a number of Russian submarines attempting to escape into the Baltic had been destroyed by the combined German and Finnish anti-submarine forces.

However, the overall situation for German U-boats generally was extremely grave. 118 had been lost in the first six months of the year. The Instructor, Langen, continued, "If you are aboard one of the new

Type XXI or XXIII U-boats, your high underwater speed is your salvation. If you are on any other type of U-boat and you fall into the hands of a hunter-killer group, you are dead."

We looked at each other in alarm.

How long would it be until the new Walther boats were actually available in reasonable numbers? The question drew no response.

We docked *U-234* at the Danzig yard on 18 August in order to have a transformer or something similar fitted to the boat, and then wandered off in groups around the beautiful, undamaged city, sightseeing. We spent long hours strolling the long alleys on the Milchkannentor, alive with people, and many pretty girls, and then in the evening occupied a table at the 'Kapitol' in the Langgasse. Every diner there received gratis a full-bellied glass of old Malaga wine. Sandmüller whispered to me, "You know what this means, don't you? He's giving it to us so that the Russians won't get it. This is a place where they have already surrendered."

The alarums, the rumours of an impending collapse of the German front line, the prospect of the Russian advance, had filled the Danzigers with a lively apprehension, and their city had an eerie, tense mood to it. Nobody mentioned the war, least of all the furloughed troops in field-grey, who alone showed a certain natural exuberance wherever they went.

It was not difficult to entice four attractive girls to join us at our table. In normal times they would never have dreamed of such a thing, for they were all decent, married women. But their men were far away at the front, somewhere in Russia the last time they had heard, and whether they were alive or dead they did not know. We wined and dined them until late into the night.

Afterwards Paul Rische said to me, "Wolfgang, I really feel for those poor, loyal women. Here they stay, waiting for their husbands who are probably long dead, and refuse to budge. Can you imagine what the Russians will do to them when they get here?"

"Shut up, Paul. It makes me sick to think about it. I told the small blonde who was sitting next to me that she should pack her bags and go right away to her relatives in Westphalia. There's still a regular train service to there, you know."

But the brave women had made their decision. Paul Rische and I spent that warm summer night wandering among the crowds on the beautiful streets of Danzig, seized by a sickening melancholia which I shall never forget.

We arrived in Kiel on 30 August, 1944, for a refit, and upon arrival I went aboard the former cruise liner *St Louis* to have a look at her radio room. The news was bad; the appalling losses of U-boats had continued and many more famous commanders had failed to return. *U-233*, our sister-boat, had been caught by an American hunter-killer group off Nova Scotia and destroyed. My old friend, Rafalski, and 29 others had been rescued, but more than half the complement of the boat were lost. That same afternoon there was a heavy air raid on Kiel and the *St Louis* was set ablaze and had to be scuttled in order to quench the uncontrollable fire. *U-234* had previously slipped out of the U-boat harbour into the relative safety of Heikendorf Bay, where we concealed ourselves in a thick smoke-screen, but even so we were lucky to escape when an enemy aircraft in difficulties jettisoned its bomb load within 30 metres of us.

Shortly afterwards, we put back into the German Werft U-boat yard where *U-234* was to be refitted and converted from a minelayer into a transport submarine.

As originally built, the boat was fitted with thirty vertical mine shafts. Twenty-four of these were so situated that there were twelve of them running through the saddle-tanks fore and aft either side of the conning tower. All of these shafts were removed in order to create two large, lateral holds amidships.

The other mine shafts were located in a line of six on the meridian of the forecasing and within a slightly raised emplacement 45 feet (13.7m) long. The forward edge of the mound was 60 feet (18.26m) back from the peak of the bow, and the rear edge of the mound was about 50 feet (15.22m) forward of the foot of the conning tower coaming.

Each shaft was 30 feet (9.13m) deep, was hollow and was open to the sea at the bottom. The diameter of each shaft was about 7 feet (2.13m) and passed vertically through the bow-room.

The original purpose of the six shafts had been to contain three sea-mines each, held in place one above the other on a frame. This framework had been removed, and a pressure-resistant steel cylinder with a lid was inserted into each vertical chamber and secured by retaining screws into the emplacement.[1]

These cylinders were now ready to receive cargo. I noted with satisfaction that a small tower had been built for the radar mattress, and a snorkel installation of the most modern design had also been fitted which had required the reconstruction of part of the starboard foredeck.

The purpose of the snorkel was to permit submerged travel under diesel propulsion, instead of the slow electric motors, by feeding air to the diesel engines through an intake mast. The device had numerous drawbacks in use. In the head of the snorkel was a float valve which shut automatically when a sea swept over the mast. This prevented the entry of water, but also cut off the air supply at the same time, so that the diesels then drew their supply from the interior of the boat. If this went on too long, it had a tendency to suffocate the crew. Coupled with this problem was the possibility of carbon monoxide poisoning in the event that the diesel exhaust discharged into the boat, as might happen if the clutches jammed.

During the day the snorkel head could be seen slicing through the waves, but obviously this was far less visible than a surfaced U-boat. When in use, the snorkel was so noisy that it masked reception through the hydrophones, the underwater listening device, and a visual watch had to be maintained at the periscope.

On the whole, however, the snorkel provided U-boat crews with sorely needed protection from Allied air supremacy over the sea and was welcomed despite all its disadvantages. All they had to do was learn how to use it.

By 16 December, 1944, Budapest had been cut off by the Red Army and on the same day the Ardennes offensive began in the west. Although initial reports from the front were highly encouraging, the crew was sceptical.

On 22 December *U-234* emerged from the yards and made a trial run under the supervision of the Germania Werft engineers before retiring to the great Schwentine bunker, where we were to spend Christmas.

Meanwhile the great air raids went on; I was surprised that the repair yards could possibly manage to keep working. The commander had confided to me that the boat was destined for the Far East and told me to see to the arrangements for anti-radar equipment to be delivered to the Yard. Finally, after one last short visit to have it fitted, we were listed for snorkel training.

Our instructor was a white-haired, pithy 61-year-old veteran of the Kaiser's War, in which he had been one of the top three U-boat commanders; Captain Max Valentiner[2] wore his "Pour Le Mérite" with singular pride, I recall. Upon being piped aboard *U-234* though, he made a dismissive gesture with his hand and said, "Now let's not get carried away, gentlemen!"

For the first time since the conversion we left for Kieler Förde for the isolated Strander Bucht. Valentiner asked the Chief Engineer and the engine room personnel if they had read and understood the Snorkel Instructions Manual and they all confirmed that to be the case.

The boat made a fast dive and came to trim at periscope depth. The crew were all tense, since it was by no means guaranteed that it would all pass off satisfactorily even with a well-trained complement.

The snorkel was raised hydraulically and the exhaust and intake tubes were opened; the boat trembled as the diesels were cut in. As an old U-boat hand it was a strange feeling to have the diesels running while we were submerged; under electric propulsion it was so quiet that you could easily hear the propellers of ships at a good distance.

In the radio room I tried out the dipole aerial fitted to the head of the snorkel mast and found that short-wave reception was excellent. The boat was progressing smoothly beneath a slight swell; in the Atlantic it would be different of course. I went into the control room to check the direction-finding equipment and the radar mattress, and I heard Valentiner tell the Chief Engineer, "Now have the snorkel cut into the sea. You'll find that it will happen a lot in the Atlantic."

Lieutenant-Commander Ernst gave the hydroplane operators the order and the captain reported that the snorkel had cut under. Initially there was no noticeable effect, even though the diesels were consuming the air from the interior of the boat. All the internal hatches were open and I thought what an advantage it was to have such a large boat as this. After five minutes had passed, the diesels were still running and there was now a partial vacuum, which was particularly unpleasant on the eardrums.

I went through the Officers' wardroom and saw the Austrian Staff Surgeon, Dr Walter, sitting there with large, wild eyes. He yelled to me, "Can you still hear anything? They're going to kill us all!"

The vacuum was becoming intolerable. I saw the boatswain, Peter Schölch, stoop to retrieve two fillings which had fallen from his teeth; the situation was rapidly becoming desperate.

I thought, Surely this can't be intentional? I ran to the hydrophones room and jerked open a cabinet, thrusting my head inside, hoping to find air still present there. Suddenly, as if from a great distance, I heard them screaming in the control room that all the men in the diesel room had collapsed; all at once the diesels were silent and the boat shuddered to a halt.

I realized immediately that we had touched bottom. Ernst had managed to ground us on a sandbank 30 metres down in the Strander Bucht; the silence was deathly, but we were very fortunate to be in the shallows. As my hearing slowly returned, I looked up into the control room where Captain Valentiner was calmly standing at the chart table, shaking his head in annoyance.

Lieutenant-Commander Ernst was gripping the ladder to the conning tower for support.

"Yes, Chief Engineer, now you begin to see what you did wrong, don't you? If you had done that in action or over deep water, you would have drowned us," Valentiner told him quietly. I couldn't hear the Chief's answer.

"Now shut the intake mast and let's go up." The tanks were blown and the boat rose, but the vacuum remained. The control room petty officer went up to the tower, and when it was reported to him that the conning tower was clear of the sea, he carefully turned on the test-cock and jumped smartly clear. The air came whistling in, but it was some time before the air intake masts could be reopened. When they were, a storm-wind swept through the boat, followed by a strange mist. Our ears popped as the drums adjusted to the change in pressure.

I listened as Valentiner delivered a blistering criticism to the Chief Engineer.

"Chief, that was absolutely disgraceful, I want you to understand that clearly. You didn't read the service manual properly, and your condemnation of Petty Officer Winkelmann was unjustified. Not until five minutes after the immersion of the snorkel mast did you give the order, 'Both diesels stop'. But that order merely means that the diesels are to be put in neutral while propulsion is supplied by the electric motors. The correct order after a long immersion of the mast is 'Cut out the diesels'. Your men waited for *this* order until they collapsed. It was sheer luck that Petty Officer Winkelmann still had the strength to disconnect the diesels without you ordering him to do so."

Valentiner took a deep breath. "I can only advise you thoroughly to revise the instructions before you embark on your long voyage and keep on practising with the snorkel."

Lieutenant-Commander Horst had had the severest possible reprimand; Valentiner had given him a dressing-down in front of the entire crew. It was his first snorkel attempt and a complete disaster. It was said in the U-boat Arm that if you snorkelled well, you lived longer, but whoever snorkelled badly, died quickly. I had the feeling that *U-234* belonged to the second category.

The captain and the First Lieutenant, Reserve-Lieutenant Klingenberg, had such a poor working relationship that at Fehler's suggestion their ways parted and Lieutenant-Commander Richard Bulla, who was on the staff of the new Luftwaffe attaché to Tokyo, General der Flieger Ulrich Kessler, who was to be one of the passengers, was made Klingenberg's replacement. Bulla had served as flying officer aboard the raider *Atlantis* and so Fehler knew him well.

Fehler had been summoned to Naval HQ to be informed that *U-234* was to take twenty-seven passengers to Tokyo. The commander told them that he considered the number to be entirely unreasonable. They would take the place of eighteen crew members; they would be a nuisance and endanger the mission. After substantial negotiations, a compromise was struck in which twelve passengers would travel and eight crew members would make way for them.

In January, 1945, we began the final preparations for the voyage to Tokyo. A Hohentwiel radar set, a Luftwaffe invention, was installed; its aerial nestled in a slot within the tower coaming from where it was raised by air pressure. This radar gave a U-boat the priceless advantage of detecting an approaching aircraft before its own radar could get a fix on the boat, but it became very hot if left working too long. The passenger Dr Schlicke, a former Director of the Telecommunications Testing Station at the Kiel Arsenal, who had been given the temporary rank of Naval Captain for the purpose of impressing the Japanese, went to Berlin and arranged a two-for-one swop to eliminate the radar-overheating problem.

The cargo was loaded under conditions of the strictest secrecy. Into the keel went the 50lb iron bottles of mercury. Elsewhere optical glass, engineering blueprints, cameras, secret documents in sealed containers and an Me262 jet fighter in its component parts were stowed in the holds amidships. Some of the forward upright tubes were packed with Panzerfäuste, anti-tank weapons and small rockets.

On one particular February morning a pall of drifting smoke hung over the ruined city and *U-234* rose and fell almost imperceptibly in the sluggish, scum-covered waters of the U-boat basin. The sunlight was thin and the wind was chill, and I shivered a little as I watched some of the hands toiling at the cargo.

After a few moments I noticed something which struck me as distinctly odd, for among the small knot of men working on the foredeck in the area of the open mine shafts there were two Japanese officers who appeared to be supervising the loading of the boat. They were seated on a crate, occupied in painting a description in black characters on the brown paper wrapping gummed around each of a large number of small containers of uniform size. These were so numerous[3] that I couldn't count them, but certainly there seemed to be well over fifty of them. Each such container was a lead cube, nine inches (25 cm) along each edge, and enormously heavy.

Once the Japanese had painted the inscription 'U-235' on the wrapping of a package, it would be carefully passed to a crew member for storage in one of the six forward mine shafts.

When I asked Captain Hideo Tomonaga of the Imperial Japanese Navy what the lead cubes contained, he told me, "It is the cargo from submarine *U-235*. That boat is no longer going to Japan.". When I enquired at the 5th Flotilla Office, they told me that *U-235* was a small type VII training boat which had never been intended for any operation out of the Baltic. So I knew that Tomonaga had lied to me.

When the loading was finished, it was estimated that the total weight of the cargo was 260 tons. Unknown to us then, 550 kilograms of this was uranium.'

The commander of the 5th Flotilla arranged a reception for the two Japanese officers, Captain Tomonaga, a submarine architect, and Air Force Colonel Genzo Shosi, an aeronautical engineer. In a ceremony aboard the hulk of the liner *St Louis*, the Japanese ambassador, Oshima, placed Tomonaga's 300-year-old Samurai sword into the care of the commander of *U-234* for the duration of the voyage. The other passengers boarding in Germany were civilian aircraft engineers Bringewald and Franz Ruf, advising the Japanese Air Force on the production of jet and rocket aircraft; Luftwaffe Colonel Fritz von Sandrath; Captain Gerhard Falk of the Naval Architecture Division, OKM; Dr (Ing) Captain Heinz Schlicke, High Frequency specialist; Squadron-Judge Kay Nieschling, travelling to hear the accusations against the German ambassador in the matter of the Sorge spy case; Lieutenant Erich Menzel of the Luftwaffe, a V-1 and aerial torpedo expert; Lieutenant Heinrich Hellendorn (Navy) and an engineering midshipman, Klug.

As for accommodation, the two Japanese, the Judge and Captain Falk slept in the deck below the NCO's wardroom, while General Kessler, when he embarked in Norway, would commute between whichever of the two beds in the Senior NCO's mess shared by the Engineer Warrant Officers happened to be empty. All the remaining guests would have to sleep where they could.

Meanwhile, they watched the city being systematically reduced to rubble. Among the smouldering brickwork, the wretched inhabitants of Kiel made their homes in the debris left by days and nights of endless bombing; from offshore at night, away from the air fleets, the lookouts on the bridges of the wallowing U-boats cupped their hands around hot mugs of coffee and gazed at the glowing ruin in the distance.

On the afternoon of 25 March, 1945, squatting low in the water with all the fuel, ammunition, provisions and cargo she had aboard, *U-234* dieseled out of the U-boat harbour into the Förde. Flotilla comrades lined the Hindenburgufer in hundreds to see them off. Their destination was supposed to be a secret, but everybody seemed to know.

By nightfall they were at anchor on the far side of the Strander Bucht waiting for the escort to take them north. *U-234* was about to embark on the most difficult part of her voyage to Tokyo and would soon be required to fight her way northwards to Norway on the surface and through waters thickly sown with mines by both belligerents, over which the enemy exercised almost complete air supremacy. It was the purpose of every Allied aircraft, and, once at the portals to the Atlantic north of the British Isles, if they got that far, of hundreds of Allied anti-submarine vessels, to hunt and harry every U-boat to destruction.

Only five persons aboard *U-234* knew that the numerous lead cubes stowed in one of the steel cylinders within the forward mineshafts contained uranium: Fehler, the captain; Ernst, the Chief Engineer, and Pfaff, the third lieutenant who had supervised the loading, together with the two Japanese. Of these five, none of the Germans knew what uranium was, and what the Japanese officers understood of the lethal effects of gamma ray emissions in the case of leakage from any of the lead containers, is unknown. If *U-234* was attacked and damaged, or struck a mine, with resultant spillage from any one of the fifty cubes containing the fiercely radioactive reactor fission products, and was subsequently beached, sank in shallow water or, worst of all, was taken or towed into a port, the consequences were likely to be catastrophic.

In the early hours of the morning of 26 March, 1945, the escort vessels appeared in company with three new Type XXIII U-boats. This group, including *U-234*, was to attempt to run the gauntlet from Kiel to Kristiansand in Norway. As Senior Officer of the little convoy, Fehler's responsibilities were onerous. Above all he was most concerned at the probability that enemy agents would have reported his departure from Kiel and that he could expect to be attacked in the Kattegat. If located there, the chances of surviving the onslaught would be poor, for the waters were very shallow and the depths offered little shelter. Accordingly, once clear of the land he reduced speed and headed for Copenhagen. The sea was thickly mined, but as soon as he was out of the Great Belt, he detached the minesweeper escort on the grounds that she was too conspicuous, and having passed the Danish capital by night, set his course to run inside Swedish neutral waters wherever that was possible.

Although *U-234* could make 17 knots in calm conditions, Fehler was obliged to proceed at 10 knots, the speed of the slowest U-boat of the convoy.

They passed through the Kattegat in good weather conditions without incident while the radar mattress revolved constantly.

At about 1500 hrs on 27 March Hirschfeld reported to the bridge that he wanted to exchange the Hohentwiel set with the reserve because it was overheating, and that there would be a blind period of ten minutes while the valves of the replacement receiver warmed up. The officer of the watch shouted down his permission and Hirschfeld wasted no time in getting the reserve set plugged in, but before the ten minutes had elapsed the aircraft warning siren wailed through the boat, and the AA [anti-aircraft] weapons were manned to a thunder of sea boots on the plating. Three machines had been sighted off the bow.

Dr Schlicke, the High Frequency specialist, was standing near Hirschfeld, who asked him if he should turn the set on immediately. Schlicke agreed, commenting that he could get a new tube in Oslo.

When at last the radar screen displayed the field, Hirschfeld saw that the enemy aircraft were within 5,000 metres, and he began to relay the decreasing range to the bridge. At 3,000 metres, he heard the commander calmly give the order to open fire.

The AA gunners failed to respond, and it remained quiet. Hirschfeld sprinted up the conning tower ladder to the bridge and heard the captain loudly berating the gun crews on the AA platforms. Everyone on the upper deck of the boat had heard the order to open fire except the gunners, and it was fortunate for them all that the enemy aircraft were equally inattentive, for they flew on in ignorance of a string of four U-boats below them.

At midnight, proceeding north in the main swept channel off Frederikshavn, they passed a southbound German convoy consisting of four steamers and a number of modern-looking torpedo-boats. Half an hour later they watched from the bridge as a cluster of flares dropped from the clouds and lit up the sea to their stern with a pale, yellow light. Then the bombers came in quickly for one of the steamers, defying the streams of molten flak that spewed at them from the escort, and suddenly, with a tremendous flash, an ammunition ship exploded in a ball of fire and vanished in splinters.

The radar aboard *U-234* showed a multitude of contacts at all points of the screen; the Kattegat was swarming with enemy aircraft. Fehler's gun crews waited quietly at their weapons and searched the heavens while the captain raged inwardly on his bridge, unable to run for it because of his responsibility to the other three U-boats, and aware that submerging in the Kattegat was hardly advisable.

The beam from Hirschfeld's ever-circling radar antenna soon detected an aircraft approaching at low altitude from the west, the trace appearing when it was 6,000 metres distant and barely skimming the surface of the sea. The gun crews were notified verbally, the other U-boats by signal lamp.

Now they could do little but fire off a lethal curtain of 2-cm tracer and lead for the enemy aircraft to fly through as he attacked. The radar targets intensified the closer an aircraft approached; in despair,

Hirschfeld directed the beam on the attacker and maintained a flow of information to the bridge.

At 3,300 metres the aircraft inexplicably pulled off its headlong course and turned away; at 6,000 metres he vanished from the screen.

Hirschfeld looked at the assistant operator, Werner Bachmann, in surprise.

'I don't think he liked the look of us,' Bachmann said, 'we gave him such a big contact that he thought we were a battleship.'

Hirschfeld shrugged. The radar indicated aircraft in all sectors of the sky, milling around as if in confusion.

After about half a hour there was a fresh approach from the west, but again when the radar beam was concentrated fully on the inbound bomber, it disengaged at 3,300 metres. The game went on all night; three times it was repeated. It couldn't have been coincidence.

By daybreak it was all over. The four U-boats cruised unscathed quietly into Oslofjord and dropped anchor at Horten.

On 29 March the resident U-boat Training Officer announced an exercise for all boats at Christiansand fitted with a snorkel. In fine conditions with good visibility and a calm sea the submarines glided out to the training lanes where all boats submerged and the exercise began. After a short while, about a mile offshore, *U-1301* (Lieutenant Commander Lenkheit) crossed into the adjacent training lane occupied by *U-234* and rammed her abaft the conning tower at the level of Number VII tank on the port side, tearing open the bunker and liberating about 16 tonnes of diesel oil into the pure waters of the fjord through a gash 5 feet square. The ramming boat sustained damage to her bow and torpedo caps, a misfortune which was to put her out of action for the remainder of the war, as her crew were to smirk quietly later.

Upon entering harbour at Christiansand, Fehler was informed by the port authority that there was no dry dock available and that he would have to take his boat to Bergen. The officers had a long discussion about this on account of two things: it was dangerous to go into dry dock with a fully-laden boat, and the voyage to Bergen would involve a three-day limp along the Norwegian coast at the mercy of any Allied aircraft, submarine or destroyer which happened to be in the area. Fehler's compromise was to obtain a suitable sheet of steel plate, anchor in a quiet spot near Christiansand, submerge the bow by 20° by flooding the forward tanks in order to lift the stern above the waterline − a difficult task with a 300-feet-long submarine − and have the crew go to work on it.

Over a period of a week in early April, 1945, and then only when a surface calm permitted it, Fehler's men succeeded in removing the bent and torn frames, replacing them with substitutes cut from the steel plate, and welding the parts together using power from *U-234*'s diesel engines.

The last of the passengers now came aboard: General der Flieger Ulrich Kessler, the new Lutwaffe attaché to Tokyo, a jovial extrovert much given to fulminating against the Nazi regime and Goering in particular; Fehler gasped in horror as he listened to the General's brand of political frankness.

During the lay-up at Christiansand, Hirschfeld attended every morning at the signals station to collect the messages for the boat. On or about 14 April he took possession of a signal which read:

> '*U-234*. Only sail on the orders of the highest level. Führer HQ.'

A short while afterwards, he was summoned to fetch an urgent signal which stated:

> '*U-234*. Sail only on my order. Sail at once on your own initiative. Doenitz.'

At this, the commander went ashore at once to organize the escort and arranged for a fast anti-submarine trawler to take them round the Skaw. On the afternoon of 16 April, 1945, with little ado, *U-234* quietly parted from the pier and dieseled out of the harbour. Once clear of Christiansand, they stopped and allowed a communications launch to come alongside, and the Regional Commander of U-boats (FdU), Captain Rösing, came on deck for a swift farewell ceremony. The crew fell in on the aftercasing; the passengers remained below.

Rösing wished them luck for the long voyage and then said, 'Comrades, when you return from this mission, we will have our final victory.' With that he left. The commander addressed his crew in the following vein: 'Comrades, you have all heard the latest news bulletins and know how it stands at home. Germany is approaching a hard time. However this war may turn out, I promise to do everything I can to bring you safely back.'

The escort arrived, and at 16 knots *U-234* followed her into the dusk. At Lindesnes Fehler signalled that she was no longer required.

'Then good luck and a safe homecoming,' was flashed to Fehler through the gloom.

With a final glance at the low mountains to starboard, the bridge watch went below and Fehler secured the hatch lid. The boat was trimmed at periscope depth and then started the long underwater voyage to the Equator by snorkel. So began at last the prime exploit of the war under the sea. A giant U-boat, equipped and provisioned for a voyage to Tokyo, and carrying a secret freight with which a war might be won, had sailed from Norway for the wide Atlantic and beyond. The pencilled course on the quartermaster's charts ran parallel to the West African coast, around the Cape of Good Hope and into the Indian Ocean to a point south of Ceylon; beyond that their wild spirit would carry them across the wide ocean to the heart of Japan. The talk was of an arrival sometime in mid-July.

On the first day out the motor of the main bilge pump caught fire. Although the flames were soon extinguished, there was an appalling electrical stink in the boat and the crew found difficulty in breathing. There was no possibility of rising to the surface in these waters, but necessity being the mother of invention, Petty Officer Winkelmann came up with the saving idea of disconnecting the snorkel from the diesel so that the engine drew on the foul air in the boat, while the snorkel discharged fresh air from the surface into the bow and stern rooms.

Off Bergen at midday the commander brought the boat to 14 metres to take in the Long Wave signals and during the precautionary periscope sweep saw a very large aircraft curving towards them at a low altitude.

U-234 dived at once to 100 metres, the crew tensing for the dreaded depth charging, but despite the excellent audibility of these depths, nothing was heard but three gentle splashes one after the other. Then silence. By intensive hydrophone observation, Hirschfeld located the emission of an occulting beam consisting of a five second hum and a longer period of silence from each of three different bearings.

After feverishly flicking through the 'Novelty Catalogue' which Hirschfeld had been given by the Radio Supplies Office in Kiel, they concluded that the aircraft had dropped three sonar buoys equipped with a microphone and a transmitter for sending back its findings from which the navigator of the aircraft could then obtain the position of the submarine by triangulation and drop his depth charges on it.

Only in the possibility that there might be a warm water layer beneath them which would refract the sonar beams was there any hope of escape. Accordingly Fehler took the boat deeper, to her maximum operating depth of 180 metres; he was lucky again, for no depth charges followed him down.

That night they narrowly escaped being run down by a steamer. The quartermaster, Jasper, had the periscope watch, and only at the last moment did he see the tumbling wash and give the order to dive deep. *U-234* passed directly beneath the belly of the freighter, the crew cringing as they imagined the suction dragging the conning tower into her mincing propellors.

At the head of the snorkel mast was a dipole for the detection of radar emissions. The device could also be used as an aerial to receive the 'Funksonne' radio navigation aid transmitted from Norway, which enabled the boat to be accurately navigated whilst submerged. On the very first occasion of its use, an argument arose almost immediately between the rival navigators of the Telegraphy and Seaman branches.

A course had been laid to snorkel through to the Atlantic Ocean by way of the Iceland-Faroes Narrows, and Quartermaster Rische had used an estimated starting position obtained by dead reckoning. This point was materially different from that calculated by Hirschfeld using 'Funksonne' bearings obtained by means of the dipole. Hirschfeld asserted that if they held to the Quartermaster's course, the boat would pass through the shallowest part of an area known as the 'Rosegarden', which U-boats were advised to avoid at all costs, since it was notorious as a spot where Allied aircraft dumped unwanted bomb loads when returning from missions. It had long been favoured for the purpose because U-boats returning to Germany from the Atlantic were known to pause there for rest and recuperation after breaking back into the North Sea from the Atlantic.

Fehler, in common with almost all Seaman branch officers, held radio navigation in low regard and dismissed Hirschfeld's protest until it was proved to him with the assistance of the echo sounder that the boat was clearly approaching the 'Rosegarden'.

It was at this juncture that Fehler decided to abandon caution and, acting in a manner contrary to his operational orders, to proceed on the surface and break out into the Atlantic as soon as possible. He had found that the snorkel was proving a mixed blessing in the high sub-arctic swell, and that it was no simple matter to keep the trim.

Reasoning that a U-boat was difficult to spot in these latitudes because of her low form and camouflage, particularly if the hull could be kept continually awash, he now intended to remain on the surface even if attacked by an enemy warship. He would trust that the natural inclination of a heavily-laden U-boat to carve through the Atlantic rollers would enable him to foil even a destroyer which would tend to climb over and around the seas, losing both the ability to bring her artillery to bear effectively and the advantage of speed.

They blew the tanks and, with a roar, *U-234* surfaced into the spume-flecked swell. The snorkel was withdrawn into its socket on the foredeck, the radar mattress was extended and set revolving, and the diesels growled into life with a puff of blue exhaust smoke to mark the effort. At full speed they hammered through the Iceland-Faroes Narrows, an area where many U-boats had come to grief. During the first night they were obliged to dive twice at the approach of aircraft, but detected them long before the fliers could get a fix.

They broke through into the vast Atlantic Ocean. The long bows pointed to the south-east and the boat surged forward into the giant combers; they had made such good progress that there was now definite talk of an arrival at Tokyo by the middle of July. In Christiansand, Hirschfeld had obtained extremely useful information regarding the location of radio beacons down the South Atlantic coasts and right across into the western Pacific from the telegraphists of an inbound boat; this would be invaluable for navigation purposes and Hirschfeld had already prepared a tentative course.

They learned of the death of Adolf Hitler and of the accession of Admiral Doenitz to be Reichspräsident at the beginning of May; they realized that this presaged the imminent end of the Third Reich.

On the evening of 4 May, 1945, Hirschfeld took down in his cursive script the order of the U-boat Command that all German submarines were to observe a cease-fire with effect from 0800 hours German Time on the following morning. All attacks were forbidden, and any current pursuit was to be abandoned forthwith. All attack U-boats were to return to Norwegian harbours.

In accordance with his secret orders, Fehler merely noted the instruction. *U-234* was not an attack U-boat, so he could proceed on his heading to the south, submerged by day and surfaced at night under the protection of his radar.

The last Long Wave transmitter, 'Goliath', at Magdeburg, had been destroyed upon the approach of enemy land forces, and naval telegraphists were now obliged to rely on Short Wave senders. When instructed to tune to the 'Special Frequency' for a message of the utmost importance, *U-234* was suddenly cut adrift from U-boat Command, for Hirschfeld found that he had been provided with a table of 'false' frequencies. Was it an error, or intentional?

For a while, Fehler was reduced to informing himself as to the war situation by listening in to English language radio broadcasts from the United States and Canada until Bachmann finally succeeded, by a patient process of elimination, in identifying the new wave-lengths.

On 8 May, 1945, U-boats at sea received notification of Germany's capitulation. Rulings newly in force prohibited the sending of enciphered messages; a signal addressed to all submarines and to the beleaguered naval garrisons at Lorient and St Nazaire required the destruction of all old ciphers and the giving up of all current and forward-dated code books.

Late that same evening the Regional Commander of U-boats at Bergen, Norway, Captain Rösing, sent Fehler a signal in the Japan cipher:

'*U-234* continue your voyage or return to Bergen. FdU.'

When shown the signal log, Fehler shook his head and said to Hirschfeld, 'Well I'm definitely not going back.'

U-234 was hammering at 16 knots to the south west on a Great Circle course in mid-Atlantic and, having eluded the anti-submarine forces protecting the exits into the ocean from the north-about routes around Great Britain, had now substantially improved her chances of reaching Tokyo with her cargo.

On 6 May, two days earlier, an American news broadcast had reported the Japanese Foreign Minister, Togo, as having made an official declaration that Japan considered herself free from all contracts and treaties concluded with the German Reich and would fight on alone; on the evening of 8 May Reuters issued a communiqué to the effect that Japan had severed relations with Germany, and that, as a consequence, German citizens in Japan were being arrested.[4]

Taking the two reports together, Fehler was now of the view that the purpose of the voyage had been frustrated, and he told his officers that he was accepting the capitulation. His immediate problem was the two Japanese officers. They were likely to consider it to be their duty to take action to prevent the cargo from falling into the hands of Japan's enemies, and Fehler informed them both of the political developments and placed them under arrest.

In return, Tomonaga and Shosi expressed understanding for Fehler's dilemma and generously wished him an honourable solution. In asking him to reconsider his decision, Shosi gave his personal undertaking that the crew of *U-234* would not be imprisoned on the completion of the voyage, but would receive especially favourable treatment. Fehler had no confidence in the Japanese Government, however; he felt sure that following the capitulation of Germany, the Eastern partner, considering German citizens on her territory to have outlived their usefulness, would correspondingly treat them no better and perhaps much worse than other Europeans who had also been unfortunate enough to fall into the hands of the Emperor.

The captain heard out the plea of the Japanese officers, but shook his head with a smile.

Subsequently it transpired that Fehler's assumption was uncharitable; on 15 May, 1945, when the diplomatic missions and party organs of the defunct Third Reich in East Asia were finally closed, German citizens were interned for the remainder of the conflict under the most hospitable and generous conditions.[5]

When Hirschfeld went to the radio room later, Bachmann told him that the two Japanese had made their way through the boat taking their leave of the crew, Tomonaga distributing among them the watches he had bought in Switzerland. At that time it was not suspected what all this might portend. The Japanese could not practise the rite of hara kiri because the captain had possession of Tomonaga's Samurai sword and they had no other weapons; before the voyage, Fehler had taken the precaution of depriving even the German passengers of their side arms so that only officers and warrant officers of the crew had service pistols.

The Allies had signalled to U-boats at sea that they were to comply with the following requirements when surrendering:

1. All torpedo pistols were to be removed and jettisoned, but the disarmed torpedoes were to be retained.
2. All AA ammunition was to be jettisoned and guns were to be lashed facing astern.
3. A black flag was to be set at the extended periscope tube.
4. Navigation lamps were to be set.
5. The exact navigational position was to be reported and all further movements were to be made whilst surfaced.

Following these there was a string of instructions for interpreting the harbour of surrender for each particular sea area. The surrender port for *U-234* was Halifax, Nova Scotia.

Upon reading this signal, the captain hesitated to transmit his advice of surrender, since Article 3 designated him as a pirate. A conference followed in the Officers' Mess at which it was considered whether, in view of the black flag requirement, the boat was likely to be sunk when offering to surrender, a possibility not thought unlikely in view of the continuous depth charging and bombing audible through the hydrophones. Alternatives to surrender appeared to exist in sailing onwards into the Pacific, either to deliver the cargo to the Japanese or to make for an uninhabited atoll in the South Seas.

The captain postponed his decision and gave the quartermaster instructions to continue sailing south. For the next five days Fehler and the first lieutenant, Bulla, who both spoke good English, sat in the wireless room every evening listening to the news bulletins from all points in order to obtain a broad view of the international situation.

163

It was evident that the Allied navies were not satisfied that all U-boats at sea had surrendered, for almost a week after the general capitulation they sent the following signal over all frequencies:

'Whoever does not capitulate now will be treated as a pirate
and put on trial.'

There was no signature, but the manner of keying indicated a British operator. Once again there was a long conference involving senior crewmen and passengers. Fehler expressed no opinion as to which course of action he preferred; General Kessler and Colonel von Sandrath wanted to proceed with the mission to Tokyo; Lieutenant Bulla and Lieutenant Pfaff wished to sail to the South Pacific. Dr Walter and Judge Nieschling, the most fervent Nazis aboard, were both for surrender.

There was no possible consensus.

On 13 May, 1945, Hirschfeld obeyed his captain's order, tuned in his transmitter and for the first time on the voyage tapped out a message:

'Halifax. Here is *U-234*'

The Canadian station answered at once in German:

'*U-234* give your position.'

Once this had been supplied, they were given a course for Nova Scotia. But Fehler had not the least intention of going to Halifax, and he now headed his submarine at high speed to the south west in order to cross into the American sector.

The diesel hands had dyed a bedsheet black and fastened it to the periscope, and the German battle flag had been hoisted at the jack on the upper gun platform. The running lights were also set, but none of the other requirements of the surrender were complied with.

The two stern torpedo tubes were loaded and the AA weapons positioned ready to fire. The radar antenna revolved in an endless circle, precluding any surprise approach from the air. *U-234* would fight if attacked.

At about 2300 hours Hirschfeld was summoned to the wireless room to see an aerial contact on the radar screen. Fehler gave the alarm, the gun crews closed up and Hirschfeld beamed the radar directly at the approaching aircraft. Just before entering the critical defensive circle of the U-boat, the machine altered course and patrolled the perimeter of the range of the guns. A white flare soared into the night sky and burst, after which the aircraft flew off. Shortly afterwards, Halifax called:

'*U-234*. Your reported position and course are not correct. Steer 340 degrees to Halifax. Report position, course and speed every four hours.'

Fehler read the signal and grinned; on his present course, every hour put Canada another sixteen sea miles astern of him.

Judge Nieschling, who lodged in the lower deck, reported to Fehler that Tomonaga and Shosi were lying in adjacent cots, their arms linked, breathing stertorously, and couldn't be awakened. An empty bottle which had contained Luminal sleeping tablets had been found on the deck plating nearby. Now the reason for their leave-taking became clear. The boatswain, Peter Schölch, was sent to search the Japanese officers' sea-bags, and in one of them found a note addressed to the commander asking him 'Should he find us alive here, to leave us alone please, and let us die.'

They had taken their action so as to avoid captivity. In closing, they requested that their bodies should not be allowed to fall into the hands of the Americans, and that their diplomatic bag should be weighted and sunk, as it held secret papers useful to the enemy. There was a will confirming the assignment of certain property to members of the crew, and for the captain a sum of money in Swiss francs to be used to inform their relatives that they were dead, but not dishonoured.

Fehler merely said, 'We will do as they have asked.'

Dr Walter later confirmed that both men were still alive; the overdose would have killed a European, but the Japanese were stronger in constitution.

Having disobeyed the Canadian's instructions to report in every four hours, Hirschfeld now began to find himself inundated with signals from the station at Halifax. Fehler waved him away when he arrived with the signals log, saying, "Let them call." Later that evening, Fehler decided to mollify them with a position report. Giving Hirschfeld a slip of paper from which to transmit, he remarked, "It's false, and send it at low volume."

Hirschfeld tapped out his call sign and Halifax responded at once, confirming good reception; but as soon as he set to the task of keying out his message, it was jammed by a very powerful transmitter which stopped and started whenever he did.

Halifax morsed:

'*U-234* I am being jammed. Change to frequency...'

Bachmann tuned the set to the frequency ordered, but when Hirschfeld resumed sending, the jamming supervened. It was no coincidence; it was deliberate. Hirschfeld reported the occurrence to the captain who said, 'Turn the set off then. That's our excuse for not reporting in!'

Not long after, the stern lookouts reported a destroyer coming up fast on the port quarter; this was the *USS Sutton*, which gave them orders by lamp to head for the Gulf of Maine and to ignore all further communications from Halifax. It seemed most probable therefore that the *Sutton* had been the perpetrator of the jamming.

Fehler sent for the doctor and said, 'Tonight we must get the Japanese overboard. If the Americans get to them, they'll do everything they can to bring them round. See to it that they die peacefully.'

The doctor descended to the lower deck without speaking, and a few hours later reported the deaths of the Japanese.

The captain acted swiftly. Each corpse was sewn into a weighted hammock, while the diplomatic pouch and the Samurai sword were bound to the body of Tomonaga and then laid on the deck under the red sunburst flag of Japan. The order was given to stop engines and the German crew observed a ten-minute silence for the fallen, after which the bodies were committed to the deep.

When *Sutton* enquired why they had stopped, a signaller flashed back that it had been 'engine trouble'.

All this happened at position 47°07'N 42°25'W.

The destroyer closed to 800 metres with all her guns bearing on the U-boat and a launch conveying the prize crew pitched and tossed its way across the gap before being swept by the swell hard against the saddle tank on the port side, nearly overturning. The helmsman managed to retrieve the situation, manoeuvred the launch round the stern of the submarine, and threw a small anchor upwards. It lodged, and the occupants heaved themselves aboard.

'God, look at the weapons they're carrying,' said Bulla, 'in one hand a machine pistol, in the other a Colt revolver and round the shoulders three crossed belts of bullets.'

With a flick of the wrist, Dr Schlicke tossed a few rolls of microfilm into the sea and watched them slowly sink. Then he said to Hirschfeld, 'And there goes the rocket that could fly the Atlantic.'

CHAPTER 4

NEMESIS

'Our lingering belief in the supremacy of German science makes it hard for us to accept the fact that German physicists could have failed so utterly.'

Professor Samuel Goudsmit,
Scientific Head,
US Intelligence Mission *Alsos*.

ON THURSDAY 17 MAY, 1945, the New Hampshire evening paper *Portsmouth Herald* carried the headline, '*U-234* with 3 Air Generals, 2 Dead Japs Due Saturday.'

It was the first of a number of reports that were to issue from this American daily concerning Fehler's U-boat, and if the information was sometimes a little inaccurate, as the quoted headline implies, the reporters involved must nevertheless have had close contacts with local US Navy sources.

On the evening of Saturday 19 May, 1945, the arrival of the surrendered submarine was announced in a headline reading: '1600 ton Nazi Sub Arrives in Portsmouth — *U-234* Brings Air Force General Ulrich Kessler and 2 Dead Japs.'

The text of the newspaper article stated:

'The 1600 ton Nazi submarine *U-234*, carrying Major-General Ulrich Kessler of the Luftwaffe, other high Luftwaffe officials and the bodies of two Japanese who committed hara kiri, glided into the Portsmouth lower harbour this morning and tied up at a mooring prepared for her by the Navy.

The big undersea craft, escorted in by naval craft, had radioed her surrender a week ago from a point 500 miles east of Greenland in the North Atlantic.

Censorship shrouded many of the details of the crew and passengers of the craft and tighter restrictions were placed on the Press than had been the case in the arrival of three Nazi subs which put in here previously during the week.'

The fact that the stated number of 'Air Force Generals' aboard *U-234* had been reduced from three to one, Kessler now being identified by name, but that the information as to the two dead Japanese had not yet been corrected, appears to confirm that the US Navy Yard at Portsmouth was the source of the reports.

Early the following week the source passed further information to the *Portsmouth Herald* which was duly published:

> 'It (*U-234*) is reportedly loaded with charts, aviation material and information headed for Japan for the purpose of aiding Japan's air war with rocket and jet planes and *other German V-type bombs*.
>
> All that material is now in United States Navy hands and will prove invaluable.'

This is the first reference from a suspected US Navy source to a 'V-type bomb'.

The US Navy Archive admits a loading list for *U-234* which includes 550 kilograms of unspecified uranium, but the manifest does not show any bombs of any description aboard the surrendered submarine.[1]

No further information of any nature has ever been elicited from US Government sources in respect of the uranium. However, the fact that matters relating to atomic energy affairs for that period remain protected under the highest security classification of the US Government even half a century later is not an obstacle to determining the physical properties of the uranium shipped aboard the German submarine *U-234* bound for Tokyo.

The application of simple nuclear physics to the known facts is enough to prove the matter conclusively. And it was in the circumstances surrounding the unloading of the submarine's cargo that the remaining facts necessary to solve the enigma were unearthed.

Not until July, 1945, did the Americans tackle the problem of unloading the cargo of *U-234*, although they knew from the captured documents seized in May what the cargo actually was.

Once the submarine was secured alongside the wharf, the six steel cylinders within the mine shafts on the foredeck were extracted with a crane and most carefully deposited on the quayside.

The boatswain, Schölch[2], was made to supervise the operation, because the Americans feared that the steel containers might be booby-trapped.

Hirschfeld was present at this proceeding in the company of other crew members, and they now witnessed the arrival of a number of scientists, who immediately began to examine the exterior of the tubes with Geiger counters.

When Hirschfeld asked the scientists what they were doing, they told him that *U-234* had been carrying a consignment of uranium for Japan. This fact had been such a closely guarded secret that only three officers, Fehler the captain, Ernst the Chief Engineer and Pfaff, who had supervised the loading in Kiel, knew of it.

At last Hirschfeld understood that it was one of the formulae for uranium, U^{235}, that the two Japanese officers had been painting on the wrappers of the lead cubes during the loading operation.

The German officers had no understanding of what uranium was, and the *Portsmouth Herald* was little better informed, claiming that the quantity of uranium on board *U-234* had been sufficient to produce an explosion to eradicate all of Portsmouth and the surrounding suburbs from the face of the earth. Naturally, even if the 550 kilos had been assembled in a lump, a melt-down could not have resulted in a nuclear explosion because the fissile part of the fuel had not been enriched from its natural proportion of 0.7 per cent in the material to at least 7 per cent. According to the American physicist, Serber[3], the least possible degree of enrichment of the isotope U^{235} necessary for an explosion *of sorts* is 7 per cent. Similarly, 550 kilos of irradiated uranium fuel does not contain fissile quantities of plutonium either.

The *Portsmouth Herald* was, therefore, guilty of a little alarmist rhetoric.

Schölch, the boatswain, knew in which of the six steel tubes the uranium had been stowed, but he did not tell the Americans that he knew this. For their part, the Americans had decided not to open any of the tubes because all were contaminated with gamma radiation to such an extent that it was impossible to distinguish by means of their instrumentation which tube held the uranium.

The problem was resolved a few days later when Lieutenant Pfaff volunteered to open the steel tubes and unload the uranium in exchange for an undertaking of immediate release, a condition to which the Americans assented.

We now have all the information necessary to determine the nature of the uranium aboard the German submarine *U-234*.

The uranium was transported in radioisotope shipping containers of lead, in the shape of a cube, with each side nine inches in length.

Natural uranium which has not been subjected to neutron bombardment in a nuclear reactor is a class IV nuclide of very low radioactivity requiring no shielding. It is its chemical toxicity rather than the absorbed dose of radiation from it which limits the body tolerance.

Alpha radiation requires no shielding for the handler since the particles are stopped within a few micrometres of tissue and present no external hazard, and the intensity of beta radiation is completely absorbed by a 7mm thickness of aluminium, glass or perspex. But gamma rays have very much greater penetrative powers than alpha or beta particles, and require a considerable thickness of lead, steel or concrete for satisfactory shielding from this extreme form of radiation.

The thickness of lead required to reduce the initial intensity of gamma radiation by a factor of ten is 1.8 inches and an additional 1.4 inches is needed to reduce it by a further factor of ten. Therefore 3.2 inches of lead is required in order to reduce the intensity of gamma radiation to 1 per cent of the initial value.

The only conceivable purpose for using radioisotope shipping containers for uranium is to contain gamma radiation from uranium isotopes.

The walls, lid and base of the lead cubes described by Hirschfeld would have been of the order of 3.2 inches in thickness allowing an interior volume of 2.6 inches cubed; the maximum quantity of uranium in each container would have been about 12 kilos.

Although there were so many containers that Hirschfeld felt unable even to guess the total number, if each held 12 kilos of uranium then there would have been at least fifty in the consignment, which agrees with his lowest figure.

Uranium emitting radiation requiring this form of biological shielding is produced by exposure to neutron bombardment in a nuclear reactor. But could 550 kilos of it have been produced in a cyclotron, the most efficient particle accelerator then available in Germany, rather than in a nuclear reactor?

Both Heisenberg and Houtermans indicated in their reports that a ton of fission products obtained by irradiating uranium by chain reaction in a reactor was equivalent to that produced by 10^4 to 10^5 cyclotrons. Germany would therefore have required a minimum of 5,500 cyclotrons; the total number available to German scientists from all sources during the war was four.

It is for this mathematical reason that the existence of the National Socialist nuclear reactor cannot be denied. Nazi Germany was undoubtedly an atomic power, and the indications are that the reactor would have gone critical in the late autumn of 1942, probably in October. Since the Chicago pile set by Fermi went critical on 2 December, 1942, Nazi Germany was almost certainly the world's first atomic power.

On 23 April, 1945, the head of the Allied Intelligence Mission *Alsos*, General Leslie R. Groves, reported to General Marshall in Washington that the possibility of the Germans having manufactured nuclear weapons was non-existent.

On or about 17 May, 1945, the disastrous failure of the *Alsos* operation was revealed when to the utter surprise and consternation of the United States Government, a German U-boat commander, condescending to accede to the Allied directive of surrender, presented the United States with both the documentary and the physical evidence not only that the Nazi Government had achieved a critical nuclear reactor, but that they had used it to produce radiological weapons which they proposed should be introduced into the conflict by Japan.

Sufficient material had been consigned to enable Japan to destroy the civilian populations of a number of major cities, condemning millions of men, women and children to death by radiation sickness, or from lethal cancers contracted during the spread of the material.

Densely populated conurbations such as San Francisco and Los Angeles would have to be abandoned to the elements for centuries, maybe for ever, while the genetic damage visited upon the descendants of the survivors down to the second and third generations would bring a blight upon the race.

The people of the United States would now resist the fury of the Japanese at their peril, and if President Truman insisted on fighting on, American troops could expect to encounter a horrific first generation of radiological weapons both in the field and from the air.

Not all German U-boats had been accounted for, and the United States Government had no means of determining whether another German U-boat might not, even now, be approaching her moorings at Yokohama in triumph, with a similar cargo of fission products radiating in lead containers in her bowel.

The weight of evidence available suggests that the decision to use the atomic bomb against Japan did not have as its primary purpose the intention to signal any implicit political warning to Moscow. The indications are rather that some hitherto unexplained factor occurring between 16 May and 30 May, 1945, suddenly dictated the chief aim of American atomic strategic policy to be the military defeat of Japan at the earliest possible opportunity and using the atomic bombs then nearing completion.

As at 15 May, 1945, no executive decision had yet been taken to use the atomic bomb against Japan. Thus the Secretary for War, Stimson, confided to his diary in the entry for that date that with regard to the deteriorating relationship between the United States and the USSR,

'over such a tangled weave of problems (i.e. China and the USSR) the S.I. secret (i.e. the atom bomb) would be dominant, and yet we will not know until after that time probably (i.e. the first bomb test on 16 July), until after that meeting (i.e. the Potsdam Conference), whether this is a weapon in our hands or not.'

It seemed to him to be:

'a terrible thing to gamble with such big stakes in diplomacy without having your master card in your hand.'[4]

Stimson harboured no hatred, racial or otherwise, for the Japanese people, and he was awake to the moral implications in US war policy likely to affect world opinion. On 16 May, 1945, he is reported to have advised President Truman that he considered 'the reputation of the United States for fair play and humanity' to be their biggest asset for peace in the coming decades and that the rule of sparing the civilian population, 'should be applied, as far as possible, to the use of any new weapons'.

During Stimson's vacational absence from office during the latter part of May, 1945, the presidential aide, James F. Byrnes, swiftly co-opted the Interior Committee to convene on 31 May since Byrnes felt that 'it was imperative there be a final decision on the question of the use of the weapon'.[5]

When the Interior Committee sat on the morning of 31 May, 1945,

'Mr Byrnes recommended and the Committee agreed that the Secretary for War should be advised that, while recognizing that the final selection of the target was a military decision, the present view of the Committee was that the bomb should be used against Japan as soon as possible, that it be used on a war plant surrounded by workers' houses, that it be used without prior warning.'

Arthur H. Compton of the Scientific Panel noted[6] of that morning's decision that, 'it seemed to be a foregone conclusion that the bomb would be used', and when the meeting reconvened that afternoon the agenda had been amended so that consideration could be given to the question of the effect of the atom bomb on the Japanese and on their will to fight.

When President Truman learned of the decision on 1 June, he admitted to Byrnes that he had been giving the matter serious thought for some days and that after considering alternative plans he had come reluctantly to the conclusion that there was no alternative. Whereas he did not give the order to drop the bomb on 1 June, it appears that he had made the decision by then.

The political activity during the last two weeks in May, 1945, was such that Stimson appears to have been a man overtaken by events. Somewhere in that period, he ceased to treasure jealously the United States' reputation for fair play and humanity. He never satisfactorily explained why. In retrospect, he was to state coldly only:

> 'My chief purpose was to end the war in victory with the least possible cost in the lives of the men in the armies which I helped to raise.'[7]

It had ceased to be his rule to 'spare the civilian population, as far as possible, to the new weapons'.

Perhaps we can now guess the reason.

The German transport submarine *U-234* surrendered to the US destroyer *Sutton* at sea on the evening of 16 May, 1945. As soon as news had reached him of what she was carrying, President Truman had no real alternative but to authorize the use of his atomic weapons, then close to completion and testing, as a means of attempting to bring the war with Japan to its conclusion at the earliest possible moment.

This was how Hitler's posthumous gift of the weapons of frightfulness to the people of Japan made the atomic attacks on the Japanese cities inevitable.

This was what the American physicist Robert J. Oppenheimer meant when he said that the atomic bombs dropped on Hiroshima and Nagasaki came from German arsenals.

Chapter 1

One of the briefest yet historically most useful publications concerning the German nuclear programme is *Atomic Bomb Scientists: Memoirs 1939-1945* by Joseph J Ermenc, Emeritus Professor at Dartmouth College, (Meckler, Westport and London 1989). Ermenc reproduces the transcripts of interviews he conducted with Heisenberg on 29 August, 1967, at Urfeld am Walchensee, and with Harteck on 6 July, 1967, at the Rensselaer Polytechnic Institute, Troy, New York.

There have been only two major attempts to deal exclusively with the German nuclear programme. The most recent is *The Quest for Nuclear Power in National Socialist Germany, 1939-1949* by Mark Walker, Union College, (Cambridge University Press, 1989). Walker ably marshalls the documentary facts, but in common with all previous American commentators excludes any mention of the Post Office project.

Both Walker and Irving fail to ask themselves what the purpose is of a low temperature reactor which produces no heat energy. Accordingly both understand the term 'nuclear weapons' only in the sense of atomic bombs and fail to see the radiological uses of nuclear power for weapons development. At p.138, Walker even goes so far as to remark that the sabotage operations against the heavy water plant at Vemork and the sinking of the ferry *Hydro* were pointless since 'by the time the first acts of sabotage took place, the threat of German nuclear weapons was only a German fantasy and an Allied bad dream.' After p. 153, Walker's contribution is propagandist and is now of little value for historians.

The first fairly comprehensive history of the project was David Irving's *The Virus House*, (Wm Kimber, London 1967), recently reproduced in paperback by Da Capo Press, New York, under the title *The German Atomic Bomb*.

Heisenberg commented on this work in Ermenc (op. cit.) that whereas it was very carefully done it had a deficiency in that Irving had failed 'to understand the spirit of the thing.' Irving was convinced that in a war, people must want to win the war and because of that they must want to make atom bombs. 'This is so obvious to him that he cannot get away from the idea, but it was not the situation.'

A supplementary work composed of reflections on the German project is *Im Umkreis der Physik*, (Karlsruhe Atomic Research Centre, 1988) by Dr Karl Wirtz who was the leader of Heisenberg's experimental team.

1. *Max Born* (1882-1970). Born in Breslau of a Jewish professional family, he specialized in the physics of crystals. His research at Göttingen in 1921 was concerned with quantum theories. Upon the accession of Hitler, Born emigrated to Britain and worked in Cambridge, accepting UK citizenship in 1939. He was awarded the Nobel Prize for Physics in 1954 for work on the wave frequency of electrons.

2. *Niels Bohr* (1885-1962). Born in Copenhagen and half-Jewish. He studied at the University of Copenhagen, and was appointed Professor of Theoretical Physics there in 1916. Bohr had spent some time in England, and in 1913 at Manchester had proposed his famous model of the hydrogen atom, the first application of Planck's quantum hypothesis to atomic structure.

   Bohr was the guiding spirit in the subsequent growth of the quantum theory of atoms and later of nuclei. He was awarded the Nobel Prize in 1922. In 1943 he left Denmark once he had been warned that there was to be a Nazi pogrom of Danish Jews.

3. *'Uber die Quanten-theoretische Umdeutung Kinematischen und mechanischen Beziehungen.'*

4. See Helwig, L W: *Die Deutsche Physik*, 1935.

5. *Carl von Ossietsky* (1889-1938). Leading German pacifist and anti-Nazi journalist, he was the Secretary of the German Peace Society in 1920 and was involved in forming the Republican Party in 1924. He became the assistant editor of the Berlin daily, *Berliner Volkszeitung*, and in 1927 the editor of *Die Weltbühne* (The World Stage), a non-partisan left-wing political organ.

   Following a scurrilous trial, he was sentenced to 18 months' imprisonment at Leipzig in November, 1931, and was amnestied in December, 1932. Disregarding advice to leave Germany the following month when the Nazis came to power, he was re-arrested in February, 1933, and sent to Papenburg-Estwegen concentration camp as an enemy of the State. Awarded the Nobel Peace Prize in 1935, an action which infuriated the Nazis and led to a prohibition on any German accepting a Nobel Prize in future, Ossietsky was paroled to a Berlin public hospital on the grounds of tuberculosis which he contracted in the concentration camp and died of the disease in May, 1938.

6. A *cyclotron* is a laboratory machine used to accelerate electrically

charged particles to the exceptionally high velocities required in nuclear investigations. One of its applications is the production of microscopic radioisotopes by bombarding a target element with protons. All the activity in a cyclotron occurs in a vacuum chamber enclosed between the flat, circular pole pieces of a large electro-magnet. The evacuated area is fitted with two hollow, flat semi-circular copper electrodes known as 'Dees'. Between the 'Dees' there is a narrow gap across which an alternating voltage is applied. Protons released from a discharge tube into the centre of the gap in a weak neutral gas are attracted into one of the 'Dees' on the negative charge and start to circulate in a bunch. The circular magnet covering the chamber gives it a constant magnetic field and the particles describe a spiral path at right angles to the field, whirling ever faster in the spiral path towards the outer edge of the chamber where they are then deflected outwards by a plate and collide with the target material.

7. On 28 January, 1939, Hahn and Strassmann further proposed in *Die Wissenschaften* that a number of neutrons might be liberated in each act of fission which by inference could of themselves initiate further fissioning, leading to a full chain reaction.

8. *Otto Hahn* (1879-1968). Born Frankfurt am Main. PhD in Organic Chemistry, Munich, 1898. Discovered radiothorium 1905 and mesothorium the following year. Lecturer in Chemistry at University of Berlin, 1907. In the Great War worked on the development of battlefield gases. Director of Chemistry at KWI and discovered fission in uranium December, 1938. Nobel Prize for Chemistry for 1944 awarded in 1945.

9. Ermenc, op. cit.

10. Heereswaffenamt. Army Ordnance Office.

11. Various sources incl. Groves (ibid.) at p.244.

12. For Sengier's part in this matter, see Harald Steinert, *The Atom Rush; Man's Quest for Radioactive Materials*, (Thames & Hudson, London, 1958).

   For the British handling of Sengier, see Margaret Gowing, *Britain and Atomic Energy 1939-1945*, (UKAEA, Macmillan, 1964), at p. 35 et seq.

13. General Leslie M. Groves; *Now It Can Be Told: The Story of the Manhattan Project,* (Harper, New York 1962), pp. 33-7 et seq.

14. Steinert, op. cit.

15. Groves, op. cit.

16. Groves, op. cit., p. 178.

17. Groves, op. cit., p. 184. Shortly before the Yalta Conference,

President Roosevelt informed Groves that if the European war was not over before the United States had its first atomic bombs ready, he wanted Groves to be ready to drop them on Germany.

18. Irving, op. cit., p.45, information received from Dr Friedrich Berkei.
19. Armin Herrmann, *Heisenberg*, Rohwohlt Taschenbuch Verlag, Reinbek 1976.
20. Wirtz, op. cit., p.33.
21. Ermenc, op. cit.
22. Herrmann, op. cit.
23. *Die Möglichkeit der technischen Energiegewinnung aus der Uranspaltung*
    Paper G39, Kernforschungszentrum, Karlsruhe.
    The German wartime uranium project reports are filed on microfilm at the Karlsruhe Atomic Research Centre, from where photocopies may be obtained. Each document of the series is listed with the prefix G. Many of Heisenberg's reports have been reproduced in the various volumes of his lifetime's work *Gesammelte Werke*, (Springer Verlag, Heidelberg 1989).
24. Ermenc, op. cit.
25. Irving, op. cit., p.63.
26. Wirtz, op. cit., p.37.
27. Ermenc, op. cit.
28. *Bestimmung der Diffusionslänge thermischen Neutronen im Schwerem Wasser.*
    Report G23 at Karlsruhe.
29. *Bestimmung der Diffusionslänge thermischen Neutronen im Präparat 38 (Uranoxyd).*
    Report G22 at Karlsruhe.
30. Ermenc, op. cit.
31. *Die Absorption thermischen Neutronen im Elektro-graphit* Karlsruhe report G-71.
32. *Ueber den Nachweis von Boron und Kadmium in Kohle* Karlsruhe reports G-46 and G-85.
33. Karlsruhe reports G-39(24) and G40(a).
34. Ermenc, op. cit. The Austrians' report is G-55 at Karlsruhe.
35. Albert Speer, *The Slave State*, Weidenfeld & Nicolson, 1981.
36. Albert Speer, *Erinnerungen*, (Propyläen Verlag, Ullstein, Berlin 1969), at p.241.
37. Andreas Hillgruber, *Staatsmänner und Diplomaten bei Hitler*, Band II 1942-1944, (Bernard und Graefe, Frankfurt 1970).
38. Ermenc, op. cit.

39. Speer, *Erinnerungen*, op. cit.
40. Ermenc, op. cit.
41. Speer, *Erinnerungen* op. cit.
42. Irving, op. cit., p. 129.
43. Ermenc, op. cit.
44. Wirtz, op. cit., p.57.
45. *Die Energiegewinnung aus der Atomkernspaltung* from *Gesammelte Werke*, op. cit.
46. Corpuscular radiation is alpha and beta particles.
47. *Biologische Wirkungen korpuskularer Strahlungen incl. Neutronen unter Berücksichtigung der Möglichkeit deren Verwendung als Kampfmittel.*
    Karlsruhe report G-374.
48. Groves, op. cit., p.232, and Professor Samuel A Goudsmit, *Alsos-The Failure in German Science,* Sigma Books, London 1947, relate this incident; see also Bothe's account of the work of the Institute *Bericht über die Arbeit des Instituts während des Krieges* 11.7.45, S Goudsmit papers.
49. Erhard Milch (1892-1972). State Secretary in the Ministry of Aviation 1933, Luftwaffe Field-Marshal 19 July, 1940. Milch was half-Jewish. He owed his spectacular career to the protection of Hermann Goering who declared of him, *Wer Jude ist, bestimme ich* (I decide who's Jewish). Milch obtained Aryanisation by having his mother sign a disclaimer of parenthood. Milch received life imprisonment for war crimes and served ten years.
50. Irving, op. cit., p.189.
51. Manfred von Ardenne, *Ein Glückliches Leben für Forschung und Technik,* (Verlag der Nation, East Berlin 1972) p.179.
52. *Ueber die Möglichkeit biologischer Wirkungen kurzwelliger Röntgen bzw. Gammastrahlen von Röntgenröhren besonderer Bauart auf grössere Entfernungen.*
    Report G-284, Karlsruhe.
53. von Ardenne, op. cit., p.159.
54. Irving, op. cit., p.264.
55. Wirtz, op. cit., p.61.
56. Goudsmit, op. cit.
57. Groves, op. cit., pp.219-20.
58. Werner Heisenberg. *Physics and Beyond*, (Allen & Unwin, London 1959).
59. Werner Heisenberg essay *Individual Behaviour in the Face of Disaster.*
    Where not specifically referenced, Heisenberg's reports and

commentaries mentioned in the text can be found in W. Heisenberg and K. Wirtz *'Grossversuche zur Vorbereitung der Konstruktion eines Uranbrenners'* in FIAT *Review of German Science 1939-45,* republished in *Series B, Gesammelte Werke von Werner Heisenberg,* (Springer Verlag, Berlin Heidelberg and New York 1984), and in Series A, the Original Works under the title *Atomenergiegewinnung.*

Chapter 2

1. Philipp Lenard, *Erinnerungen eines Naturforschers*, Heidelberg, 1943 p.202.
2. Dr Henry Picker, *Hitlers Tischgespräche im Führerhauptquartier*, Seewald Verlag, Stuttgart, 1976 p.148.
3. Klaus Hoffmann, *Otto Hahn*, Verlag Neues, Berlin 1978. p.227.
4. Klaus Hoffmann, op. cit.
5. *Soldatenzeitung*, Berlin, 16 March, 1962.
6. As above, the actual words reported to have been used by Hitler were: *'Das wäre ja noch schöner, dass mein Postminister die Atombombe erfunden hätte.'*
7. A table of the average rates of capture of neutrons whose natural velocity has been slowed by a moderating substance.
8. Fritz Georg Houtermans, *Zur Frage der Auslösung von Kernketten reaktionen*, Lichterfelde-Ost, Berlin, August, 1941.

   Document G94 at Karlsruhe Atomic Research Centre as amended by Review document G267 published August, 1944, cf. in particular the latter at pp. 20 and 25. Also see Appendix 4.

   In an inconclusive exchange of correspondence between Professor Manfred von Ardenne and myself in March, 1991, the Professor sent me a document which purported to be a true copy of Houtermans' 1941 paper. My attention was drawn in the covering letter to the mention of plutonium which Houtermans had made. Comparing this document with the original obtained from the Karlsruhe Nuclear Research Centre, I noticed that all reference to methane in moderating a low temperature reactor had been omitted from Professor von Ardenne's reproduction.
9. Armin Herrmann, *Heisenberg*, Rohwohlt Taschenbuch Verlag, (Reinbek 1976).
10. Ermenc, op. cit.
11. Ermenc, op. cit.; also Ruth Moore, *Niels Bohr, Ein Mann und*

sein Werk verändern die Welt. (Munich 1970, p.278).

12. Robert Jungk *Brighter Than a Thousand Suns:* Victor Gollancz
     Ltd, Penguin Books, New York, 1982. Jungk, a Swiss,
     interviewed Houtermans after the war in Switzerland.

     In the BBC *Horizon* television documentary *Hitler's Bomb*
     broadcast on 23 February, 1992, the American physicist Hans
     Bethe stated that in late 1943 he came into possession of a
     diagram drawn without explanation by Heisenberg during his
     conversation with Bohr.

     The diagram consisted of a square with three protruding
     strokes along one side, which Bethe thought might have
     represented a schematic nuclear reactor, the protruding strokes
     representing the control rods. Thus Heisenberg had gone as far
     as he dared to indicate that it was from the nuclear reactor itself
     that the world had most to fear.

13. Klaus Hoffmann, op. cit., reported as *'Beeilt Euch! Wir sind
     nahe dran!'* Wigner's special interest was very low temperature
     reactor design.

14. Manfred von Ardenne, *Ein Glückliches Leben für Forschung
     und Technik,* Verlag der Nation, East Berlin, 1972; pp. 156-157.

15. Von Ardenne, op. cit., p. 430

16. Albert Speer, *Erinnerungen*, Polyproplären Verlag, Ullstein
     Berlin, 1969, p. 241.

17. Heinrich Hoffmann (1885-1957) was Hitler's official
     photographer, confidant and friend. Hitler would often visit
     Hoffmann's house in Munich for relaxation. They had first met
     in 1920, and Hoffmann soon joined the inner circle of intimate
     companions. It was in Hoffmann's photography shop that Hitler
     met Eva Braun who worked there. Hoffmann was the only man
     allowed to photograph Hitler and he was his constant attendant
     on the road to power and at the battle front. His collection of
     photographs from the Nazi period eventually totalled over 2½
     million. It was Hoffmann's idea that Hitler should receive a
     royalty in respect of every postage stamp that bore his image, a
     matter agreed in 1937 with the Postmaster Ohnesorge. By this
     means the Führer accrued enormous wealth. Tried as a profiteer
     in 1947, Hoffmann was deprived of his fortune and served five
     years' imprisonment.

18. Dr Henry Picker, op. cit.

19. See Appendix One.

20. See *inter alia*: 'Agreement Respecting the Availability of
     Manufacturing Copyrights and Raw Material between Germany

and Japan bilaterally', Political Archive, Auswärtiges Amt, Bonn.

Article 1 reads: 'The Government of the German Reich and the Imperial Japanese Government will each place bilaterally at the disposal of the other for use during the war all design rights proper to war devices as well as all raw materials necessary for the war economy.'

Article 2 ...(in respect of the above) 'no price shall be calculated or paid by either Government to the other...'

Article 4 ... (such) 'to be determined following the achievement of the common victory.'

The projected treaty was initialled on 8 November, 1942, and ratified on 2 March, 1944.

See also Bernd Martin, *Deutschland und Japan im Zweiten Weltkrieg*, Musterschmidt Verlag, Göttingen 1969.

21. Charles Gibson, *Death of a Phantom Raider*, Robert Hale Ltd., London 1987 p.172.
     The *Doggerbank* was formerly the 5152 GRT Bank Line motor ship, *Speybank* captured in the Indian Ocean by the raider, *Atlantis* (Captain Rogge) on 31 January, 1941.

22. Peenemünde's purpose had been deduced by British aerial photographic reconnaissance.

23. Professor Samuel Goudsmit, *Alsos - The Failure in German Science*, Sigma Books, London, 1947, pp.32-3.

24. Rudolf Lusar, *Die deutschen Waffen und Geheimwaffen des Zweiten Weltkriegs und ihre Weiterentwicklung*, Lehmanns Verlag, Munich 1958.

25. Professor Samuel Goudsmit, op. cit.

26. Andreas Hillgruber, *Staatsmänner und Diplomaten bei Hitler, Band II, 1942-44* Bernard und Graefe, Frankfurt 1970.

27. The weapon was a 3-metre long barrel with a number of external chambers along its length. When the gun was fired, the projectile was impelled forward by pressure from a gas cartridge. As it passed each chamber, it triggered a cartridge positioned there which gave further velocity to the shell. This was repeated throughout its transit of the barrel. The muzzle velocity was significantly greater than that of standard artillery and gave the weapon a great range.
     The projectile weighed 140 kilos and was stabilized by wings which opened once the shell was in flight. It carried a 25 kilo warhead a distance of 160 km. Using 25 to 50 of these weapons, salvoes repeated at five-minute intervals would have subjected London to an unbroken hail of from 300 to 600 rounds per hour.

Hitler showed much excited interest in the 'England Gun' and demanded that the development should be proceeded with immediately. The prototypes were tested near Magdeburg and on Wollin Island in the Pomeranian Bight, but German forces were driven back beyond the effective firing range of 160 km before the weapons could be brought into operation.

28. The actual description used by Hitler was: *'hat eine so gewaltige Wirkung, dass in einem Umkreis von drei bis vier Kilometer von der Einschlagstelle alles menschliche Leben vernichtet würde.'*

29. David Irving, *The German Atomic Bomb*, Simon and Schuster, 1967 New York; published more recently in Da Capo Press, New York (paperback), at p. 241.

30. Cherwell papers.

31. Wilfred von Oven, *Finale Furioso-Mit Goebbels bis zum Ende*, Tübingen 1974.

32. Public Records Office; PREM 3/89

33. PRO/CAB 79/77 Meeting of Chiefs of Staff 8 July, 1944.

34. PRO.../CAB 84/64 Instructions to the JPS 16 July, 1944.

35. See Martin J. Sherwin, *A World Destroyed- The Atom Bomb and the Grand Alliance*, Alfred A. Knopf, New York 1975 and MED document 15 TSfolder 25 tab M, United States National Archive.

36. Towards the end of the war, US Chiefs of Staff devised a plan to use unpiloted old US bombers loaded with up to 10 tons of high explosive to be aimed at industrial targets in Germany. Although British Chiefs of Staff agreed to the plan, the War Cabinet opposed it on the grounds of the possible German scale of retaliation against London.

   Following the death of President Roosevelt, Churchill notified President Truman that the British 'would not dissent' from the use of the pilotless bombers if the United States thought that it would speed the end of the war, adding pithily that, 'we shall make no complaint if misfortune comes to us in consequence'. Truman was left with little alternative but to respond that the project would not be pressed forward in Europe.

   PREM 3 473 PM to President. Truman: T472/5 14.4. 1945; Truman to PM No5 T500/5 17.4.45

37. Hirschfeld, *Das Letzte Boot*, op. cit., p.203.

38. Report of Karl Ritter, Diplomat for Special Affairs in the Foreign Ministry, 20.5.1944 to 28.12.1944, as reported in Bernd Martin, op. cit.

Chapter 3

1. One of these six steel tubes received the uranium. If the ultimate intention had been to extract plutonium from the irradiated uranium, the tube would have been flooded so as to permit the radioactivity level to decrease and to reduce the heat emissions. This would also have reduced the danger to the crew of the submarine.

   This was not, however, the case. The tube was sealed dry, and it is obvious that the purpose was to maintain the load in as high a state of energy as possible, confirming that the uranium was to be used in radiation-emitting weapons.

2. Fregattenkapitän der Reserve Max Valentiner was a U-boat training instructor at Kiel throughout the Second World War. He had taken Hirschfeld's previous boat *U-109* through her acceptance trials in December, 1940.

   During the First World War he had been the commander of *U-38* and was a notorious U-boat ace. He was at the centre of the international controversy regarding the misuse of Austria's flag by German submarines. Germany was not at war with Italy although Germany's ally Austria was. Valentiner seems to have been one of the first U-boat commanders to have used this ploy. During his sinking of the 8,210 ton Italian liner, *Ancona*, on 7 November, 1915, off Bizerta, Valentiner fired a torpedo into the foundering vessel while passengers were still abandoning ship, thereby occasioning heavy loss of life. Many of the passengers were neutral Americans. US Secretary of State, Lansing, said of Valentiner's conduct that, 'for cold blooded inhumanity, an equal could scarcely be found in the annals of modern war', and the incident was branded, 'more atrocious than any of the other attacks which had previously taken place.'

   A further dubious sinking by him occurred off Crete shortly afterwards when 334 lives were lost during the attack on the P&O liner *Persia*.

   During the month of November, 1915, alone, Valentiner sank 14 Allied merchant ships of 47,460 tons, not including the two liners.

3. Correspondence from Wolfgang Hirschfeld to the author, 21.1.91.
4. These Reuters reports were premature, since it was not until 15

May, 1945, that diplomatic relations were finally broken off.

5. Internment Camp (Japan) Reports, Militärgeschichtliches Forschungsamt, Freiburg; IIIM30 1-4, 30/9 31/2-3.

Chapter 4

1. Following publication of his first book *Feindfahrten* (Neff Verlag, Vienna 1982), Wolfgang Hirschfeld received from Washington at the beginning of 1983 a request for an interview from Laurie Rackas of the Cable News Network Inc (CNN) in connection with a proposed television documentary, 'Japanese Nuclear Research'.

   Mrs Rackas stated that apart from the loading list already mentioned, she had not been able to obtain anything further from the US Navy Archive and had been told that all matters relating to atomic affairs even fifty years back were still subject to the highest degree of official secrecy.

   In its own way, of course, this sort of secrecy merely confirms that this was no straighforward consignment, since the US authorities were quite open about accounting for supplies of uranium metal seized by their land forces in Europe.

   The CNN was interested in knowing the purpose for which the Japanese wanted the uranium, and whether they were in a position to put an atomic explosive together (i.e. an atom bomb).

   When Mrs Rackas was asked by Hirschfeld if the collective conscience of the American people remained uneasy at the memory of the atomic attacks on the civilian populations of Hiroshima and Nagasaki, Mrs Rackas replied, without stating the reason for saying so, that the question should really be addressed to the crew of the German submarine *U-234*, since those attacks had been brought to pass, if unwittingly, by the surrender of their submarine to the US Navy.

2. Both Schölch and Pfaff became US citizens after the war.
3. R. Rhodes: *The Making of the Atomic Bomb*, Simon & Schuster, London, p.461.
4. Henry L. Stimson Diaries, Sterling Memorial Library, Yale.
5. Dean Acheson: *Present at the Creation*, W. W. Norton, 1969.
6. A. H. Compton: *Atomic Quest — A Personal Narrative*, New York 1956, p.238.
7. Stimson: *The Decision to Use the Bomb*, Harper's Magazine, February 1947, p. 107.

Oberkommando des Heeres
(Chef der Heeresrüstung und
Befehlshaber des Ersatzheeres)

Berlin W 35, den   *15. 10.*   194 *2*
Tirpitzufer 72—76
Fernsprecher:
Ortsverkehr: Sammelnummer 3) 00 12
Fernverkehr: ///// // //// /897631

Auftrag-Nr Wa Prüf 11 **KAP/L 88 011-5371/42 ET 200**

Auftrag-Nr bei allen Schriftstücken stets angeben!

Bb.-Nr   *959* /42 g**Kdos** Geheime Kommandosache   11. 11. 1942

Kriegsauftrag

Firma   **Forschungsanstalt der Deutschen
Reichspost
z.Hd.v.Herrn Postrat K u b i c k i**

W.-Nr

Berlin - Tempelhof

Ringbahnstr.125

Es   Auf Ihr Angebot vom
wird Ihnen hiermit der Auftrag übertragen auf

1.) Durchführung grundsätzlicher Untersuchungen über die
Leistungssteigerung von Flüssigkeits-R-Antrieben durch
Verwendung von Treibstoffgemischen höchsten Energie-
gehaltes.

2.) Untersuchung der Möglichkeit der Ausnutzung des Atom-
zerfalls und Kettenreaktion zum R-Antrieb.

Preis = Festpreise
vorläufigen (Richt-)Preise Los   FUB für   Konstruktionsauftrag
Stück-bz. usw.

Der Preis versteht sich: _ _ _ _ _

Zahlungsbedingungen: _ _ _ _ _

Dem Auftrag liegen die —)entgegenen — in Ihren Händen befindlichen — „Besonderen
Bedingungen für Kriegsaufträge des Heereswaffenamts (Ausgabe vom März 1941)" und die
weiteren, hierin genannten Unterlagen zugrunde.

Since the contract, of which a facsimile is shown opposite, placed by the Heereswaffenamt with the German Post Office was *prima facie* to investigate atomic propulsion systems for rockets, it is necessary to show that that could not have been the case.

The two leading personalities in the development of the V-2 rocket programme were Captain, later Colonel, Walter Dornberger and the Baron Wernher von Braun.

Dornberger was appointed to undertake experiments with liquid-fuel rockets when the Army first thought of the idea in 1930. Wernher von Braun accepted a research position as a civilian employee of the army in October, 1932, and was subsequently permitted to pursue a degree in physics at the University of Berlin; he graduated at the Faculty of Military Science following his work into the problem of liquid-fuel propulsion for rockets. For the practical part of this research, he was appointed to superintend the newly inaugurated army testing ground for liquid-fuel rockets at Kummersdorf near Berlin. Later, when the need was recognized for acquiring an extensive test and development range, a suitable site was purchased at Peenemünde on the Baltic coast north of the town of Wolgast in 1935.

In March, 1936, the prototype rocket, A4, later to become universally known as the V-2, was unveiled. This 12 ton missile stood 14 metres high, and, driven by a power plant burning for 65 seconds with a thrust of 25 tons, would carry a 1-ton explosive warhead a distance of 155 miles, which meant in effect that England fell within its range from the Low Countries or France.

Its power plant had been painstakingly developed by a team of scientists and engineers under Dornberger and Von Braun over a period of twelve years. By 1942 they had succeeded in the satisfactory assembly of a liquid-fuel system for large rockets unrivalled in the world. Much of its technology remains unsurpassed to this day.

The V-2 was powered by a 75/25 mixture of ethyl alcohol and water known as 'ethanol', and liquid oxygen. The two liquid components of the fuel were stored in separate tanks in the belly of the rocket and were drawn into the combustion chamber by fuel pumps driven by a small turbine. This device had blades with an overall diameter of 19 inches and developed the equivalent of 5,000 hp. It was powered by hydrogen peroxide acting on the catalyst, sodium permanganate, which when mixed produces superheated steam at 500°C. The V-2 rocket owed its success to the invention of this miniature turbine and the chemical compound providing the superheated steam; every large liquid-fuel rocket since has its fuel supplied to the combustion chamber by this method.

On 3 October, 1942, in the presence of General Leeb, head of the Heereswaffenamt, the first V-2 successfully to complete a programmed flight covered by a distance of 192 km. Whereas Hitler remained unimpressed this performance, since it was a single success among many failures, Speer was eventually able to record on 22 November, 1942, that 'the Führer takes note of the production plans for the V-2 and believes — providing the necessary numbers can be turned out within the time scale — that this weapon can be made to influence England very strongly.'

Hitler finally underwrote the order for mass production on 22 December, but the rocket retained only the second rating of priority *SS (Sonderstufe)*, and was not accorded the highest priority *DE (Dringende Entwicklung)* until 7 July, 1943, and even then against the advice of Goering.

The Peenemünde records first mention the concept of the A9/10 two-stage intercontinental rocket on 29 July, 1940.

The A9, carrying the 1-ton warhead, was basically a V-2 rocket with wings. It was 26 metres in length and 4 metres in diameter, and was designed to be launched in partnership with a detachable propulsion unit, the A-10. After the first stage had burned for 50 seconds, and the joined projectile had attained an altitude of 180 km, separation would occur. The A-10 would fall away and return to earth at the end of a 2500 m^2 parachute canopy, while the A-9 would proceed to a height of 350 km under its own power at a speed of 10,000 kilometres per hour and then begin its descent in a shallow glide at a speed of about 7,800 kilometres per hour. Arrival in the United States would follow 35 minutes after the launch.

As from early October, 1942, however, Colonel Dornberger ordered all development work on the A-9 to be suspended until further notice in order to concentrate all his resources on the V-2. On resumption in June, 1944, only a limited outlay was allocated to the project. The first successful flight of the A-9 first stage took place on 24 January, 1945, but the A-9/A-10 programme was then abandoned.

It will be recalled that when in September, 1939, a research group for nuclear weapons investigation was set up by the Heereswaffenamt, the purpose of the project was described as 'an investigation of new energy sources for R (Rocket) propulsion' and the suffix for 'R propulsion' was used as a means of cloaking the nature of the research.

On 15 October, 1942, the Oberkommando des Heeres issued a war contract to the Research Institute of the German Post Office at its Headquarters at Ringbahnstrasse 125, Berlin Tempelhof. The contract, which is numbered 3 of 9 for invoice purposes, was subject to the provisions of the Special Conditions for Heereswaffenamt War Contracts, March, 1941. The Führer's ruling that no new weapon development was to be undertaken which would not result in the weapon being ready for deployment in the short term was in force at this time, and in April, 1942, Goering had also signed a decree prohibiting research work which had no immediate relevance to the war effort.

Yet all historians who have mentioned the document have accepted that it must have been intended to initiate atomic rocket propulsion technology.

It will be observed that the contract bears a reference which is to be quoted in all cases of correspondence:

Wa Prüf 11 HAP/L SS 011-5371/42 ET200

This formula indicates that the contract was placed by the Weapons Testing and Development Section of the Heereswaffenamt (*Abteilung 11 der Amtsgruppe für Entwicklung und Prüfwesen des Heereswaffenamtes-Wa Prüf 11*) at the Heeresanstalt Peenemünde (HAP) and that it had been accorded the second priority rating SS (*Sonderstufe*), so that it was equal in status to the V-2 rocket development programme.

The contract is in two parts and it is certainly the case that the first part relates to the investigation of means of increasing the efficiency of rocket fuel blends.

The second part reads: '*You are hereby contracted...to investigate the possibility of the fullest use of atomic decay (i.e. radioactivity) and chain reactions for R-propulsion.*'

When Houtermans described the possible applications of the radioactive material produced in his postulated nuclear reactor, he had foreseen that the radioisotopes might have applications in the fields of applied chemistry, biology, medicine and physiology, but not for powering a large rocket.

In fact, since there is no feasible way of altering the atomic decay rate of uranium radioisotopes, radioactive decay is not a practical means of large-scale power production.

As regards the question of using an on-board reactor to power a war rocket, Colonel Dornberger stated in his book 'V-2' (Hurst and Blackett, 1954, p. 140): 'We dreamed, too, of atomic energy which would at last give us the necessary drive for flight into the infinity of space, to the very stars.'

But it *was* merely a dream, because no atomic rocket plant has ever been designed which is anywhere near light enough to be a flight engine. The weight problems are formidable. All modern experimental reactors for nuclear rocket engines are comprised of enriched U^{235} metal powder embedded in the moderator graphite. On the grounds of the fantastic expenditure alone, the very idea of using a reactor to power a rocket for use against an enemy is ludicrous.

These points, of course, would have been sorted out in a two-minute telephone conversation with a physicist; no war contract would have been necessary to obtain an opinion on the matter.

Lieutenant Krafft Ehricke, a tank platoon leader wounded at Dunkirk and a veteran of the assault on Moscow, who had once spent six months as an assistant under Professor Heisenberg, was seconded to Peenemünde and worked under Dr Walter Thiel on the development of the methyl-alcohol rocket fuel. In *The Rocket Team* (Frederick Ordway III and Mitchell Sharpe; William Heinemann, London 1979), Ehricke stated to the authors that Dr Thiel passed him some reports in November, 1942, which included a design for a nuclear steam turbine drawn up by Heisenberg and Pose at Leipzig. Thiel asked him to look into the matter and report back. Ehricke made his own evaluation and recalled advising his senior officer that a nuclear rocket engine would probably need to be made up of enriched U^{235} with a solid moderator (i.e. graphite), probably with methane or hydrogen as a propellant, both of which of course are highly flammable. Thiel agreed, but the matter ended there; the discussion was purely academic.

When Ehricke spoke to Heisenberg on the subject in 1944, the physicist told him that he considered the most immediate military application of the nuclear reactor would be for submarine propulsion.

Dornberger stated in the conclusion to his book (op. cit., p. 237) that he thought he ought to mention the extent to which

> 'we had considered the use of atomic energy for rocket propulsion. After 1943 we had approached Professor Heisenberg for information about the practical possibilities. He could give us no firm promises of any description.'

The very curious fact therefore emerges that Colonel Dornberger, who was the Head of the Department which had placed the atomic propulsion contract with the Post Office Research Institute, omits to mention that contract or its findings.

The reason is, of course, self-evident. When the suffix 'for R-propulsion' is deleted from the relevant text, it then reads,

'You are hereby contracted to investigate the possibility of the fullest use of atomic decay and chain reactions.'

This was, therefore, the contract issued by the V-Weapons Development Centre at Peenemünde, which had nothing to do with rocket propulsion, but placed Hitler's radiological weapon project with Dr Wilhelm Ohnesorge.

APPENDIX 2

Within twenty years of a ten-week visit to their country by Einstein in 1922, the Japanese had set up teaching and research institutes for physics in all parts of Asia and the Pacific region which were under their influence. Following their military conquests of European colonies in the Far East, they came into possession of observatories and laboratories which in some respects excelled the standards of corresponding institutions in Japan.

Their leading physicists in the field of atomic research were Yoshio Nishina, who had spent a number of years in Copenhagen with Nils Bohr, the close associate of both Heisenberg and Houtermans; and Ryokichi Sagane, who had studied the subject of cyclotrons under the inventor of the apparatus, E. O. Lawrence at Berkeley.

In 1928 Nishina worked together with Klein, the American physicist, to establish a theory for the Compton Effect using Dirac's relativistic theory of the electron. The Compton Effect describes the result of a collision between a photon and a free electron in which the electron recoils and a photon of longer wavelength is emitted. It is one of the most important means by which X-rays and gamma rays interact with matter and can be accurately calculated in theory. Nishina's resulting calculation has been described as one of the brilliant successes of the Dirac theory.

In April, 1940, the Director of the Aviation Technical Research Institute of the Imperial Japanese Army commissioned a survey of all accessible uranium concentrations within Japan's potential sphere of control and particularly in Korea and Burma.

When he was presented with the report six months later, he learned that deposits in those countries would be enough to fulfil Japan's requirements for an atom bomb. Shortly afterwards, Nishina began cross-section measurements at the Riken laboratory in Tokyo in anticipation of receiving the authority of the Army Air Force to instigate atom bomb research, which permission he duly received in April, 1941.

Nishina's initial calculations indicated that 10 kilos of the U^{235} isotope of at least 50 per cent purity should be enough to make a bomb, subject to cyclotron tests to confirm his estimate. These would have revealed that 50 per cent enrichment was enough (just) for an atom bomb, but that 10 kilos were insufficient.

The interest of the Japanese Government in the project waned in 1942 once it was realized that the separation of the U^{235} isotope for the purpose of making the bomb would require an enormous labour force, stupendous investment, one tenth of Japan's annual electricity requirement and half the nation's copper output for a year.

Nishina persisted, however, and he built a small gaseous thermal diffusion plant to investigate whether it would be possible to enrich the U^{235} isotope in uranium to about 2 per cent in order to achieve a reactor using ordinary water as a moderator. Following this, consultations were soon under way as to the best means of processing several hundred tons of uranium ore.

The Japanese Imperial Navy had funded a second project under Arakatsu at Kyoto University in the meantime and had engaged in prospecting for uranium for an unknown purpose.

Despite the pessimism of the Japanese Government for the project, it is recorded of Nishina that at a meeting with the Army Liaison Officer, Major-General Nobuuji, on 7 February, 1942, he stated that he had 'great expectations'. It may have been at this time that the first approaches were made by German sources as to the possibility of technical cooperation; once Japanese physicists had seen that they stood no chance of developing an atomic bomb in time to influence the outcome of the war, they may have considered it to be in their interest to give material assistance to Germany within the spirit of the projected treaties for economic and technical co-operation in war projects.

Following the surrender of Japan in August, 1945, the American General Staff issued instructions on 5 September, 1945, for the destruction of all enemy war equipment (except equipment not essentially or exclusively for war and which was suitable for peacetime civilian use).

A cable from the Joint Chiefs of Staff on 30 October to Pacific area commanders called on them to intern all persons engaged in atomic research and to impound all facilities. Once this had been done, the five cyclotrons installed in universities at Osaka, Kyoto and Tokyo were destroyed.

In the wake of the resulting worldwide scientific furore, the Americans announced that the acts of destruction had not been intentional at all, but had arisen as a result of a clerical error, and Groves (op. cit., chapter 27) devotes over five pages explaining how it all came about, but nevertheless admits (p. 367) that he cannot piece together the chain of events coherently.

It would have been far simpler to have explained that, not four months previously, Japan had been prepared to use Nazi Germany's radiological weaponry against the civilian populations of the United States, or even that the Wehrmacht had been experimenting on the Heidelberg and Paris cyclotrons with a view to producing milligramme quantities of short-lived radio-isotopes as a special ingredient to spice up the ordinary ordnance; but probably the climate was not right.

ALSOS

American Intelligence Mission to Germany and former German-occupied territories in western Europe, the principal purpose of which was to ascertain if Nazi Germany had made nuclear weapons.

As a result of poor intelligence methods, *Alsos* failed to discover that Germany had developed radiological weapons, some of which had been shipped to Japan by U-boat. *Alsos* officers also falsely believed that German scientists did not understand the principle of the atomic bomb.

ARYAN PHYSICS

A Nazi doctrine inspired by the physicists Lenard and Stark, which refuted all twentieth century developments in atomic science including Einstein's theories of relativity, and quantum theory, labelling them 'Jewish pseudo-science'.

ATOM

The smallest part of an element which can take part in a chemical reaction. The atom is now conceived as a microplanet orbited by a cloud of electrons. The central part of the atom is the nucleus which is composed of neutrons and protons bound tightly together by nuclear forces into a roughly spherical volume. The number of electrons, which are negatively charged, and protons, which have positive electrical charge, is equal.

ATOMIC BOMB

A nuclear explosive device which uses the principle of the fast fission chain reaction. See *Uranium Bomb* and *Plutonium Bomb*.

BORON

The most widely used neutron absorbent for controlling a nuclear reactor. It has a relatively high neutron capture cross-section and its melting point is 2300°C. The element is brittle with a hardness comparable to diamond, is inexpensive and common.

CADMIUM

An excellent material for neutron absorption, but which has a relatively low melting point of 320°C. It cannot be used on its own for reactor control or to shut down a reactor with a temperature greater than its melting point. It is soft and lacks strength and, when used in a working nuclear pile, must be clad in aluminium or stainless steel for strength and for protection against corrosion. It has a relatively complex isotopic structure and depletes rapidly.

CHAIN REACTION

A cascade of collisions between neutrons and incident U^{235} nuclei initiated by a single fission. In a *fast fission* reaction, the avalanche of fissions in a critical mass of uranium occurs instantaneously. In a *slow neutron* reaction, neutrons are slowed by a moderating substance such as heavy water or pure carbon, and this procedure is used to harness the energy of nuclear fissions for power purposes in a nuclear reactor.

CONTROL RODS

The activity of a reactor may be controlled by means of absorbers which capture some of the neutrons in the reactor core and thus prevent the chain reaction from diversifying too rapidly. Cadmium and boron rods are the most commonly used materials for regulation. Shut-off rods are used for quick submersion into the reactor core to close down the reaction. These rods are invariably of boron.

CORE

The part of the reactor which contains the uranium fuel and moderator making up the chain reaction assembly.

CORPUSCULAR RADIATION

Particles emitting alpha and beta radiation. Alpha rays are ejected in a stream from many radioactive substances, but have little penetrating power. Beta radiation is a stream of energetic electrons or positrons emitted by the nucleus of a radioisotope during beta-decay. It is a form of ionizing radiation and can penetrate a very thin metal foil.

CRITICAL MASS

The minimum mass of a fissile material necessary to sustain a chain reaction. A considerable number of variables are involved in the calculation of the figure. The critical mass will be lower where the number of U^{238} atoms in a lump of uranium has been decreased by separation; the nature of the reflector and its thickness are also important. The best physical arrangement for a critical mass is a sphere. It would be impossible to create a critical mass no matter how much uranium was used, if it were to be distributed in a thin film over a large surface area.

CROSS SECTION

A measure of the probability of a particular collision process, for example, between a beam of neutrons and a substance through which the beam is passed. One possible reaction may be the absorption of a number of neutrons by the U^{238} nuclei upon which the neutrons are incident. The value of the cross section will depend on the energy of the neutrons as well as the nuclei considered.

CYCLOTRON

A laboratory apparatus for the acceleration of protons and positive ions. See fuller description in References to Chapter One, No.6.

ENRICHMENT

In uranium, to increase the abundance of the U^{235} isotope in the natural element by depleting it physically of quantities of the companion U^{238} isotope.

There are many ways in which the U^{235} and U^{238} isotopes can be separated from each other, but only two methods were actually experimented with to the prototype stage in Nazi Germany, and both made use of uranium in its gaseous form UF6 (uranium hexafluoride):

Isotope Sluice: Professor Erich Bagge

The third prototype of this invention was found later to have an isotope separation factor four times greater than a single stage of the gaseous diffusion system used by the Americans. Two early prototypes were destroyed in air raids. Relying on Maxwell's velocity-distribution theory, which states that lighter isotopes travel faster than heavier isotopes in a molecular beam, Bagge's principle was to aim a narrow stream of the uranium hexafluoride gas through two shutters revolving at an optimum speed to permit one group of molecules only to pass while diverting the other group into a collection receptacle.

Ultracentrifuge: Dr Wilhelm Groth

The ultracentrifuge was two connected centrifuges, each consisting of five chambers separated by baffles arranged in such a way that only a heavier gas concentrating near the wall of the chamber could pass into the chamber above, and only a lighter gas near the axis of the chamber could pass into the chamber below. The very high speed of the cylinders was typically more than 50,000 revolutions per minute, which imbued the centrifuges with a tendency to explode. During the operation of the ultracentrifuge, the rate of rotation of one of the two centrifuges was periodically altered so as to create a sudden drop in pressure, thus causing a gas stream to oscillate, pushing (or pulling) the gas near the outer chamber wall of one chamber into the central chamber of the upper. Groth was inspired by a demonstration of the layout and mounting of ultracentrifuge installations in the laboratory of the University of Uppsala in Sweden which he visited in November, 1942.

Whereas Dr Groth's ten ultracentrifuges cost the German Government 600,000 Reichsmarks, a full-scale enrichment plant would have required up to a thousand of the machines. In modern technology, 5½ tons of natural uranium is required to produce 1 ton of uranium enriched to 3 per cent U^{235} and 97 per cent U^{238}. The best reported performance of one of Groth's machines for a day's production was 7½ grams of uranium with the U^{235} isotope enriched from 0.7 per cent to 0.735 per cent.

Probably the best design was Professor Manfred von Ardenne's electro-magnetic mass separator, which was very similar to the apparatus used by the Americans. In this equipment, uranium hexafluoride molecules in a gas with an overall positive electrical charge are released into an evacuated flight tube where they come under the attracting influence of the negative potential of an accelerating electrode in the shape of a disc with a small aperture at its centre. A beam of fast-moving ions passes through the aperture and comes under the influence of a magnetic field produced by a deflection magnet. Here the U^{235} molecules are subject to a greater deflection than U^{238} molecules by reason of their lighter mass.

The efficiency of the enrichment is improved substantially by repeatedly passing the enriched gas through the same process so that the enrichment improves with each traverse.

HOMOGENOUS/HETEROGENOUS REACTORS

A *homogenous* reactor is one in which the uranium fuel and moderator are mixed so as to present a uniform medium to the neutrons. Criticality cannot be achieved in homogenous reactors at ordinary temperatures because of the occurrence of large resonances in the absorption cross section of materials, in particular the U^{238} energy bands. A *heterogenous* reactor has the uranium fuel arranged in a geometrical configuration and is not inseparably mixed with the moderator.

GAMMA RADIATION

Electro-magnetic radiation emitted as a result of a decrease in the mass of a nucleus, i.e. at fission. Being electrically without charge, the radiation has a much greater penetrating power than alpha or beta particles and is not deflected in a magnetic or electrical field. A considerable thickness of lead, steel or concrete is required for satisfactory shielding from its effects.

JEWISH PHYSICS

A Nazi doctrine intended to denigrate all advances in atomic physics made during the twentieth century.

KAISER WILHELM GESELLSCHAFT
Kaiser Wilhelm Gesellschaft zur Förderung der Wissenschaften. The research institutes of the Kaiser Wilhelm Foundation for the Advancement of Science was funded during the war by the Reichs Ministry of Education and Science. Each Kaiser Wilhelm Institute (KWI) had a Director as well as departmental heads who often held a university professorial title.

MODERATOR
A substance used in a reactor core to slow down neutrons emitted in fissions. Liberated neutrons possess an energy of about two million electron-volts (eV). In thermal reactors they require much reduced energy (of about 0.025 eV at 20°C) in order to cause further fissions themselves in collisions with U^{235} atoms. This deceleration is achieved by elastic collisions between the neutrons and the molecules of the moderating substance. Neutrons are liable to capture by U^{238} resonances at energies of between 6-100 eV.

Specific Moderators:
Dry ice (CO_2) see pages 34-35; 38-42
Electrographite (solid carbon) see page 43
Heavy water (D_2O) see pages 25-26; 43; 45
Liquid Methane (CH_4) see pages 106-107
Pentene (C_5H_{10}) see page 77
Water (H_2O) see pages 26; 28-29; 105-106

NEUTRON
An elementary particle of zero charge bound within the nucleus of an atom. When a *slow* neutron approaches close to the nucleus, the nuclear forces act and disturb the equilibrium of the nucleus which then splits into two or more fission fragments. The large majority of neutrons liberated at fission are emitted instantaneously (within 10^{-8} seconds), and have an energy of about 2 MeV. These are known as *prompt* neutrons.

0.75 percent of all neutrons liberated emerge from the fragmented nucleus later, and generally have a much longer lifetime than prompt neutrons. These are known as *delayed* neutrons.

A *thermal* neutron is any neutron which has been slowed from its initial velocity at emission to an energy in the region of 0.025 eV at normal temperature by scattering interaction with the moderator in a nuclear reactor.

NSDAP
National Sozialistische Deutsche Arbeiter Partei. The Nazi Party.

NUCLEAR DOPPLER EFFECT

The phenomenon causing an increase in the width of the resonance capture peaks of U^{238} resulting from a rise in temperature in the reactor core. As a result slow neutrons are captured by the U^{238} isotope over a much wider range of their energies. The converse is true for a decrease in temperature, so that if the core environment is refrigerated, the resonance capture peaks not only of the U^{238} molecules, but also of the hydrogen molecules in carbon compounds are severely narrowed. This makes a chain reaction with simple carbon moderators easy to achieve.

PLUTONIUM

An artificial element with atomic number 94 produced in a nuclear reactor by a decay process following the absorption of a neutron by the U^{238} atom in uranium. Fourteen plutonium isotopes are known varying in mass from 232 to 246. All are highly radioactive.

Plutonium Pu^{239} is fissile and has a critical mass of about 5 kilos. It is far cheaper to obtain in sufficient quantity for an atom bomb than is U^{235}.

5 kilos Pu^{239} approximately is produced during the fission cycle of a reactor for every 20 tonnes of U^{238}.

PLUTONIUM BOMB

The weapon consists of a uniform layer of high explosive surrounding a layer of U^{238} which encloses a core of 5 kilos plutonium at a sub-critical density. When the high explosive detonates a massive uniform pressure of millions of pounds p.s.i. is created which compresses the core material to a supercritical density, this causing an implosion. The gun device used to explode the *uranium bomb* is not suitable because the speed of assembly of a critical mass of plutonium is required to be many powers more sudden in order to preclude a premature explosion known as 'fizzle'.

RADIOACTIVITY

The emission of high energy particles or a stream of electromagnetic radiation following the fragmentation of a nucleus after bombardment with neutrons, protons or gamma rays in a particle accelerator or in a nuclear reactor. The activity of radioisotopes decreases exponentially with time, and the time required for a particular quantity to decay to half its value is the half-life.

RADIOLOGICAL WARFARE

The military exploitation of radioisotopes. A radiological weapon is a weapon, other than a nuclear explosive device, designed to cause destruction, damage, death and injury by the dissemination of radioactive material. Such weapons are permitted in international law even though biological and chemical weapons are outlawed. Nuclear reactors create waste products as the uranium fuel is consumed through controlled fission. Reactor waste contains any number of highly lethal radioactive materials which can be incorporated into a crude but highly efficient weapon of mass destruction.

RADIOLOGICAL WEAPONS MATERIALS
A single bomb containing 50 kilos of mixed isotopes of plutonium of atomic mass 238 to 242 inclusive would comprise aggregate activities of the order of 500,000 curies. (One curie is equivalent to 3.7 x 1010 disintegrations per second).

The inhalation or ingestion of 1 milligram of plutonium would result in the almost certain death of the victim within weeks, and even a microgram would result in later high susceptibility to pulmonary cancer.

50 kilos of plutonium contains 50 million milligrams, or 50,000 million micrograms. Only 30 kilos of this matter in an aerosol would be enough to cover a city of 100 square kilometres to a height of 3 metres. In addition to plutonium radionuclides, Strontium-90, Strontium-89 and Caesium-137 occur in the inventory of fission products. Cobalt-60 is an extremely energetic radiator of gamma and beta radiation and has a half-life of just over five years. This material could be abundantly produced in a reactor by irradiating quantities of the stable isotope.

RMfVP
Reich Propaganda Ministry.

REFLECTOR
A material completely enclosing the reactor core against which neutrons escaping at the perimeters, which would otherwise be lost to the operation of the reactor, rebound. Common reflector materials are heavy water, ordinary water, graphite, beryllium and natural uranium.

RESONANCE
A phenomenon in which neutrons induce different reactions according to their energy. Within a particular range of their energies, there is a high probability that a neutron will be absorbed by the nucleus of an atom and so form a compound with it.

In order to sustain the chain reaction in uranium, neutrons must be prevented as far as is possible from being captured by the U^{238} resonances. This is achieved by slowing the neutrons down rapidly to energies outside the optimum capture bands in a suitable moderator. In the case of very cold reactors, the temperature of the reactor atmosphere reduces the width of the resonances.

SEPARATION OF ISOTOPES
See *Enrichment*

SHIELDING

A reactor has an outer shield of concrete completely surrounding the reactor vessel which protects personnel against neutrons and gamma radiation. Between this outer shield and the reflector is a *thermal* shield of iron or steel of a thickness of approximately 6 inches, which attenuates the radiation and slows the neutrons. The presence of fast neutrons and gamma radiation in the outer shield would result in heat production and possible structural damage.

STABILITY

The stability of a reactor is its tendency to hold a steady power level without action by the control system. When the reactor departs from the condition in which the reaction continues at stability, (the critical condition), the indication is known as reactivity.

URANIUM

A lustrous metal with the appearance of iron. It is the heaviest known natural metallic element with a density of 19.04 gm/ml as compared to lead with 11.34 gm/ml. It is fairly abundant.

After mining, the ore is leached and then recovered by solvent extraction and roasting to form a crude concentration known as 'Yellow Cake' which assays at between 60-90 per cent U_3O_8 (uranium oxide). Over 1000 tons of this material was captured by the Germans at Oolen in Belgium in May, 1940.

In further chemical processes, the concentrate is dissolved into hot nitric acid to form uranyl nitrate, which is purified by solvent extraction and then calcined to form essentially pure UO_3 (uranium trioxide). This in turn is converted by a hydrogen reduction process into UO_2 (uranium dioxide). UO_2 may be reduced with calcium to form powdered, metallic uranium. For the production of uranium metal or hexafluoride gas, UO_2 is hydrofluorinated into UF_4.

If the gas is required, the UF_4 is injected into a chemical reactor containing calcium fluoride granules at a temperature of 460°C, where the gaseous uranium hexafluoride is generated.

The metal is produced by mixing UF_4 with magnesium metal raspings and compressing. The mixture is then baked at 900°C. Following a reaction between the UF_4 and the magnesium, molten uranium falls into a catchpot for moulding.

See also pages 71; 116-117

URANIUM BOMB

A nuclear explosive device using the principle of fast fission for the chain reaction. The explosive substance consists of two subcritical lumps of highly enriched uranium which, when fired together by conventional explosive within a gun-type assembly, instantaneously form a supercritical mass. This takes place within a tamper usually of beryllium. A radium source is attached to one of the subcritical lumps to 'spark' the chain reaction. A supercritical lump of weapons grade uranium would have a mass of about 14 kilos.

VAN DE GRAAF GENERATOR

A high voltage electrostatic generator capable of producing potentials of millions of volts. It consists essentially of an endless insulated fabric belt moving vertically which collects ions from discharge needles in its metal base and carries them through an insulated support cylinder for deposition in a smooth metal storage sphere. The voltage of the sphere increases with the increasing accumulation of ions. The voltage may be discharged as a spark, or drawn off to power an accelerator tube.

ARDENNE, Manfred von — *Ein Glückliches Leben für Forschung und Technik* Verlag der Nation, East Berlin 1972.

ERMENC, Joseph J. — *Atomic Bomb Scientists-Memoirs 1939-1945* Greenwood Press, Westport, CT. 1989.

GOWING, Margaret — *Britain and Atomic Energy 1939-1945* UKAEA and Macmillan 1964.

GOUDSMIT, Samuel A. — *Alsos - The Failure in German Science* Sigma Books, London 1947.

GROVES, Leslie — *Now It Can Be Told* Harper & Row, New York 1962.

HERMANN, Armin — *Heisenberg* Rowohlt Taschenbuch Verlag, Reinbek 1976.

HIRSCHFELD, Wolfgang — *Das Letzte Boot-Atlantik Farewell* Universitas Verlag, Munich 1989. *Feindfahrten* Neff Verlag, Wien 1983.

HOFFMANN, Klaus — *Otto Hahn* Verlag Neues Berlin 1978

IRVING, David — *The German Atomic Bomb* Da Capo Press, New York; published in England under the title '*The Virus House,*' William Kimber, London 1967.

JUNGK, Robert — *Brighter Than A Thousand Suns* Victor Gollancz, London 1982; Scherz Verlag, Bergn.

PICKER, Dr H. — *Hitlers Tischgespräche im Führerhauptquartier* Seewald Verlag, Stuttgart 1976.

SPEER, Albert

The Slave State
Weidenfield & Nicholson 1981.
Erinnerungen
Polyproplaen Verlag, Ullstein, Berlin
1969.

SPRINGER, VERLAG

*Gesammelte Werke von Werner
Heisenberg* Berlin, Heidelberg 1984

WALKER, Mark

*The Quest for Nuclear Power in
National Socialist Germany 1939-1945*
Cambridge University Press 1989.

WIRTZ, Dr Karl

Im Umkreis der Physik
Karlsruhe/Kernforschungszentrum,
1987.

INDEX

Built first American nuclear reactor, Chicago, December 1942, 19, 54, 92, 171

Flügge, Siegfried, Dr, (born 1912). Dr. Göttingen. Lecturer Frankfurt and Leipzig 1936-1937. At KWI for Chemistry, Berlin Dahlem, 32, 50, 84, 85, 89, 98

Frank, Hans, (1900-1946, executed). NSDAP Attorney, President Law Academy, Governor-General occupied Poland, 72, 118

Friedman, Aleksandr, (1888-1925). Russian astronomer. Pavlovsk Univ. 1913, Prof theoretical mechanics, Perm Univ. 1918

Fromm, Fritz, General. Commander German Ersatzheer, 57

Fünfer, Erwin, Dr. Asst to Bothe, W at KWI, Heidelberg, 44, 70, 76, 78, 79

Geib, Karl-Herrmann. Chemist, pupil of Harteck, P, 70

Geiger, Hans, Prof, (1882-1945). Dr Munich 1906. Univ Manchester 1907-1912, Director Reich Bureau of Standards 1912. Prof Kiel 1925. Inventor of the Geiger counter 1928, 11

Gerlach, Walther, Prof, (1889-1979). Prof Tübingen 1916. Prof. experimental physics Frankfurt 1920. Prof Munich 1929. Plenipotentiary for Nuclear Science December 1943-May 1945, 72, 73, 76-78, 80-82, 86, 87, 93

Gerwig. President Post Office Research Inst, 75

Goebbels, Josef, Dr phil, (1897-1945 suicide). Reichsminster for Enlightenment and Propaganda, 114, 127, 128, 131

Goering, Hermann, Reichsmarschall, (1893-1946 suicide). Chief of Luftwaffe, Head of Reich Research Council 1942-1945, 51, 58, 65, 75, 78, 87, 117, 158, 188, 189

Görnnert, Fritz, Dr. Personal aide to Goering, H, 65

Goudsmit, Samuel, Prof, (1902-1978). Dutch-American physicist, PhD Leiden, 1927. Emigrated USA 1928. Scientific Head, *Alsos* Mission 1944-1945, 66, 87, 88, 90-92, 127, 168

Gowing, Margaret, official historian, UKAEA, 52

Groth, Wilhelm, Dr. Physical-chemist, Asst to Harteck, P. Developed ultra-centrifuge 1944, 16, 20, 88, 196, 197

Groves, Leslie, General US Army, (1896-1970). Head of Manhattan Project, Chief of Military Intelligence of Enemy Activities, 1942-1947, 1, 18, 53, 87-89, 91, 136, 171, 193

Gugelmeier, Lieutenant, German Navy. Signals Officer, Lorient, 4

Haber, Fritz, Prof, (1868-1934). Physical chemist. Technical Institute, Karlsruhe 1894, Prof Karlsruhe 1906. Director KWI Chemistry Berlin Dahlem 1911. Devised Zyklon-B pesticide during Great War as by-product of chemical weapons research. Emigrated Britain 1933, 15

Hahn, Otto, Prof. (Biographical details 177), 14, 31, 51, 55, 68, 73, 85, 86, 88, 93, 98, 100, 101, 104, 111, 114

Halifax, Lord (1881-1959). British Foreign Secretary 1938-1940, 109

Halban, Hans von, Dr. French physicist, 14, 33, 50, 84, 85

Hanle, Wilhelm, Prof. Asst Esau, Uranium Club, independent Göttingen work group, 16, 20, 42, 43

Harteck, Paul, Prof, (1902-1985). Austrian physical-chemist. Univ. Vienna 1921-1923, PhD Berlin 1926, Asst Prof Univ Breslau 1928-1933, Asst Prof to Director of KWI Physics-Chemistry Berlin Dahlem; Rockefeller Scholarship, Cavendish Laboratory, Univ. Cambridge 1933-1934. Director Inst. of Physical Chemistry, Hamburg 1934-1945, 15, 16, 20, 21, 31, 34, 35, 38-42, 45, 47, 48, 51, 52, 55, 58, 60, 68-71, 73, 74, 77, 81, 88, 93, 112, 117, 126

Hassell, Ulrich von, (1881-1944 executed). Veteran career diplomat, 1908-1938. Resistance worker 1938-1944. Warned 1942 by von Weizsäcker, E. of Gestapo surveillance. Implicated in conspiracy of 20 July, 1944, 76

Haxel, Otto, Prof, (born 1909). Prof Univ. Munich/Tübingen 1936, physicist with German Admiralty research establishment, Kiel, 59

Heims, Heinrich. NSDAP lawyer, stenographer to Bormann, M., 118, 119

Heinert, H. Radio engineer, collaborator with Ardenne, M von, 98

Heisenberg, August, (1869-1930). Father of Heisenberg, W, 6, 7

Heisenberg, Werner, Prof, (1901-1976). Theoretical physicist. Nobel prize for physics 1932. Head of Inst. for Theoretical Physics, Leipzig 1932-1941: Director at KWI of Physics, Berlin Dahlem 1942-1945. Leader of group of three anti-Nazi saboteurs 1939-1945, 4, 5, *numerous references* 6-93, 107, 109-111, 171, 175, 181, 190, 191

Hellendorn, Heinrich, Lieutenant, German Navy. Passenger *U-234*, 123

Hernegger, F, Dr. Austrian physicist, 47, 105

Herold, P, Dr. Research Director, I. G. Farben, 39

Himmler, Heinrich, Reichsführer SS (1900-1945 suicide). Dipl. Agr, 13, 51, 121, 122

Hirschfeld, Wolfgang, Warrant Officer (Telegraphy) Germany Navy (born 1916). In charge telecomm-unications section, *U-234*, 1-5, 141-154, 155-157, 159-167, 169-171, 185

Hitler, Adolf (1889-1945 suicide). Austrian. Führer and Chancellor of the German Reich 1933-1945, 6, 10-12, 18-20, 35-38, 44-47, 50, 54, 55, 57, 62, 76, 77, 90, 91, 93-95, 98, 101, 102, 104, 111-115, 118, 119, 121, 123, 127-132, 135-137, 139, 140, 161, 174, 181, 187, 189, 191

Hoffmann, Heinrich. Hitler's personal photographer, 114. Biographical details, 181

Houtermans, Fritz, Prof (born 1903) biographical details 103-108. PhD experimental physics Göttingen 1932. Senior atomic physicist, laboratory of Ardenne, M von 1941-1944: set the world's first self-sustaining chain reaction, Berlin, 1942, 44, 45, 49, 50, 52, 68, 84, 89, 111, 112, 114, 116-118, 125-127, 171, 189, 191

Hubble, Edwin, (1889-1953). American astronomer, 9

Irving, David, (born 1938). British historian, 52, 80, 175

Jasper, Warrant Officer, German Navy, *U-234*, 160

Jensen, Johannes, Prof. Physicist, Asst. to Harteck, P. at Hamburg, 1939-1945. Nobel prize for Physics 1963, 112

Jensen, Peter, Prof. Physicist, Asst to Bothe, W at Heidelberg. Third member of Heisenberg, W's group of three anti-Nazi saboteurs, 42, 44, 47, 49, 50, 110

Joliot-Curie, Frederic, Prof. (1900-1958). French physicist. Nobel prize for physics, 1935, 14, 17, 68, 69, 84

Jones, Reginald, Dr, (born 1911). Dr Univ. Cambridge 1934. British physicist FRS, 92

Joos, Georg. Physicist, Asst Esau, A, Uranium Club, independent Göttingen work group, 16, 20, 42, 43

Kaltenbrunner, Ernst (1903-1946, executed). Succeeded Heydrich as Head of RHSA (Reich Security Headquarters) 1942, 121

Kammler, Hans, Dr (Eng.), (1903-1945 in action?). SS-Obergruppenführer Head of WvHA (Chief Office of Economic Administration); Director V-Weapon Development and Testing 1943-1945, Head Fighter Plane Staff, 123

Nishina, Yoshio. Japanese physicist, 191, 192

Ohnesorge, Wilhelm, Dr (Eng.) (1872-1962). Dr Univ. Kiel 1901. Biographical details 94, 95. Reichspostminister 1937-1945. Headed Nazi Germany's atomic weapons project, 50, 75, 88, 97, 98, 100-102, 112-114, 118, 120, 126, 127, 181, 191

Oliphant, M. Prof, (born 1901). Australian physicist, 16

Oppenheimer, Robert, Dr, (1904-1967). American physicist. Head of atomic weapons development laboratory, Los Alamos, 1, 59, 130, 174

Oshima, Hiroshi, (born 1886). Japanese Military Attaché Berlin 1934. General 1934-1938. Ambassador to Berlin 1940-1945, 154

Ossietski, Carl von, 12. Biographical details 176.

Otterbein, Dr. Official at Post Office Central Headquarters, 125

Oven, Wilfred von. Biographer of Goebbels, J., 127

Pash, Boris, Colonel, US Army. Military head, *Alsos* Intelligence Mission, 87, 88

Patterson. American Under-Secretary for War, 1945, 1

Pfaff, Carl-Ernst, Lt. German Navy. Third lieutenant, *U-234*, 155, 164, 170, 185

Philipp, Kurt, Prof. chemist, Asst to Hahn, O at KWI Chemistry, Berlin Dahlem, 100

Picker, Henry, Dr. Landrat, stenographer at Reichs Chancellery, staff of Bormann, M, 115, 118, 119, 121, 123

Planck, Max, Prof, (1858-1947). Prof Berlin 1892. Nobel prize for Physics 1918, President of KW Foundation 1928-1937, 16, 44, 66, 96, 100, 101

Popitz, Johannes, (1884-1945 executed). Career bureaucrat, Prussian Ministry of Finance, 1933-1944. 1943 involved in Himmler plot for coup d'etat. Implicated in plot of 20th July 1944. Execution delayed by Himmler during attempted negotiations with Allies, 76

Portal, Sir Charles, (born 1893). Chief Air Staff 1940-1945, 132

Pose, Heinz, Prof. Physicist, Asst. Diebner, K at Gottow, 71, 190

Rackas, Laurie. American television journalist, CNN, 185

Rafalski, Fritz. Warrant Officer (Telegraphy) *U-233*, 145, 149

Rajewski, Boris, Dr phil nat, (1893-1974). Prof Frankfurt 1934. Director KWI Biophysics until 1945, 68, 77

Reichwein, Adolf, (1898-1944 executed). Prof Civics and History, Halle 1930. Schoolteacher. Implicated in plot of 20th July 1944, 76, 77.

Reimann, Viktor. Biographer of Goebbels, J., 127

Rexer, Ernst, Prof. Physicist, 71

Riehl, Nikolaus, Dr. Director I.G. Farben, 38, 71

Rische, Paul. Warrant Officer, German Navy, *U-234*, 144-146, 148, 160

Roosevelt, Franklin, (1882-1945). President of the United States 1933-1945, 37, 136, 145, 183

Rosbaud, Paul, Dr. Scientific journalist, 80, 81, 87

Rösing, Captain, German Navy. Regional Commander U-boats, Norway, 158, 162

Ruf, Franz. Passenger, *U-234*, 154

Rust, Bernhard, (1893-1945, suicide). Schoolteacher, Hannover 1909. Reichsminister for Education, Science and National Culture, 1933-1945, 11, 13, 51, 53, 57

Rutherford, Lord, (1871-1937). New Zealand physicist, Nobel prize for Physics 1908. Director of Cavendish Laboratory, Cambridge Univ. 1919, 16, 45

Sagane, Ryokichi. Japanese physicist, 191

Sandmüller, Warrant Officer (Eng.) German Navy, *U-234*, 144-145

Sandrath, Fritz von. Colonel, Luftwaffe, passenger *U-234*, 154, 164

Teller, Edward, Prof, (born 1908). Göttingen 1931-1933, Copenhagen, 1934, London 1935-1941. Prof George Washington Univ. 1941. Involved US atomic weapons project, 130

Telschow, Ernst, Dr phil, (born 1889). Chemist. General Admin KWG 1931, Sec-Gen KWG 1937-1945, 56, 65

Thiessen, Adolf, Prof. Head KWI Phys-Chem & Electrochem, Berlin Dahlem, 55

Thiel, Walter, Dr, (died, air raid, 1943). Rocket engine designer, Kummersdorf; Deputy to Braun, W von, at Peenemünded, 121, 190

Tizard, Sir Henry. Chairman Cttee of Scientific Survey of Air Defence and Director of Imperial College of Science and Technology, 17, 18

Todt, Fritz, (1891-1942, suspicious accident). Autobahn and military fortifications engineer, Reichsminister for Armaments and War Industry, 1940-1942, 50, 51, 53

Togo, Shigenori. Japanese Foreign Minister, 162

Tomonaga, Hideo, Captain, Japanese Imperial Navy, (died 1945, suicide). Submarine architect, passenger *U-234*, 153-155, 162-166

Truman, Harry, (1884-1972). President of the United States 1945-1952, 1, 172-174, 183

Valentiner, Max, Captain, German Naval Reserve. Biographical details 184. 150-152

Vögler, Dr Albert, (1877-1945, suicide). Steel industrialist and scientist. Introduced synthetic rubber and petrol to Hitler in 1933. Co-Founder and Gen. Dir. Verein Stahlwerke AG: President KWG 1941-1945, 51, 56, 58, 65, 72, 76

Walker, Mark. American historian, 91, 175

Walter, Dr, Naval Staff Surgeon, *U-234*, 151, 164-166

Wecklein, Anna. Mother of Heisenberg, W, 6

Weisskopf, Viktor, Prof. German-American physicist, 8, 59

Weizsäcker, Carl-Friedrich con, Prof, (born 1912). Theoretical physicist, son of Weizsäcker, E. PhD Leipzig 1933 under Heisenberg, W. Second member of Heisenberg's group of three saboteurs of Nazi science, 8, 22, 24, 28, 41, 46, 47, 50, 51, 56, 58, 63, 66, 73, 81, 93, 103, 105, 109-111

Weizsäcker, Ernst von (1882-1951). Under Secretary of State, German Foreign Ministry. Anti-Nazi but sentenced at Nuremberg for alleged war crimes on basis of signing documents.

Wheeler, Joh, Dr, (born 1911). American theoretical physicist, 46

Wiederöe, Rolf, Dr. Norwegian laboratory engineer, 74-75

Wiehl, Emil. Economic Attaché, German Foreign Ministry, 116

Wigner, Eugene, Prof, (born 1902). American-Hungarian theoretical physicist. Dr (Eng) Inst. Technology, Berlin, 1925. Emigrated USA 1930, 111, 181

Winkelmann, Wilhelm. Petty Officer (Eng), *U-234*, 152, 159

Wirtz, Karl, Dr (born 1910). Experimental physicist, in charge Heisenberg's experimental team, KWI Berlin Dahlem, 22, 40, 50, 55, 58-60, 70, 73, 76, 79-83, 93

Wissmann, Wilhelm, Lt-Cdr. Commander U-boat depot ship *Waldemar Kophamel*, 147